THE BIG GUIDE 2:
IRISH CHILDREN'S BOOKS

Edited by Valerie Coghlan and Celia Keenan

ACKNOWLEDGEMENTS

Thanks are due for much help in various ways with *The Big Guide 2* to the following: Sydney Blain and the Church of Ireland College of Education, Helen Carr, Rex Coghlan, Martin Maguire, Liz Morris, Ivan O'Brien, Lynn Pierce, Rachel Pierce, Claire Ranson, Julie Rowan, Mary Sedgwick, the Library staff of St Patrick's College, Drumcondra, and in particular to Terry O'Sullivan, Paul Rowan of Computer Support, St Patrick's College, Drumcondra, Bernadette McHugh and the staff of the National Reading Initiative, and especially to Rosemary Hetherington, President of CBI, 1999–2000. Particular thanks are due to P.J. Lynch for the cover illustration for *The Big Guide 2* and to Michael O'Brien of The O'Brien Press for professional advice.

First published 2000 by Children's Books Ireland,
19 Parnell Square,
Dublin 1

ISBN: 1-872917-06-2

British Library Cataloguing-in-Publication Data
A catalogue record for this title is available from the British Library

CBI receives
assistance from

The Arts Council
An Chomhairle Ealaíon

1 2 3 4 5 6 7 8 9 10
00 01 02 03 04 05 06 07

Typesetting, layout and design: Lynn Pierce
Cover illustration: P.J. Lynch
Colour separations: C&A Print Services Ltd.
Printing: Brookfield Printing Company, Dublin.

THE BIG GUIDE 2:
IRISH CHILDREN'S BOOKS

Detail from cover of
The Big Guide to Irish Children's Books,
illustration by P.J. Lynch.

CONTENTS

INTRODUCTION

Recent developments in writing for children have provided the impetus for *The Big Guide 2: Irish Children's Books*, which follows *The Big Guide to Irish Children's Books* (1996). There is, however, a number of significant differences between the two publications. Four years ago a publication that outlined the scope and range of Irish publishing for young people was required. Until then, the only information available about this was in articles in periodicals and a few reference books. Recent years have brought changes in publishing and this will be evident from the articles contained here. More commentary is available about books which have an Irish relevance, and indeed the length of the bibliography in *Big Guide 2*, relating to sources of information about the topic, is witness to this.

Big Guide 2 is arranged under a number of headings and chapters which reflect recent developments and areas under consideration by commentators in the fields of education, English and Irish studies and social history. It considers not only books published in Ireland, but also books by Irish authors/illustrators published elsewhere and in translation. Books with Irish 'themes' are also discussed in these pages; indeed, the extent to which Ireland features in books by non-Irish authors/illustrators published outside Ireland is remarkable. Most chapters are followed by lists of recommended books in recognition of the value placed on a similar form of listing by readers of the previous *Big Guide*.

Big Guide 2 does not set out to be a comprehensive listing of all books published in Ireland or by Irish authors. That information is available elsewhere. It is the intention of the editors and the publisher that it will provide a focus on what is happening in the areas of writing, publishing, and critical analysis of books with an Irish relevance for young people. It is also hoped that it will provide food for debate, discussion and indeed argument!

'Books, Classrooms and Curricula', the opening section, provides a focus on what is happening in the changing classroom in Irish schools. The National Reading Initiative inaugurated by the Department of Education and Science in 2000, with its aim of improving national levels of literacy, has done much to raise the profile of books and reading, both in schools and in the community. Changes in school curricula, especially the introduction of the revised Primary School Curriculum (1999), with its increased emphasis on using 'real' books in the classroom, and funds given to primary and post-primary schools to purchase books has meant that it is now possible for teachers to see their classrooms and school libraries as places where books are available and as a vibrant and essential part of the educational process. However, to be effective the selection of books must be informed and here there is need for greater emphasis on the professional education of librarians, teachers and booksellers.

'Emergent' readers now have a far greater selection of Irish-published material on which to cut their literary teeth. In common with trends elsewhere, much of this is in series format and is written by established authors. Some excellent poetry anthologies have been published, including some by children themselves. However, apart from Paul Muldoon, no Irish poet with an international reputation has published for children, either in Irish or in English. Little or no drama for children has been published in the English language either, but there is somewhat more in Irish. Children's theatre is, however, increasing in popularity, and credit must be given to theatre groups, which tour schools and work with children, and to the Ark, a cultural centre for children, for making a great contribution in this area. The Lambert Puppet Theatre, too, has offered to generations of children enchanting, dramatised versions of classic fairy and folk tales.

It is necessary to stand back a little from the present to understand recent developments, and the section 'The Past is a Foreign Country' provides a context out of which current writing has evolved and offers suggestions on what might constitute 'a classic' in terms of Irish writing for or adopted by children. Writing about the past still dominates Irish publishing, although a number of writers who have made a significant and original contribution seem to have stopped writing in this genre. There are some welcome new voices whose work challenges and excites, but there is also a tendency for some of this writing to become textbook-like, as if pre-designed for the classroom. It would seem a pity if 'real' books were to become textbooks, and hence unreal. The over-reliance on study guides to novels also needs to be avoided, but used judiciously they can be very helpful. Some otherwise very good guides have a weakness in that their recommended reading lists fail to mention good books from other publishing houses.

At a time when Ireland is changing significantly, moving from a largely rural economy of small farmers to a more sophisticated, Europeanised society based on the successful development of ICT industries, issues revolving around 'Culture, Identity and Image' are likely to occur in writing for young people. Indeed, there is a strong argument for saying they should be a focus of attention, especially in writing for older children and young adults. There is, however, a great desire to be even-handed, to be politically correct on the part of Irish publishers and writers, and this leads to a fiction that at times fails to address issues as robustly as it might. Nowhere is this more evident than in writing about Northern Ireland.

Despite Ireland's economic growth there are still many who are marginalised in society for one reason or another. With some exceptions, their voices are not heard in the pages of Irish children's books. Possibly writers need more time to create a distance, to adjust to recent changes and their ramifications before they can properly address them. Certainly, there is still a tendency to look to an Ireland of the past, whether this is in picture books or in the ever-popular historical fiction. It would be untenable to argue that books are not an important medium for bringing a sense of the past to younger generations, but books should also offer a vision for the future. In the previous *Big Guide,* the shortage of fiction of a futuristic type was commented upon. While there is still a shortage of futuristic fantasy and science fiction, there has been a move away from the 'swirling mists' and Celtic twilight high fantasy that dominated the form for some time. Now there is hardly a druid to be seen. Instead, a new kind of urban, original and challenging fantasy has emerged, which owes more to le Fanu and Bram Stoker than to the Tuatha de Danaan.

Picture books and information books on Irish matters are still in short supply. There may be economic reasons for caution about such books on the part of publishers, but the interest in matters Irish that is evident in many strands of life should encourage greater risk-taking in these areas. While information books are not specifically discussed in these pages, it must be noted that a few high quality publications have appeared recently in the areas of Irish history and culture.

Where there are weaknesses in Irish writing and publishing for children some of them may be attributed to the fact that there is little public critical debate or discussion in this area. Most sections of the media pay little attention to children's books. When books for young people are reviewed, frequently the discussion tends to take the form of a plot summary to which is added some bland comment. This is in part due to the slight allocation of space in some publications for reviews, which does not allow reviewers to extend their comments. The number of reviewers' voices heard is limited, and at times those reviewing do not have a sufficient knowledge of what might be expected from a children's or a young adult's book. There is a particular lacuna in the area of picture book reviewing, where reviews frequently consist of a synopsis of the story and pay little attention to the visual qualities of the book. That the reviewer will often know the reviewed may at times impose restraints. Thus more constructively critical reviewing from outside Ireland would be healthy.

While there are areas for concern in Irish writing and publishing for children, there is much about which to be positive. Design and overall production values have risen. The fact that Ireland can sustain two well-regarded children's book awards is positive, although book awards is one area where more discussion by both adults and children may be generated. The number of Irish-published books in translation and the variety of languages into which they are translated is impressive, and signifies the remarkable developments in Irish writing and publishing which have taken place in the relatively recent past.

To the contributors who cheerfully, willingly and unstintingly wrote for *Big Guide 2* considerable thanks are due. Their dedication and enthusiasm in the face of tight deadlines have considerably eased the editorial burden.

The Editors

BOOKS, CLASSROOMS AND CURRICULA

ENCOURAGING THE RELUCTANT READER – PRIMARY

By 'reluctant' I mean the primary schoolchild who can read but chooses not to. If asked why, the response is likely to be that reading is boring, or that it takes too long, or that there are better things to do, or that it's tiring, but, grudgingly, it might be alright as a second choice activity!

In 1996 the National Centre for Research in Children's Literature (NCRCL) at Roehampton Institute, London, published the findings of a survey of the leisure reading habits of young people. A total of 8,834 young people between the ages of four and sixteen were questioned, and the result is the most comprehensive British study yet in this area. (It is envisaged that a comparable study will take place in Ireland, under the aegis of CBI, in the near future.) This study showed that across all age groups surveyed, nearly twice as many boys as girls regarded themselves as 'reluctant' readers. Interestingly, this has not always been the case. Kimberly Reynolds, Director of the NCRCL, notes that over a hundred years ago the situation was reversed, and the problem then was how to stop boys reading!

Over time the content of boys' books has changed to become increasingly preoccupied with action-packed stories with little emotional or intellectual content. Reynolds argues that it may well be that the increasingly macho content of these books didn't sustain boys sufficiently and they lapsed into reluctance. If Reynolds's hypothesis is correct, we must guard against replicating past mistakes by ensuring that the books we recommend do not disappoint.

Michael Rosen, a well-known poet who writes for children, argues from his research that boys do read but tend not to choose fiction. Rosen sees the 'domestic-isation' of fiction, with its high emotional demands on the reader, as a turn-off for boys.

Cup Final Kid, illustrated by Jeff Cummins.

So when selecting books to entice reluctant and predominantly (though not exclusively) male readers, what should we bear in mind? Here it is interesting to return to the NCRCL research. It confirmed that boys more than girls:

- ► are influenced by the book cover
- ► choose hobby-related books
- ► read more comics
- ► prefer to read about male rather than female characters
- ► like adventure, funny and horror stories (in that order)
- ► dislike poetry
- ► prefer information books (hobby-related, mainly sport and technology)
- ► like to access information on CD-ROM

▶ like books with lists of facts

▶ are attracted to books with lots of pictures

So what Irish titles are available to tempt the taste buds? The intervention that occurs when children begin to tackle texts other than their class readers can be critical. This is the time to encourage children to view themselves as readers and to view reading as a pleasurable and worthwhile pastime. To achieve this they must be exposed to attractively packaged books with appropriately pitched text, theme and illustration. Since the first *Big Guide to Irish Children's Books* was published, there has been a proliferation of Irish-published books for beginner and newly independent readers. Poolbeg Press publish *Goldcrest Readers* for beginners, followed by the *Wren* series for emerging readers. O'Brien Press publish the *Panda* series for beginners and the *Flyers* series as a 'second step' in reading. Both Mentor and Mercier Press have a series labelled 'suitable for the six to nine year olds'. The common features of these series are brightly coloured covers, short blocks of large print and cartoon-

The Children of Nuala, illustrated by Amanda Harvey.

type, black-and-white illustrations on most or all pages. Chapters are introduced in the books for emerging readers. In general, the authors are established writers, many of whom already write for a variety of age groups. This development in publishing for the youngest readers is to be welcomed. Ireland now has a rich and varied diet with which to nurture emerging readers.

The difficulty for the author, in particular when writing for the beginner reader, is to create a story that is in tune with the cognitive and emotional development of the child (hooked, as many are, on Pokémon and The Simpsons), but expressed in phonically regular words and short sentences. It seems to me that most of the books published for the beginner reader are pitched a little too high and are too difficult at a time when the child really needs to experience success. Morag Styles uses the terms 'spare and rich' to describe the prose in Ted Hughes's *The Iron Man*. This spare but rich style seems to be very appropriate to reluctant readers, who need texts that challenge, engage and enrich without being too difficult in terms of readability.

It is encouraging to see books for young readers making an appearance in the list of Bisto award-winners. In 1998, Sam McBratney's *Bert's Wonderful News* (illustrated by Brita Granström) and Pat Boran's *All the Way from China* (illustrated by Stewart Curry) were shortlisted. *Fierce Milly* by Marilyn McLaughlin (illustrated by Leonie Shearing) won the 1999 Eilís Dillon Memorial Award for best newcomer.

The *Blue Bananas* and *Yellow Bananas* series for beginners, published by Mammoth, are different in that they have colour pictures throughout. Irish author Maddie Stewart's *Peg* (illustrated by Bee Willey), in the *Blue Bananas* series, has a simple repetitive rhyming text that tells a warm-hearted, folksy tale in a way which is accessible and worthwhile.

Now that the child can read, it is important to sustain the facility. It is at this stage of childhood (second/third class) that the child's range of activity broadens out away from home and classroom, and where peer philosophy begins to dominate. Without concerted adult intervention, enjoyment of reading can easily be quashed and skills hard won can be lost. Short and funny is a good place to start when selecting books. Herbie Brennan's *Eddie the Duck* (illustrated by Ann Kronheimer) is about a wisecracking duck who is an amalgam of all the trench-coated New York detectives we've ever seen in any movie. 'A cool blonde sidled up. "Want some company, big boy?" she asked.' Well, Eddie is a duck so it's all very tongue in cheek and innocent, but children will appreciate the movie-genre reference and be amused and flattered by it. In terms of readability, the text and plot are undemanding and this book could be great fun for reluctant readers to read aloud – hiding behind their best Mafia accents. Another very funny book is Roddy Doyle's first book for children, *The Giggler Treatment*. The fact that the author has oodles of street cred as author of *The Commitments*, *The Snapper* and *The Van* should enhance the attraction of this book. *The Irish Legends* series published by Blackwater Press is accurately described as 'wild and wacky'. These are retellings of well-known legends in comic form and are highly entertaining and very accessible. Each page is laced with speech bubbles, interspersed with short pieces of simple text and generously sprinkled with cartoon-type pictures. Aislinn O'Loughlin is a writer to look out for. Her titles include *Shak and the Beanstalk*, *The Emperor's Birthday Suit* and *A Right Royal Pain*. She wrote these books when she was teenager, and they have a light, humorous touch and a quirkiness and sharpness that should strike a chord with reluctant readers aged eight and up.

Shak & the Beanstalk, illustrated by Marie-Louise Fitzpatrick.

Eddie the Duck, illustrated by Ann Kronheimer.

Martin Waddell's appeal for reluctant readers is that he gets straight to the point – no long preambles or elaborate scene-setting. He is a wonderful, unsentimental storyteller who never uses two words where one will do. His *River Rock* stories, about Little Obie growing up in an isolated cabin at Cold Creek, sound so authentic in incident and relationships that we feel enriched for having met Obie. Waddell's football stories have the same authenticity. In *Napper goes for Goal*, the reader knows that the writer understands schoolboy football: the moves, the psyching out, the hacking, the bravado, the tension. *Cup Final Kid*, also by Waddell, is a football story for younger readers, while Peter Regan's *Riverside* series would be enjoyed by older readers. Sam McBratney is another great storyteller whose books are very accessible. He has a magical touch and his breezy, confident style will keep the reader enthralled. McBratney has written for a wide age range, from the award-winning *Guess How Much I Love You?* for younger readers to the award-winning *The Chieftain's Daughter*, for older readers, which is surely a classic.

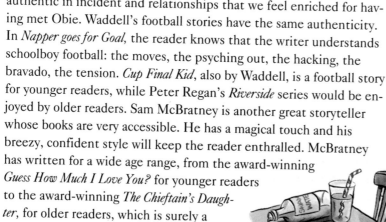

Picture books are a must and there should be a clear and general under-standing in the classroom that they are not the sole preserve of younger readers. Every child should have access to books illustrated by such skilful and varied illustrators as P.J. Lynch (*The Christmas Miracle of Jonathan Toomey*), Marie-Louise Fitzpatrick (*The Long March*), Niamh Sharkey (*Tales of Wisdom and Wonder*) and Jane Ray (*The Story of the Creation*), to name but a few.

Research shows that boys like information books, but, as yet, this need is not being met to any great extent by Irish publishers. Poolbeg have published a 'faction' series by Arthur McKeown, which comprises stories woven around historic events, such as the Battle of the Somme or the sinking of the *Titanic*. These are labelled *Easy Readers*, which they are, but the designation might be off-putting for an older reader. Nevertheless they are clearly presented, have frequent breaks in text, are liberally illustrated, have reasonably large print, contain lots of factual information and have an accessible feel. Mercier have published books by Ellen Regan on famous ship mysteries, such as the *Titanic* and the *Lusitania*. Again, I would quibble with the age labelling. These are tagged for readers aged six to nine years, which is a bit optimistic both in terms of readability and subject matter. (It would have been an interesting development if both these series had been produced as straight information books without the narrative element.)

Books to dip into in order to extract nuggets of information with which to impress your friends seem to appeal to boys. Pierce Feirtear's *Brainstorm* series, published annually by Blackwater, contains facts, quizzes, puzzles and true life stories, and their variety and challenge should appeal to those who feel defeated by large chunks of uninterrupted text. Dipping into *Kids Can Cook* by Sarah Webb can yield very tangible benefits – something nice to eat! But there is still a huge gap in the information book market. Where can Irish children read hard facts about their GAA sporting heroes, their soccer stars, their world-acclaimed singers, musicians, writers, actors, sports personalities, their environment, their heritage and themselves at the beginning of a new millennium?

Terry Deary's immensely popular *Horrible Histories* series (sold over one million copies to date) now includes a special edition on Ireland. Serious historians may cringe at the 'History in sound bites' approach, and the oversimplification of complex and sensitive issues might leave some adults squirming in their seats. But what we are trying to do in our classrooms is encourage independent readers who have developed their own personal tastes, so this series should be available simply because it is so popular. A million children can't be wrong!

The male respondents to the NCRCL survey were so anti-poetry (terms like 'rubbish', 'crap' and 'very soppy' are pretty unambiguous!) that I thought long and hard about including it. I can only conclude that the respondents cannot have been exposed to a broad range of modern and classic poetry in a conducive environment.

Television tie-ins are immediately interesting to children, but we must make sure that the book lives up to the hype, that the content doesn't disappoint.

For children who find reading slow and tiring, videos, audio tapes and CDs may be a welcome option. The choice here is limited. *Under the Hawthorn Tree* by Marita Conlon-McKenna and *The Secret of the Ruby Ring* by Yvonne MacGrory are available on video. The incomparable storyteller Liz Weir's *Boom Chicka Boom* is available on CD and tape, and *The Boyne Valley Book of Irish Legends*, narrated by well-known personalities, is available on tape. They are all available in local bookshops.

To encourage and support the reluctant reader it is necessary to make available to them the widest possible range of satisfying reading material in all appropriate genres and media. But that alone is not enough. In addition we must:

▶ Keep ourselves informed about children's books and libraries (see resources at the back of this Guide).

▶ Read aloud and give time for silent reading – give time and advice on book selection.

▶ Mount attractive displays featuring books, authors, genres or illustrators (contact publishers for promotional material, and contact Poetry Ireland for information on their Writers in Schools scheme).

▶ Encourage every child in our classes to record all leisure reading, not just novels, in a simply tabulated reading diary. Do not draw comparisons between readers. Dispense bribes if necessary – something small and edible works wonders!

▶ Timetable small group discussions entitled 'Book Talk'. These discussions could be fuelled by the content of the reading diaries. Pool ideas about good books. Peer recommendation is much more powerful than anything you can advise.

▶ Teach children their way around books and libraries, giving them accurate terminology.

▶ Arrange regular book festivals to include author visits, book creation, storytelling, etc. Hype them up, get help and don't be shy about vigorous PR!

Finally, never underestimate the power of your own enthusiasm for reading to motivate your class. It does rub off, even if they do think you are mildly eccentric! Remember, all it takes is one book to turn a reluctant reader into a committed reader. The trick is to find that one book and make the match. Good luck!

REFERENCES

→ *Books for Keeps*, issues no.106 and no.114.
→ Coghlan, V. and Keenan, C. (eds). *The Big Guide to Irish Children's Books*. Dublin: ICBT, 1996.
→ Maby, Deborah. 'Boys Read Less Than Girls: True or False?' In *Books For Keeps*, No. 106, September 1997.
→ Styles, Morag. 'Ted Hughes, 1930–1998'. In *Books For Keeps*, No. 114, January 1999.
→ *Young People's Reading at the End of the Century*. Children's Literature Research Centre, Roehampton Institute, London. British Library Report 14. London: Book Trust, 1996.

RECOMMENDED TITLES

Pat Boran/Stewart Curry (illus.)
ALL THE WAY FROM CHINA
Poolbeg Press

As part of her schoolwork, eight-year-old Shelly has to write a letter to her Chinese pen-pal, Tomi Wong. Though normally fluent, Shelly has difficulty composing a letter as she is feeling unhappy and disoriented since she and her mother moved to the city, leaving their father behind in Tralee. Finally she writes, but pretends she still lives in Kerry because that's where her heart is and she cannot come to terms with her changed circumstances. With the gentle support of her mother and her own intelligence and literary talents, she begins to come to terms with her new situation, and there is a twist at the end.

Not just reading practice, this is a challenging and worthwhile read told in simple language. It is in the Poolbeg *Wren* series.

Roddy Doyle/Brian Ajhar (illus.)
THE GIGGLER TREATMENT
Scholastic Children's Books

When adults are mean, dishonest, rude, unfair or domineering towards children, they get the Giggler treatment. This means that the Gigglers – small furry creatures – will place dog poo where the guilty party will step on it as a punishment for their meanness. This book has definite appeal to a reluctant reader: it's short, has an attractive cover, lively illustrations, large print, short paragraphs, direct speech and a definite Yuck! factor. But it is much more than this. It is an empowering and sympathetic book. The reader is literally given a voice and is allowed to argue with the author. The author makes a point of suspending the action at intervals to connect with the

The Giggler Treatment, illustrated by Brian Ajhar.

reader to make sure he/she is following the story. Encouragement is offered in the form of a surprise promised at the end of the chapter. One chapter is only one word long! There is an off-the-wall, Father Ted-ish kind of humour, a humour that is not nastily or cynically anti-adult in the mode of Roald Dahl, but is sympathetic and generous. Highly recommended.

Malachy Doyle/Amanda Harvey (illus.)
THE CHILDREN OF NUALA
Faber and Faber

This reads like a traditional folk tale, which it isn't, but it borrows very successfully from the story of the Children of Lir. It comes about that a broken-hearted woman marries a frozen-hearted man. Now there's a challenging theme! Disaster follows and the man, blinded by his jealousy of the woman's children, turns them into swans. Over time, the gentle routines of farm life and the love of a good woman melt the man's icy heart and he becomes truly human. But first he must throw off the evil influence of his cruel father. As is usual in all folk tales, the story comes to a satisfying conclusion. I recommend this book because it tells a tough, uncompromising tale in simple language while still managing to capture the passion and beauty of the story. The dark, brooding presence of the man is exceptionally well caught in the black-and-white line drawings. Don't let the cover put you off – the story is more robust than the illustration would suggest.

Frank Murphy/Kieron Black (illus.)
THE BIG FIGHT
O'Brien Press

This is a simple retelling of the story of the Táin Bó Cuailgne. It is a fast-paced, exciting story about Queen Maeve's overriding greed and the resulting carnage. The text is liberally illustrated with strangely menacing characters. The author does not patronise the reader by dumbing-down the traditional story with all its violence and intrigue, and the attention to detail in an effort to remain faithful to the original is truly impressive. As a story, it has stood the test of time and should be a satisfying and fascinating read for an emerging reader. This is No. 3 in the *Flyer* series.

The Big Fight,
illustrated by
Kieron Black.

Jane Ray
THE STORY OF THE CREATION
O'Brien Press

The text for this book is adapted from the Book of Genesis and retains all of the simple, elegant, dignified language of the Bible. Children's familiarity with the story and the rhythmic cadence of the narration should assist the reading. Children with a particular interest in nature, religion or art will be drawn to this book. For adults, its most striking feature is its absolutely stunning illustration; it won the Smarties Book Prize in 1992. The rich golden pages are teeming with life and variety and the illustrations appeal both aesthetically and scientifically. But I have a sneaking suspicion that beautifully illustrated books such as this appeal much more to adults than to children, so do not be disappointed if it is rejected. Given the increasingly multicultural profile of our schools, before recommending this book we need to be aware of the perspective of the reader and caution should be exercised. But despite these two caveats, this exquisite book should be in every classroom.
(See also: *Noah's Ark* and *The Happy Prince* by Jane Ray.)

The Story of the Creation,
illustrated by Jane Ray.

Martin Waddell/ Susie Jenkin-Pearse (illus.)
THE GET-AWAY HEN
Puffin Books

Martin Waddell/David Parkins (illus.)
THE PERILS OF LORD REGGIE PARROT
Walker Books

Martin Waddell/Sophie Williams (illus.)
THE ORCHARD BOOK OF GHOSTLY STORIES
Orchard Books

I selected these three books by Martin Waddell to demonstrate his suitability across a wide age range. *The Get-away Hen* is an ideal text for a beginner reader. Most of the individual words are ones with which a child will already be familiar, but they are skilfully woven to create an interesting and engaging story that can be appreciated on many different levels. The illustrations are solid and reassuring, in keeping with the personality of the main character, Brown Hen. A technical problem causes all systems to fail in the battery farm and Brown Hen makes a break for freedom in order to find out what life is about. Her optimism and innate sense of self-preservation bring her to a better life where she finds the ingredient that has been missing from her life so far: the need to love and be loved. Rich and spare at its best!

The Perils of Lord Reggie Parrot is an amusing book for the emerging reader. Lord Reggie falls on hard times when his wicked aunt tries to trick him out of his money. He is assisted by poor Skinny Atkins, and eventually all ends happily and fortunes are restored. But the humour is produced by the constraints imposed by Reggie's and Skinny's differing social standing. Skinny Atkins cannot speak his mind because 'there are things you don't do if you are poor'. This is his constant litany as he acts as dogsbody and saviour to the hapless and pompous Lord Reggie. Because the author allows us in on the joke, the reader can see where the real power resides and enjoy a condescending little snigger at Lord Reggie's expense.

Ghostly Stories is a collection of seven original ghost stories (and one other based on William Allingham's poem 'The Fairies'). They read like traditional stories from a long oral tradition. The language is repetitive and musical with internal rhyme reminiscent of Irish syllabic verse. It has been written to be read aloud and you might

The Orchard Book
of Ghostly Stories,
illustrated by
Sophie Williams.

encourage reluctant readers to do just this – if they dress up as seanchaithe. The stories are thought-provoking rather than scary and should produce rich discussion. It is appropriate that the collection is dedicated to Liz Weir, a magical storyteller herself. The book is sumptuously illustrated with full-page colour spreads of evocative, gauzy paintings.

Arthur McKeown/Eoin Stephens (illus.)
BATTLE OF THE SOMME
Poolbeg Press

This is the story of a County Antrim farmer, Roy, who leaves his wife and young family in 1914 to fight with the British Army. He is posted to France and is not 'home by Christmas' as widely anticipated. Instead he finds himself enduring inhuman conditions in the trenches until finally he loses his legs in an explosion at the Battle of the Somme and dies alone, screaming in agony. This is an uncompromisingly bleak book, as is entirely appropriate for such a serious period in our history. The story is told in a direct, matter-of- fact tone in short, easy to read sentences and short chapters. The chilly black-and- white illustrations on every page add to the sombre atmosphere. The final section, where Roy's grandson and his family visit France, is effective in linking these horrific events to the present day. The cover and content should have strong boy-appeal. (See also: *Famine* and *Titanic* by the same author.)

Herbie Brennan/Louise Voce (illus.)
LETTERS FROM A MOUSE
Walker Books

this book is a series of letters from s. mouse of hayes bros. ltd., office suppliers, to a customer. at night, when the hayes brothers have gone home, s. mouse, an actual mouse, takes over the office and

composes these letters on a computer. He shows scant regard for punctuation and even less for capital letters, very much in the style of this review. eventually he discovers the CAPS LOCK KEY AND FOR A WHILE ALL COMMUNICATION IS IN CAPITALS. THE STORYLINE IS THAT HE FOILS THE ESCAPE OF ROBBERS ONLY MINUTES BEFORE THEY WERE SET TO MAKE THEIR ESCAPE TO SOUTH AMERICA. This is a lively read that doesn't take itself too seriously and its novel presentation may attract reluctant readers, in particular those who are similarly challenged in terms of punctuation!

Peter Regan/Terry Myler (illus.)
RIVERSIDE,
THE CROKE PARK CONSPIRACY
The Children's Press

This is a light-hearted, uplifting book about four teenagers, Jimmy, Chippy, Mad Victor and Flintstone, who play soccer for Riverside Boys, Bray, County Wicklow. The trouble begins when the council gives the local GAA club permission to use the pitch in the People's Park, which is where Riverside play. In an effort to get even with their arch-enemy, Councillor O'Leary, the boys agree to play in her GAA tournament. They know, but she doesn't, that they are overage and their plan is to reveal this at a strategic time in order to discredit her publicly. But things don't go quite as planned. The story is easy to read and progresses at a satisfactory pace. We get occasional glimpses of another side of the boys' lives: Jimmy is an aspiring writer who de-

spises his father; Mad Victor lives with his alcoholic uncles; Chippy is a shrewd and unscrupulous business man. But these realities are presented unsentimentally, almost as asides, and essentially this is a funny football story. This is one of the *Riverside* series of football stories.

Riverside,
The Croke Park Conspiracy,
illustrated by Terry Myler.

Larry O'Loughlin/John Leonard (illus.)
THE GOBÁN SAOR
Blackwater Press

This is a comic retelling of the traditional tale of the Gobán Saor, the master builder. The Gobán Saor builds a fine house for a rich man. The rich man tries to cheat him out of his pay. The disgruntled builder begins to dismantle the house. The rich man pleads with him to finish the house and he agrees, for a fee ten times the original price. The Gobán Saor rides off, but not before he discredits the rich man in front of all the visiting dignitaries. Clearly a man not to be crossed! This book is bursting with life and vitality. Accomplished cartoons, speech bubbles, short pieces of text, variety in text size and page layout all combine to provide a lively, easy read. (Part of a series.)

The Gobán Saor,
illustrated by
John Leonard.

TITLES REFERRED TO IN ARTICLE AND IN RECOMMENDED LIST

A SELECTION OF SERIES FOR BEGINNER AND EMERGING READERS (6–9)

→ Mammoth: *Blue Bananas, Yellow Bananas, Mammoth Story Books*.
→ Mentor Press: No series title, labelled 6–9.
→ Mercier Press: No series title, labelled 6–9.
→ O'Brien Press: *Pandas, Flyers,* Yellow Flag books.
→ Poolbeg Press: *Goldcrests, Wrens, Easy Readers*.
→ Puffin Books: *Ready Steady Read, Young Puffin, Colour Young Puffin*.
→ Walker Books: *Sprinters, Racers, Walker Story Books*.

A SELECTION OF SERIES FOR THE OLDER BUT RELUCTANT READER (8+)

→ Blackwater Press: *The Irish Legends* series, *Brainstorms*.
→ Children's Press: *Riverside* series.
→ O'Brien Press: Red Flag books.
→ Poolbeg Press: *Scream, Shiver, Chiller, Nightmares* (collections of short stories).
→ Scholastic Children's Books: *Horrible Histories*.
→ Wolfhound Press: *Screamers*.

TITLES

→ Boran, Pat/Curry, Stewart (illus.). *All the Way from China.* Dublin: Poolbeg, 1998. 1-85371-853-X Reading Age Guide 7–9
→ Brennan, Herbie/Voce, Louise (illus.). *Letters from a Mouse.* London: Walker Books, 1997. 0-74454-761-X Reading Age Guide 8+
→ Brennan, Herbie/Kronheimer, Ann (illus.). *Eddie the Duck.* London: Puffin, 1998. 0-14-038632-7 Reading Age Guide 8+. See also: *Eddie and the Bad Egg.*
→ Doyle, Malachy/Harvey, Amanda (illus.). *The Children of Nuala.* London: Faber and Faber, 1998. 0-571-19316-1 Reading Age Guide 8+
→ Doyle, Roddy/Ajhar, Brian (illus.). *The Giggler Treatment.* London: Scholastic Children's Books, 2000. 0-439-99794-1 Reading Age Guide 8+
→ Fitzpatrick, Marie-Louise. *The Long March.* Dublin: Wolfhound Press, 1998. 0-86327-644-X Reading Age Guide 8+

→ Hughes, Ted/Adamson, George (illus.). *The Iron Man*. London: Faber and Faber, 1968. 0-571-14149-8 Reading Age Guide 10+

→ McBratney, Sam/Granström, Brita (illus.). *Bert's Wonderful News*. London: Walker Books, 1998. 0-74456-396-8 Reading Age Guide 7–9

→ McBratney, Sam/Jeram, Anita (illus.). *Guess How Much I Love You?* Dublin: O'Brien Press, 1994. 0-86278-390-9 Reading Age Guide 6–9

→ McBratney, Sam. *The Chieftain's Daughter*. Dublin: O'Brien Press, 1993. 0-86278-338-0 Reading Age Guide 10+

→ McKeown, Arthur/Stephens, Eoin (illus.). *Battle of the Somme*. Dublin: Poolbeg Press, 1999. 1-85371-931-5 Reading Age Guide 9+

→ McLaughlin, Marylin/Shearing, Leonie (illus.). *Fierce Milly*. London: Mammoth, 1999. 0-74973-731-X Reading Age Guide 7–9

→ Murphy, Frank/Black, Kieron (illus.). *The Big Fight*. Dublin: O'Brien Press, 1999. 0-86278-451-4 Reading Age Guide 7–9

→ O'Loughlin, Aislinn/Fitzpatrick, Marie-Louise (illus.). *The Emperor's Birthday Suit*. Dublin: Wolfhound Press, 1997. 0-86327-597-4 Reading Age Guide 8+

→ O'Loughlin, Aislinn/Fitzpatrick, Marie-Louise (illus.). *A Right Royal Pain*. Dublin: Wolfhound Press, 1996. 0-86327-514-1 Reading Age Guide 8+

→ O'Loughlin, Aislinn/Fitzpatrick, Marie-Louise (illus.). *Shak and the Beanstalk*. Dublin: Wolfhound Press, 1997. 0-86327-574-5 Reading Age Guide 8+

→ O'Loughlin, Larry/Leonard, John (illus.). *The Gobán Saor*. Dublin: Blackwater Press, 1997. 0-86121-867-1 Reading Age Guide 8+ (See: other titles in the series.)

→ Ray, Jane. *The Story of the Creation*. Dublin: O'Brien Press, 1996. 0-86278-483-2 Reading Age Guide 8+

→ Regan, Ellen/Dobson, Peter (illus.). *The Titanic and The Mystery Ship*. Dublin: Mercier Press, 1999. 1-85635-256-0 Reading Age Guide 8+

→ Regan, Ellen/Dobson, Peter (illus.). *The Mystery of the Lusitania*. Dublin: Mercier Press, 1999. 1-85635-255-2 Reading Age Guide 8+

→ Regan, Peter/Myler, Terry (illus.). *Riverside, The Croke Park Conspiracy*. Dublin: The Children's Press, 1997. 1-90173-704-7 Reading Age Guide 10+ (See: other titles in the series.)

→ Stewart, Maddie/Willey, Bee (illus.). *Peg*. London: Mammoth. 1999. 0-74973-260-1 Reading Age Guide 6–8

→ Sharkey, Niamh (illus)/Lupton, Hugh. *Tales of Wisdom and Wonder*. Bath: Barefoot Books, 1998. 1-90122-315-9 Reading Age Guide 8+

→ Waddell, Martin /Jenkin-Pearse, Susie (illus.). *The Get-away Hen*. London: Puffin Books, 1993. 0-14-036955-4 Reading Age Guide 6–8

→ Waddell, Martin/Parkins, David (illus.). *The Perils of Lord Reggie Parrot*. London: Walker Books, 1997. 0-74-455406-3 Reading Age Guide 7–9

→ Waddell, Martin/Williams, Sophie (illus.).*The Orchard Book Of Ghostly Stories*. London: Orchard Books, 2000. 1-86039-421-3 Reading Age Guide 9+

→ Waddell, Martin/Cummins, Jeff (illus.). *Cup Final Kid*. London: Walker Books, 1996. 0-7445-5240-0 Reading Age Guide 7–9

→ Waddell, Martin/Lennox, Elsie (illus.). *Little Obie and the Kidnap*. London, Walker Books, 1991. 0-7445-5450-0 Reading Age Guide 8+

→ Waddell, Martin/Mitchell, Barrie (illus.). *Napper Goes for Goal*. London: Puffin Books, 1981. 0-14-031318-4 Reading Age Guide 8+

→ Webb, Sarah/Myler, Terry (illus.). *Kids Can Cook*. Dublin: The Children's Press, 1997. 1-901737-03-9 Reading Age Guide 8+

→ Wojciechowski, Susan/Lynch, P.J. (illus.). *The Christmas Miracle of Jonathan Toomey*. Dublin: Poolbeg Press, 1995. 1-85371-535-2 Reading Age Guide 8+

Peg,
illustrated by Bee Willey

REAL BOOKS IN THE LOWER PRIMARY CLASSROOM

Why do we teach children to read and write? There are two, radically different answers to that question. The first is because we want them to grow up in possession of a highly practical, useful skill, which will help them to get ahead in life. They will be able to read menus, the small print on life insurance forms, fill out their car tax renewals, apply for jobs, go through bank statements. The second reason for teaching children to read is because we would like them to have access to a source of unlimited knowledge and moving aesthetic experiences. We want the child to be able to absorb new concepts, to grow in understanding of the world, to see things with the eyes of other people, to reflect on and understand himself.

When the child enters school, we set about equipping him to travel to this magical kingdom of stories. We work hard in the early weeks on pre-reading. We do word-recognition activities and sequencing activities and exercises to develop left/right co-ordination. Any infant teacher will tell you how important this work is. But if the work is not balanced by daily reading of stories and picture books, we are in danger of overwhelming the child before he can make the journey. He stands at the edge of a long, winding road, the distant kingdom just visible in the misty mountains – but he can't move. He is weighed down with word bags and word boxes, workbooks and pre-readers, a rucksack strapped to his back containing books one to twenty in the reading scheme. Not to mention his dismay at the sight of little Jenny or Joe, trudging on, ten paces ahead of him.

We, as teachers, need to keep the magical kingdom firmly in our sights. We must show the child the enjoyment that can be had from the written word. From his earliest days in school he should be surrounded by real books. I use the term 'real books' to mean any book, story, picture book or poetry book that was written purely for its own sake – not to practice the twenty words in stage one of the scheme. As E.B. White, author of *Charlotte's Web* and *Stuart Little*, wrote, children 'accept, almost without question, anything you present them with, as long as it is presented honestly, fearlessly and clearly.' Later in the same essay he continues: 'Children ... love words that give them a hard time, provided they are in a context that absorbs their attention.'

So, what kind of real books will we read with the children? We need to find

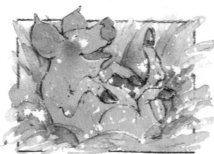

The Pig in the Pond,
illustrated by
Jill Barton.

good stories – stories that reflect what life is like for the child. A good story will relate to all aspects of the child's personality, not just the positive, 'sunny' bits. It will show a hero (or someone the child can identify with) overcoming obstacles, finding solutions. If we read meaningful books with children we are saying: you may be small, you may be powerless, you may have this or that fear or anxiety, but you will get there, you are unique and important.

Teachers use readers with good reason: we want to teach necessary reading skills. The publishers of these readers endeavour to make the books attractive, colourful, entertaining and realistic. But some readers have been compiled to teach reading, irrespective of meaning. Some have nothing to say about life with a capital 'L'. Unfortunately, a large number of these readers reflect an artificial world where the worst thing that happens is the family dog runs off with a cuddly toy. These are 'safe' stories. They say nothing to us as humans about our fears, our limits or our dreams.

Reading is a fantastic skill – one of the most important skills a human being will achieve. But the acquisition of this amazing skill can become devalued when what the child has learned to read adds nothing of importance to his life. This sets the child up for disappointment and failure. How does he know how valuable this skill is when he has no proof? And the problem is that we, as teachers, don't have much time before the 'off' switch is flicked. We must provide the proof quickly, as it is the nature of children to be impatient. In fact, it is part of the human condition, but as adults we train ourselves (with varying degrees of success) to see the big picture, to wait, to practice. We learn not to expect instant gratification, though it can be a difficult lesson. Imagine if you were required to learn Russian every day for the next five years because you are going to go on a fantastic holiday there at some distant time in the future, when you're older, when you've saved up the fare, when you've learned enough of the language. How long would you stick at it?

We cannot expect children to absorb the concept that learning to read will enrich their lives at some future time in some other place. Yes, let them practice the skills required using whatever well thought out approach the teacher chooses, but all the time, and I mean daily, we must read them great stories. Stories that entertain, that arouse curiosity, stories that are fun to listen to, stories that enrich their lives. Once we have decided to open the door of the magical kingdom, the possibilities for exploration within the classroom situation are endless. Firstly, however, we need to ask ourselves what we are looking for when choosing books to use in class. A vast amount of children's books is published each year and it can seem an impossible task to choose books which you know will 'work' with your class. In their excellent and practical book, *Picture Books for the Literacy Hour*, Guy Merchant and Huw Thomas list five criteria on which to assess picture books:

▶ 1. Visual appeal
▶ 2. Interest level

▶ 3. The book as a story
▶ 4. Use of language
▶ 5. The book's values

Depending on the particular needs/interests of the children in your class, these criteria could be arranged in any order of importance. My own experience of teaching in a disadvantaged area meant that I looked for books with a high interest level and strong visual impact, which related directly to the children's lives. I occasionally found that storytime required De Niro-like method-acting and physical energy as I tried to keep the interest-level high for the children, some of whom had no family tradition of reading and no real experience of active listening. Remember, we are competing with TV, video, playstation, etcetera, so choose carefully.

So, you have chosen great stories for your class, you've ensured that the children were sitting comfortably on soft cushions in the reading corner, you've read the text (putting on all the voices and singing where required!), the pictures have been discussed and analysed and the book is closed. What next?

Firstly, it is most important to realise that you've already done your job. You have brought the children with you into the magical kingdom. If you never look at that story again, it won't matter, it has lived in their minds. However, many teachers find that the enthusiasm and interest sparked by a story can be sustained and expanded to great effect over different subject areas and a variety of activities for some days. If you do plan to use a book in this manner, then a formal structure or outline is useful. You may like to look at a programme, such as *Real Books for Schools* (O'Brien Press), which suggests an explorative approach and follow-up activities across the curriculum for a wide range of novels and picture books. In the aforementioned *Picture Books for the Literacy Hour*, the authors give a photocopiable sheet that shows their way of looking at what a book has to offer in the way of text, sentence and word levels. You may decide to work out an exploration of your own and record your findings for future reference. As long as you are being led by the interest of the children and the relevance of the story, you will not fail. And as long as you are reading stories, you cannot fail in teaching reading. That's what it's all about. You are showing children the way to the magical kingdom.

REFERENCES

→ E.B. White, 'The Art of the Essay'. *Paris Review*, Vol.48, Autumn 1969
→ Merchant, Guy and Thomas, Huw (eds). *Picture Books for the Literacy Hour*. London: David Fulton Publishers, 1999. 1-85346-627-1

Izzy and Skunk,
illustrated by
Marie-Louise Fitzpatrick.

RECOMMENDED TITLES FOR JUNIOR CLASSES

Marie-Louise Fitzpatrick
IZZY AND SKUNK
Blackwater Press and
David & Charles Children's Books

Izzy has many fears: spiders, the dark, falling down and more besides. Luckily, though, she has Skunk to protect her, and when he's there her worries subside. One day, Skunk disappears and Izzy sets off to find him, thus facing her fears alone. A beautifully illustrated hardback that addresses the very real fears of the young child.

Martin Waddell
LITTLE MO, SMALL BEAR LOST,
FARMER DUCK, AMY SAID,
WELL DONE, LITTLE BEAR,
ROSIE'S BABIES, WHO DO YOU LOVE?
THE BIG BIG SEA
Walker Books

THE PIG IN THE POND
O'Brien Press and Walker Books (big book)

There is hardly an important psychological theme in childhood that has not invited the masterly touch of Martin Waddell. Add to that the brilliant artists/illustrators he has collaborated with and you'll find that virtually any Martin Waddell picture book is a feast for the eyes, the intellect and the soul! Teachers who are planning their SPHE scheme for the year should look at the themes explored here.

In *Little Mo*, the heroine takes some faltering steps towards independence, finds herself surrounded by the boisterous Big Ones, then learns, through perseverance, the joy of being alone.

Small Bear Lost also deals with the theme of being alone, but this time Small Bear is lost and lonely. He has to travel a long way to get home, but after low points and heart-rending pictures, he makes it.

In *Amy Said*, we have an exploration of making mistakes, making a mess and just being little. The beauty of this book is the warmth of knowing that Amy and her brother are in Gran's house and 'Gran never gets cross!'

In *Well Done, Little Bear* we also have a message of reassurance. Beautifully illustrated, with our familiar Little Bear on an adventure with Big Bear. He bounces and leaps, full of confidence until – *Splosh*! He falls in the river. But Big Bear is there to pull him out. 'I'll be there when you need me,' he says.

When a new baby arrives in the family, there's bound to be worries and sibling jealousy. *Rosie's Babies* addresses this issue with gorgeous, true-to-life illustrations and shows that everybody has their special place in the family unit.

The exuberant *Pig in the Pond* endorses originality, positive thinking and daring to be different. It shows the child the rewards of not following the herd, of challenging the system. (It is now also available in big book format, which does justice to Jill Barton's marvellous pictures.)

Both *Who Do You Love*? and *The Big Big Sea* show us the way life should be. *Who Do You Love*? is a wonderful bedtime book. A little kitten plays her favourite bedtime game of listing those she loves. It almost invariably invites the reader to play the same game, with cuddly consequences! *The Big Big Sea* describes a moonlit walk that a mother and her daughter take by the sea. It is a magical book that captures a perfect time of beauty, peace and love. As Mum says: 'Remember this time. It's the way life should be.'

The marvellous *Farmer Duck* is now available as a big book. It has also been published in Story Play format, re-played by Vivian French. This would work well as a drama activity for juniors and would really bring the text alive. The lines are colour-coded on each page, so 'finding your bit' is made easy.

Flora McDonnell
I LOVE BOATS
SPLASH!
Walker Books

As in *I Love Animals*, *I Love Boats* is a feast of colour, movement and vibrancy. A large, glossy book that would invite discussion and much observation from infant classes. *Splash!* is of equally high standard and conveys beautifully the heat and sunshine of the African plains as baby elephant cools down.

Let's follow
the baby
down to
the ...

Splash!,
illustrated by
Flora McDonnell.

Richard Edwards
YOU'RE SAFE NOW, WATERDOG
Wolfhound Press

This is a familiar theme – the loss of a toy – but the story is given a new twist as Matt had already begun to outgrow Watt the dog. One day, Watt is left behind on the riverbank, but no one goes back to look for him. This little chap does not make his way back home. Instead, he is discovered by Hattie and brought back to the safety and comfort of her house. Here, he is cuddled and loved in his new home. Beautifully illustrated by Sophie Williams.

Sam McBratney
JUST YOU AND ME
THE DARK AT THE TOP OF THE STAIRS
Walker Books

Just You and Me addresses a common theme of childhood – sharing, or, rather, not wanting to share! Little Goosey and Big Gander Goose know that a storm is coming and look for shelter. Everywhere they look, someone else is there already. They are invited in, but Little Goosey doesn't want to share. Finally, they find a place. After the storm, they discover they did share after all. And it wasn't so bad!

The Dark at the Top of the Stairs deals with childhood fears and the mixture of curiosity and terror they arouse. After much pestering, wise old mouse leads his three young mice up the dark stairs to face the monster. Afterwards, the three little ones decide they've had enough fear-facing for one day! Again, superb, strong illustrations by Ivan Bates.

Mary Murphy
PLEASE BE QUIET!
IF ...
I LIKE IT WHEN
Mammoth

Vividly illustrated in bold colours, Mary Murphy's *Penguin* series is a must for toddlers and children who've just started school. Common themes of childhood, such as trying to be quiet when the baby's sleeping, helping at home, tickles and looking for lost toys. The lift-the-flap books are particularly popular.

RECOMMENDED TITLES FOR DEVELOPING READERS

The children have left the infant classroom and are just beginning to read alone. This is a crucial time in their development, both psychologically and academically. It is also a peak time for imaginative play and for learning. At this stage, the classroom should be full of interesting books: information books, picture books and stories, anthologies of poetry. There is a huge sense of achievement for a five or six year old on reading their first 'real' book. We, as teachers, should ensure that the child has easy access to age-appropriate stories that will entertain and challenge, not overwhelm or discourage.

Irish publishing companies are now producing plenty of material for the new, developing and confident reader. Teachers and parents are probably familiar with the O'Brien Press' series of books, graded according to age level, with flags of different colours denoting the age range. The newly emerging reader may start with *Pandas* and progress through *Flyers* and on up to green flag books (for 13+). Mentor and Poolbeg have also categorised their books according to ability. In Poolbeg, the range is named after birds, so you might start with a *Wren* and move on to a *Goldcrest*!

Children from first class upwards are developing their personal sense of humour and it seems to be a peak age for jokes (some not very funny!) *The Giggle Club* (Walker) is a collection of new picture books containing funny stories and unusual characters. Anita Jeram has written and illustrated *Contrary Mary* and *Daisy Dare* for this collection. Martin Waddell gave us *Yum, Yum, Yummy* and Sam McBratney wrote *The Caterpillow Fight*. These are bound to be popular with young readers.

Martin Waddell
THE OWL AND BILLY STORIES
Walker Books

The Owl and Billy Stories is a collection of stories about Billy and his friend, Owl. When Spaceman moves in to the flats where the Old People live, Billy learns a lot of new things, like Space Signals and Moon Games. Pretty soon, Billy is able to go to school and leave Owl playing with Spaceman until he gets back. A great book for developing readers.

Lucinda Jacob
SANDY THE GREAT
Poolbeg Press

This is a Poolbeg *Wren* so it could be read aloud to young children, but developing readers would be well able to manage it alone. We meet Katie as she becomes the proud owner of a new, rather frisky, hamster. Katie enjoys choosing his name and arranging his cage, but finds the responsibilities of pet-ownership rather less fun when Sandy goes missing. The characters are well-drawn, including an irritating brother, a best friend – Carol – and a much-maligned mother who is proved right in the end (Yes!). This was declared a sure hit with my own seven-year-old, who didn't speak or eat until she'd finished it. Gripping stuff indeed!

Sam McBratney
BERT'S WONDERFUL NEWS
Walker Books

For many children, the traditional family, headed by happily married Mummy and Daddy, is not even a thing of the past, it's a complete fiction. It's refreshing, therefore, to read *Bert's Wonderful News* and to share in the joy and hope of new relationships. As a character, Bert is so vividly drawn you could almost touch the mud on his knees! The bane of his life is Geraldine Greer. We read of her teasing and the way she's always getting him into trouble at school. She even committed the crime of telling the whole class his important news, which Bert had been saving for newstime! But even Geraldine can't spoil the news about Dad's friend Liz. A warm and skilfully wrought story that brings stepmothers in from the cold!

Bert's Wonderful News,
illustrated by Brita Granström.

Sandy the Great,
illustrated by Lucinda Jacob.

Some Things Change,
illustrated by
Mary Murphy.

TITLES REFERRED TO IN ARTICLE AND IN RECOMMENDED LIST

→ Brennan, Herbie. *Letters from a Mouse.* London: Walker Books. 0-7445-132-8
→ Edwards, Richard. *You're Safe Now, Waterdog.* Dublin: Wolfhound Press. 0-86327-605-9
→ Fitzpatrick, Marie-Louise. *Izzy and Skunk.* London: David & Charles Books. 1-86233-150-2
   Dublin: Blackwater Press, 2000.
→ French, Vivian. *Playscript Farmer Duck.* London: Walker Books. 10-7445-7267-3
→ Jacob, Lucinda. *Sandy the Great.* Dublin: Poolbeg Press. 1-85371-916-1
→ Jeram, Anita. *Contrary Mary.* London: Walker Books. 0-7445-4782-2
→ Jeram, Anita. *Daisy Dare.* London: Walker Books. 0-7445-4415-7
→ McBratney, Sam. *Just You and Me.* London: Walker Books. 0-7445-5515-9
→ McBratney, Sam. *Bert's Wonderful News.* London: Walker Books. 0-7445-6396-8
→ McBratney, Sam. *The Caterpillow Fight.* London: Walker Books. 0-7445-5282-6
→ McBratney, Sam. *The Dark at the Top of the Stairs.* London: Walker Books. 0-7445-3746-0
→ McDonnell, Flora. *Splash!* London: Walker Books. 0-7445-7733-0
→ McDonnell, Flora. *I Love Boats.* London: Walker Books. 0-7445-4373-8
→ Murphy, Mary. *If ...* London: Mammoth. 0-7497-3869-3
→ Murphy, Mary. *Please Be Quiet!* London: Mammoth. 0-7497-3241-5
→ Murphy, Mary. *I Like it When* London: Mammoth. 0-7497-3119-2
→ Waddell, Martin. *Who Do You Love?* London: Walker Books. 0-7445-7742-X
→ Waddell, Martin. *Rosie's Babies.* London: Walker Books. 0-7445-2335-4
→ Waddell, Martin. *Amy Said.* London: Walker Books. 0-7445-5227-3
→ Waddell, Martin. *Well Done, Little Bear.* London: Walker Books. 0-7445-7298-3
→ Waddell, Martin. *Small Bear Lost.* London: Walker Books. 0-7445-4458-0
→ Waddell, Martin. *Yum, Yum, Yummy.* London: Walker Books. 0-7445-5478-0
→ Waddell, Martin. *The Pig in the Pond.* Dublin: O'Brien Press. 0-86278-373-9
→ Waddell, Martin. *The Big Big Sea.* London: Walker Books. 0-7445-2521-7
→ Waddell, Martin. *The Owl and Billy Stories.* London: Walker Books. 0-7445-4198-0
→ Waddell, Martin. *Little Mo.* London: Walker Books. 0-7445-2244-7
→ Waddell, Martin. *Farmer Duck.* London: Walker Books. 0-7445-1928-4

POETRY IN THE CLASSROOM

An early engagement with poetry alerts children to the richness and power of language, its playfulness and possibilities. It encourages an appreciation and enjoyment of language and a desire to explore and manipulate it.

The experience of poetry often begins in the language games and nursery rhymes that initially invite a physical response and later oral participation, but such a foundation cannot always be assumed. For many children, engagement with poetry is confined to a school setting. But while poetry may be a vibrant and daily experience in many classrooms, it is not so in all. For a large number of children, their experience of poetry remains a textbook model. In 1990, the Review Body on the Primary Curriculum proposed that more imaginative strategies should be identified, particularly in the teaching of fiction and poetry.

In 1996, in an article on poetry in the first *Big Guide to Irish Children's Books*, Tom Mullins wrote that things were changing in relation to children's engagement with poetry; experience over the last number of years has proved this to be the case. There has been a growth of interest in poetry. It would appear to be more fashionable amongst the general public and has, to some degree, shed its élitist image. Education in this country is also in a period of significant change. At second-level the new Junior Certificate programme has made it possible to expose young people to a greater variety of literature, including a broad range of poetry. The introduction of the Revised Primary Curriculum in 1999 has brought with it a fresh look at how children learn and how their learning needs can best be met.

The Revised Primary Curriculum in English strongly recommends that 'hearing and reading poetry should be an intrinsic element of [children's] language experience and one that is a source of joy and fulfilment'. To achieve this, access to

I Am the Crocus.

a selection of poems, which relate to their own experience as well as stimulating their imagination, is suggested. There is an emphasis on introducing children to 'rhymes, riddles and jingles' from an early stage so that they will recognise that poetry 'has to do with a very special use of words, their meanings and connotations'. The curriculum statement is very specific about the elements of poetry which children should be able to explore, understand and apply in their own writing, but it is clearly expected that this learning will be embedded in a meaningful engagement with poetry.

The end result of children's interaction with poetry in the classroom must be to enable them to become discriminating about poetry. They must be able to understand their own preferences and yet be willing to explore beyond these, able to differentiate between quality poetry and the patronising, second-rate verse that is sometimes directed at the child reader. The teaching of poetry must also foster readers who know that different kinds of poetry fulfil different needs, readers who are able to select the right poem for the right occasion and to suit a particular mood or feeling.

In 1971 primary teachers were advised that poems published in class readers were not sufficient to provide an adequate classroom repertoire. The current revised curriculum is more specific, calling for the broadest range of poetry in terms of cultural and historical origins. It is essential that a classroom context include both traditional and modern poetry from Ireland and abroad, which encompasses a variety of styles and forms and covers a range of themes. Access to twentieth-century Irish writing as well as contemporary writing specifically for children is also recommended. The most important concern, however, is that children should be offered poetry of the highest quality. These guidelines offer a challenge to teachers to provide a stimulating and enjoyable engagement with poetry, which will support the development of a long-term interest. The experience of reading poetry at primary level should also form a very solid foundation for a deeper engagement with and exploration of poetry at second-level and beyond.

Meeting this challenge in the context of classroom reality, where demands on teachers' and pupils' time are many and various, requires a high level of commitment. Little wonder that many a hard-pressed teacher has relied on the selection of poetry offered by publishers as part of a reading scheme. Ready availability of books from which to make a broader selection is an essential factor in encouraging exploration. In spite of the recent growth in publishing for children in Ireland, the provision for poetry remains limited. Publications considered here may be divided into three categories, the first of which is anthologies. These have much to offer in terms of classroom practice. A good anthology will provide a significant number of poems from which to make an appropriate selection. It has the potential to offer the greatest variety – different poets, past and present, encompassing a range of themes and subjects and many different styles of writing. An anthology may offer a choice of poems that will appeal across a wide age range. It may include a number of works by individual poets, allowing for a deeper level of engagement, while also offering the possibility to compare the work of different poets. Working with anthologies of poetry in a classroom setting also provides a model of collection for children and encourages them to see ways in which individual or class favourites may be preserved.

Three anthologies worthy of note are available on the Irish market. *Rusty Nails and Astronauts* and *The Poolbeg Book of Irish Poetry for Children* both contain a selection of poems that will appeal across a broad age range, from the earliest years through early second-level and beyond. *The Rattle Bag* could be appropriately explored in the second-level classroom. All three anthologies have avoided thematic divisions. Various reasons for this are offered in the editors' introductions. It is an effort to move away from the textbook image of the poetry book and to allow readers to make their own connections. It also underlines what Dunbar and Fitzmaurice, writing in the introduction to *Rusty Nails and Astronauts*, maintain is a characteristic of poetry: the ability to transcend all kinds of boundaries. The poems in *Rusty Nails and Astronauts* appear to be randomly arranged, although the editors point out that there is a number of instances where poems with an obvious connection have been placed side by side. *The Rattle Bag* also shies away from traditional divisions. The poems are arranged in alphabetical order by title or first line. Shaun Traynor, on the other hand, chooses to categorise his selection for *The Poolbeg Book of Irish Poetry for Children*, though again he avoids the thematic approach. Instead the poems are arranged into three sections – a short selection of poetry from ancient Ireland, a large number from poets of the past and a final selection from poets of today. This arrangement means that where a poet is represented by a number of pieces they appear consecutively, providing a closer look at the work of an individual poet. The move away from thematic divisions may make the search for suitable poetry for cross-curricular integration more time consuming, but perhaps more interesting. It will undoubtedly highlight the importance of poetry in its own right and not merely as a starting point for other curriculum work.

Traynor's anthology contains an interesting variety of poems. All the familiar names of the past are included: Yeats, Kavanagh, Stephens, Goldsmith, Joyce and more. Many are represented by their well-known poems, but Traynor has also included a number of less familiar pieces. The selection of poems from today includes the work of eighteen poets. The poetry in this anthology ranges from the whimsical to the profound. The biographical index for each section is a very useful element and likely to be of particular interest in terms of poetry in the classroom. The index for section one contains especially helpful information about the six poems from ancient Ireland.

Traynor's book is the most particularly Irish of the three anthologies under discussion. However, in terms of its content, Dunbar and Fitzmaurice correctly claim in their introduction to have firmly rooted their selection in Ireland, while including a significant representation from other countries. The works contained here span seven hundred years and are significantly greater in quantity. This is a vibrant and engaging collection, which invites a celebration of poetry. Included are poems for every occasion, the kind of poems which will evoke a variety of responses, from the physical enjoyment of rhyme and rhythm to thoughtful reflection. A particularly appealing aspect of this book is the inclusion of a considerable number of poems in the Irish language. They are accompanied in each case by a translation in English, which is so faithfully and delicately executed that little of the sense or feeling of the poem is lost to a non-Irish speaking audience.

The Rattle Bag, edited by Seamus Heaney and Ted Hughes, contains the largest number of poems of the three anthologies – almost four hundred. As might be expected of these two editors, the selection is wide-ranging and of the highest quality. It includes works from many of the greatest poets in the English language and a few surprises too, such as the anonymous 'Frankie and Johnny!' The language and style in many of the pieces operate at a sophisticated level, requiring several readings by the younger reader.

Attractive presentation and design are crucial if children are to be lured into choosing poetry books as part of their personal reading preferences. It is important to encourage them to see poetry books as possible sources of enjoyable and entertaining reading. The titles of the Wolfhound and Faber anthologies would arouse curiosity in the young reader about their contents, whereas Poolbeg's title is directed more towards the mediating adult. The inclusion of illustration is an interesting aspect of *Rusty Nails and Astronauts*. The combination of full-colour and black-and-white pictures, specially commissioned from Marie-Louise Fitzpatrick, which include some interpretive examples as well as decorative borders, makes this an inviting book that is likely to encourage exploration and interaction. There are also illustrations in the Poolbeg anthology. They are not interpretive in style but take the form of gentle and unobtrusive motifs, which recur throughout. They add a degree of interest to the book, particularly for child readers. *The Rattle Bag*, in size and appearance, is accessible to the older reader. With no illustrations inside at all, the images must be created solely in response to the poets' words.

Rusty Nails and Astronauts, illustrated by Marie-Louise Fitzpatrick.

Collections of work by individual poets form another category of poetry books currently available and offer different possibilities for classroom practice. They present an opportunity to engage with the work of an individual poet across a range of themes and subjects. They offer a particularly appropriate and effective context for exploring a poet's special use of language and imagery and the variety of ways in which they work to convey mood or feeling, to suggest alternative perspectives and to explore a variety of themes. A collection also allows for the close observation of a poet's particular style and the elements that might encourage recognition in future encounters.

Much of the poetry which children encounter in school is poetry written initially for an adult audience, although there has been a small but welcome increase in the number of respected modern poets who address themselves directly to a child audience. Writing poetry specifically for children can present problems. Striking a balance between addressing the child's perspective and still providing a challenging and stimulating experience of poetry is difficult. It would be easy to underestimate the child's ability to engage with poetry in a sophisticated way. Lazy writing panders to a perceived popular appeal, reducing humour to vulgarity under the guise of anarchy and subversion, and providing little or none of the richness of language that the young reader deserves. This kind of writing results in momentary entertainment, but offers little in terms of lasting enrichment. Unfortunately, Colin Fletcher's *Worst Class in the School* falls into this category. This kind of collection is unlikely to contribute to the exploration of poetry in the classroom. However, not all whimsical and light-hearted verse is out of place in a classroom setting. Children are often tempted into the world of poetry through humour. Father and daughter Larry and Aislinn O'Loughlin, better known for their work in children's fiction, have collaborated to produce *Worms Can't Fly*. Some of the entries are engagingly humorous. Some demonstrate clever wordplay likely to encourage experimentation by children.

Gordon Snell also indulges in a degree of wordplay in his collection of animal poems. Entitled *The Thursday Club*, it presents the stories of a variety of animals over a series of weekly meetings of the Thursday Club. Each animal has a part to play. The book is introduced and explained totally in verse. It contains riddles and tongue-twisters as well as narrative accounts from all the animals. Written with great humour and filled with a sense of fun, these are the kind of poems to invite young children into an early enjoyment of poetry. Particularly engaging is 'The Sssnakes' Hisss'.

Writers who take their young audience very seriously are represented in a number of current publications. Paul Muldoon's two lengthy narrative poems call to mind the earlier references to the revised primary curriculum, which suggests a particular place for poetry in the language experience of the child and also an encounter with poetry of the highest quality. Both *The Noctuary of Narcissus Bat* and *The Last Thesaurus* are full of the kind of wordplay in which children delight. This kind of

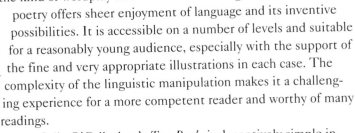

poetry offers sheer enjoyment of language and its inventive possibilities. It is accessible on a number of levels and suitable for a reasonably young audience, especially with the support of the fine and very appropriate illustrations in each case. The complexity of the linguistic manipulation makes it a challenging experience for a more competent reader and worthy of many readings.

The Noctuary of Narcissus Bat, illustrated by Markéta Prachatická.

Julie O'Callaghan's *Two Barks* is deceptively simple in appearance. The cover illustration might give the impression that this collection of poems is written for quite a junior audience. On the contrary, however, it is a collection of very perceptive poetry, powerful in its understated simplicity. This is a poet with a deep understanding of her intended audience. There is a relevance and reality about her work, which covers a wide range of everyday themes from 'Babysitting' to 'Poetry Soup!' It is a perfect example of a poet inviting a fresh look at the familiar.

Matthew Sweeney is another very perceptive writer who treats his young audience with respect. His latest collection of poems is contained in *Fatso in the Red Suit and Other Poems*. The title alone is likely to attract the attention of the child audience. Sweeney's poetry displays the same insight that was evident in his previous book, *The Flying Spring Onion*. With a quirky sense of humour he explores everyday situations from different points of view. He demonstrates great understanding of a child's perspective and the lunacy of the adult world when seen from that perspective. He has the ability to combine offbeat humour and serious subject matter in a manner that reaches out and draws the reader into a new understanding. Particularly powerful inclusions in this collection, especially when thinking in terms of poetry in the classroom, are 'Only the Wall' and 'The New Boy'.

One of the key elements of children's engagement with poetry in the classroom is the opportunity to develop a personal response. One of the most effective ways to achieve this is to experience and experiment with poetic forms of writing. Exposure to a wide range of poetry is an absolute prerequisite for this level of response. It is also very helpful for children to have an opportunity to hear and read poetry written by other children. In many cases this happens in a class or school context as children share their explorations with each other, modifying and refining their understanding in the process. In recent years, however, publications of poetry by children have become available. Four are referred to here, although it is likely that there are many more around the country, available to schools at local level. Two of the four mentioned were compiled as a result of national competitions, while the other two represent more locally based initiatives. None are the product of mainstream publishers, but all display a commendable standard of production and attractive presentation. Martin Drury, writing in the introduction to *Telepoems '97*, distances the project from the idea of a competition by stating that it is 'more a celebration of a human impulse to fashion oneself and the world in poetic terms'. However, the one hundred poems contained in this collection were chosen from a total submission of forty-four thousand; somewhere along the way standards for inclusion must have been applied and entries selected. The poems cover a wide range of topics. Many display freshness and perceptiveness, and an encouraging enthusiasm for poetic expression. *I Have a Dream, Irish Children Writing for RTÉ's Millennium Eve* is a response to a more focussed competition brief. It contains prose passages as well as poetry, drawing attention to the difference between these forms of writing. Enterprises such as these always carry the risk of intentional or accidental copying and require vigilance on the part of selectors. *Telepoems '97*, for example, contains a poem that bears a very close resemblance to a poem by Allan Ahlberg. Two collections compiled as a result of local initiatives include *I am the Crocus*, produced as part of the Wicklow County Council Writer-in-Residence Programme, and *I Am*, produced as part of an Art in Education programme by fifth- and sixth-class pupils in Scoil Íosagáin, County Donegal, and in St Mura's national school. Some of the poetry in both of these collections was clearly written to a particular pattern or structure, which leads to certain repetitiveness. The poems are best read singly over a period of time. These publications demonstrate the enthusiasm of children for poetry and their openness to expression in this form.

I Have A Dream, illustration by Kevin Guilly.

Conditions for engaging children positively with poetry in a meaningful way are favourable. School curricula strongly endorse the value of poetry. The number of well-produced poetry books that will stimulate the child's imagination is increasing.

Poetry is a fundamental part of being human and a vital element in the child's educational experience. For many children, initiation into the world of poetry will take place in a school setting. If properly presented and mediated, poetry will provide them with lasting benefit and enjoyment.

I Have A Dream,
illustration by Ailbhe Hogan.

REFERENCES

→ Barber, Irene. 'Action and Adventure Stories'. In *The Big Guide to Irish Children's Books*, edited by Valerie Coghlan and Celia Keenan, p.20. Dublin: The Children's Book Trust, 1996.
→ Drury, Martin. In Introduction, *Telepoems '97*. Dublin: The Ark, 1997.
→ Graves, Donald H. *A Fresh Look at Writing*, p.340. Britain: Heinemann, 1994.
→ Huck, Charlotte S. and Hepler, Susan and Hickman, Janet. *Children's Literature in the Elementary School*, p.405, 4th Ed., Part 2, Chapter 8. Florida: Harcourt Brace, Jovanovich Inc., 1987.
→ Mullins, Tom. 'Poetry Books'. In *The Big Guide to Irish Children's Books*, edited by Valerie Coghlan and Celia Keenan, p.104. Dublin: The Irish Children's Book Trust. 1996.
→ Mullins, Tom. 'Poetry Books'. In *The Big Guide to Irish Children's Books*, edited by Valerie Coghlan and Celia Keenan, p.104. Dublin: The Children's Book Trust, 1996.
→ *Primary School Curriculum, Teacher's Handbook*, p.103, Part 1. Dublin: An Roinn Oideachas, 1971.
→ *Primary School Curriculum, English, Teacher Guidelines*, p.84. Dublin: The Stationery Office, 1999.
→ Traynor, Shaun. *The Poolbeg Book of Irish Poetry for Children*. Dublin: Poolbeg Press, 1997.
→ 'What are Children Really Reading?' In *Children's Books in Ireland*. Dublin: CBI Spring 1998.

RECOMMENDED TITLES

Shaun Traynor
THE POOLBEG BOOK OF IRISH POETRY FOR CHILDREN
Poolbeg Press

Almost one hundred poems, from ancient Ireland to the present day, are contained in this anthology. It is attractively presented with many familiar entries alongside a range of less well-known works from recognised poets. The simple layout, with a single poem on every page, makes it very accessible to the child reader. Decorative motifs throughout the book add visual interest. According to the editor's introduction, all of the poems were tested on nine- and ten-year-old school children. They would also appeal to children outside this bracket, either younger or older. The inclusion of informative biographical detail is useful for a classroom context.

Robert Dunbar and Gabriel Fitzmaurice (eds)/ Marie-Louise Fitzpatrick (illus.)
RUSTY NAILS AND ASTRONAUTS, A WOLFHOUND POETRY ANTHOLOGY
Wolfhound Press

This is a delightful selection of close to two hundred poems, spanning seven hundred years of writing, randomly arranged in a joyful celebration of poetry.

A wide-ranging assembly of poems 'that transcend boundaries', this anthology has something to offer to children of all ages. The illustrations by Marie-Louise Fitzpatrick and the very attractive presentation make it an ideal choice for classroom use.

Seamus Heaney and Ted Hughes (eds)
THE RATTLE BAG
Faber and Faber

Almost four hundred poems are presented as the editors' personal favourites. Listed alphabetically according to title or first line, there are no chronological, thematic or other divisions; each poem stands individually on its own merits. It is a dense and weighty volume, nearly five hundred pages long. A classic anthology of high quality writing with all the major poets of the English language well represented, it also includes translated poems and traditional poetry from other cultures, for example, the Hunter Poems of the Yoruba. This challenging selection of poetry is best explored in second-level classrooms and beyond.

Julie O'Callaghan
TWO BARKS
Bloodaxe Books

This is a most engaging collection of poems, rooted firmly in the contemporary world of modern teenagers. The direct and straightforward use of language ensures accessibility. Understated and succinct, the poems convey the poet's remarkable insight into the perspective of her young audience. Entertaining and at the same time thought-provoking, this collection would be very relevant in second-level schools. It would also have something to offer to pupils at the upper end of primary school.

Matthew Sweeney/ David Austen (illus.)
FATSO IN THE RED SUIT
AND OTHER POEMS
Faber and Faber

Sweeney is a poet who displays great insight into the thoughts of a young audience. This collection of poems demonstrates the poet's ability to view the ordinary events of the world in a fresh and interesting way. Occasionally macabre, and frequently humorous in an offbeat way, Sweeney provides much food for thought for the perceptive reader. Suitable for upper primary and second-level pupils. Sweeney's work is also included in *We Couldn't Provide Fish Thumbs* (Macmillan).

Paul Muldoon/Markéta Prachatická (illus.)
THE NOCTUARY OF NARCISSUS BAT
Faber and Faber

Paul Muldoon/Rodney Rigby (illus.)
THE LAST THESAURUS
Faber and Faber

These are two lengthy poems full of intricate wordplay, which introduce children to the fun of words and the playful possibilities of language. The pocket-size format, together with the clever and appropriate illustration by the artists, makes for very appealing presentation on both counts. They are suitable on different levels for primary and second-level pupils.

Gordon Snell/Anthony Flintoft (illus.)
THE THURSDAY CLUB, ANIMAL POEMS
Dolphin

Full of rhythm and rhyme, this collection hosts a very impressive range of animals, each with a poem to present. Subtitled *Stories in the Forest* in the introduction, the collection is divided into four meetings of the animal members of the Thursday Club. Big Bill, the woolly dog, acts as master of ceremonies, choosing the order of storytellers. A most enjoyable invitation to the world of poetry, this collection also contains much wordplay, tongue-twisters and riddles. The endearing collection of animals on the front cover draws the young reader in, while the highly amusing illustrations of individual poems encourage participation.

Fatso in the Red Suit and Other Poems,
illustrated by David Austen.

Scoil Íosagáin and St Mura's National Schools
I Am
Scoil Íosagáin

This is a very interesting piece of work from fifth- and sixth-class pupils in Scoil Íosagáin and in St Mura's. A moving introduction by principal Sinead McLaughlin explains the origins of this collection. It is the result of an Art in Education programme, which was initiated to help the pupils cope with the loss of two of their classmates in the Omagh bombing of 1998. It explores and celebrates difference in the community, 'offering pupils new experiences and inviting them to look closely at who they are and where their place is'. The result is a collection of prose and poetry full of personal expression. The encouragement of guiding adults is obvious in the pattern and structure of the writing, and, from a teacher's perspective, the response evoked by a variety of stimuli is interesting. Some of the haiku are particularly impressive. This is a book to dip into and reflect on, suitable for upper-primary and second-level classrooms. The subtle and delicate cover illustration is also worth a mention.

I Am.

TITLES REFERRED TO IN ARTICLE AND IN RECOMMENDED LIST

→ Dunbar, Robert and Fitzmaurice, Gabriel (eds)/Fitzpatrick, Marie-Louise (illus.). *Rusty Nails and Astronauts: A Wolfhound Poetry Anthology*. Dublin: Wolfhound Press, 1999. 0-86327-671-7.

→ Fletcher, Colin/Curry, Stewart (illus.). *The Worst Class in the School*. Dublin: Poolbeg Press, 1999. 1-85371-936-6

→ Heaney, Seamus and Hughes, Ted (eds). *The Rattle Bag*. London: Faber and Faber, 1982. 0-571-11976-X

→ McNaughton, Colin. *We Couldn't Provide Fish Thumbs*. London: Macmillan, 1997. 0-330-35236-9

→ Muldoon, Paul/ Rigby, Rodney (illus.). *The Last Thesaurus*. London: Faber and Faber, 1995. 0-571-17580-5

→ Muldoon, Paul/ Prachatická, Markéta (illus.). *The Noctuary of Narcissus Bat*. London: Faber and Faber, 1997. 0-571-19226-2

→ O'Callaghan, Julie. *Two Barks*. Newcastle-upon-Tyne: Bloodaxe Books, 1998. 1-85224-427-5

→ O'Loughlin, Aislinn and Larry. *Worms Can't Fly*. Dublin: Wolfhound Press, 2000. 0-86327-786-1

→ Snell, Gordon/ Flintoft, Anthony. *The Thursday Club Animal Poems*. Britain: Dolphin, 2000. 1-85881-831-1

→ Sweeney, Matthew/ Austen, David (illus.). *Fatso in the Red Suit and Other Poems*. London: Faber and Faber, 1995. 0-571-17903-7

→ Traynor, Shaun. *The Poolbeg Book of Irish Poetry for Children*. Dublin: Poolbeg Press,1997. 1-85371-726-6

→ Wheatley, David (ed.). *I Am the Crocus*. Wicklow: Wicklow County Council, 1998. 0-9533904-2-X

→ Scoil Íosagáin and St Mura's National Schools. *I Am*. Buncrana: Scoil Íosagáin, 1999. 0-9536144-0-9

→ *I Have a Dream, Irish Children Writing for RTÉ's Millennium Eve*. Dublin: Marino Books, in association with RTÉ, 1999. 1-86023-106-3

→ *Telepoems '97*. Dublin: The Ark, A Cultural Centre for Children,1997. 0-9526682-1-1

REAL BOOKS IN THE CLASSROOM – OLDER READERS

In recent years, great efforts have been made by educational publishers to improve the emotional appeal and overall quality of their reading schemes. However, the Primary School Curriculum 1999 is quite clear that 'the class reader on its own will not cater adequately for the child's reading needs'. These needs, it says, will be 'fulfilled through the experience of engaging with a wide and varied range of texts'. While some educational publishers have responded to this challenge by producing reading schemes which include 'parallel reading books' written by established authors of children's fiction, there are commentators, like Henrietta Dombey, who would argue that 'no scheme-book can teach a child that the words on the page can be savoured, or can yield richer meanings on a second reading'. Though they are now being strongly encouraged to use 'real books' as the basis for some, if not all, of their classroom reading material, teachers may continue to use reading schemes. This is because, in some cases at least, teachers believe that, whatever their weaknesses, the schemes were 'graded' and so it could be assumed that a child entering any particular class *should* at least have attained the level of reading ability of that class reading book.

The Crowlings, illustration by David Wyatt.

'Real books' are written as fiction and not as graded reading material focussed on the educational needs of readers, therefore the teacher can make no such assumption and may be reluctant to choose the year's texts based largely on what the incoming class was reading the previous year. Perhaps the month of September could be used by the teacher not only to assess the reading level of the class, but also to ascertain the interests of the children in a particular genre of fiction? The selection of the novel for the first term would then be based on a month's observation of the class's reading ability and interest. The teacher might also consider encouraging the pupils to take the novels home for a week before beginning any formal work on them, which would give every child a chance to enjoy the story at his/her own pace. It would also give parents an opportunity to familiarise themselves with fiction suitable for their child's interest and ability. If we wish young people to become *readers*, we must encourage them to read for pleasure in a non-class situation. In schools, the focus can be on group discussion and debate, analysis of characters and plot, a focus that may well enhance the child's understanding of the novel, but this is a totally different reading experience from the solitary pursuit of reading for one's own enjoyment.

Teachers who have chosen to use novels with their students will vouch for the increased interest in reading. This is understandable as children will want to read when they can identify with the emotional and real-life situations of the characters in the books. A book such as William Trevor's *Juliet's Story* could be read by children in classes ranging from third to fifth, and could be understood and appreciated on many different levels. A story about the true power of story, this novel challenges children of different ages to consider, among other things, the effects of death on a small community, the condition of the elderly, the birth of a sibling, jealousy, friendship and neighbourliness. Teachers with more than one class group and the resulting mixed reading ability could also use a book such as this across a wide range of subjects. They would find it particularly useful to initiate class discussions on some of the topics which are to be taught in Social, Personal and Health Education (SPHE). Matthew Sweeney's *The Snow Vulture* is another novel which, with senior classes, would lend itself to discussion of sibling rivalry, jealousy, parent/child relationships, good and evil. But any cross-curricular element of works of fiction, however welcome to the teacher, must be seen as being of considerably less importance than the actual pleasure the children will derive from reading these books as stories.

Teachers who choose to use works of historical fiction as their class reading material will appreciate that, while their students are undoubtedly acquiring a deeper level of understanding about the historical period, the most significant benefit is the enjoyment of the book. Michael Morpurgo's *The Ghost of Grania O'Malley* might make late sixteenth-century Ireland come to life, but it is first and foremost an adventure/mystery/environmental story, which will hold the interest of children from fourth class and up. The heroine, Jessie, who first meets the ghost of Grania, is a superbly drawn character whose disability and real-life problems with school and family will captivate the reader. Likewise, while pupils will better appreciate the suffering endured during the years of the Great Famine from a reading of Marita Conlon-McKenna's *Under the Hawthorn Tree* or Ann Pilling's *Black Harvest*, it is their identification with the child characters in these books that will stay with them. Whether they are making the journey through famine-torn Ireland with Eily, Michael and Peggy, or experiencing with twentieth-century Colin, Prill and Oliver the sufferings of three children during famine times, the historical detail is of less importance to the young reader than his/her empathy with the reactions of the characters in the story.

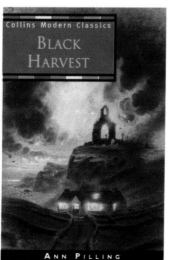

Black Harvest, illustration by David Wyatt.

The many books which use as their backdrop the turmoil and upheavals of the wars and rebellions of the early twentieth century have in common strong central child characters whose involvement in the various struggles, while central to plot, is not the main concern of the story. The young reader will see Jimmy in Gerard Whelan's *The Guns of Easter,* Alan in John Quinn's *The*

Summer of Lily and Esmé or Rosie in Ann Carroll's *Rosie's Troubles* as sympathetic, ordinary children whose family relationships and personal concerns are real and engaging. Students are often far more concerned with Jimmy's disappointment that he couldn't attend the Fairyhouse Races or with Rosie's amazement at the unfamiliar smells and clothes than they are with the accurate and vivid descriptions of the massacres at Mount Street Bridge or Croke Park in Whelan's and Carroll's books respectively. That a study of these books may also lead to a greater awareness of historical world events in the students is but a welcome incidental.

Teachers who have used these books in their classrooms will testify to the fact that the children actually enjoy these novels, they enjoy debating and arguing the relative merits of the characters and, most of all, they want to know what happens next. They also love meeting the authors as this gives them an opportunity to ask questions about the initial ideas and the inspiration that led to the book, about the time spend editing and redrafting, all of which allows them to discuss the book from a different perspective. In the days preceding and following the visit, posters, book covers and other material can be displayed not only in the classroom, but in the corridors and the library, generating an interest in books throughout the entire school that can be used to great effect. The Writers in Schools scheme, run by Poetry Ireland from Dublin Castle, is the most cost-effective means of inviting authors to the classroom because the author's expenses are part-funded by this organisation. If the school authorities are unable or unwilling to fund their share of the cost, the children can be encouraged to raise the necessary money in a variety of ways: through classroom bakes or toy sales or by collecting aluminium cans to be sold to recycling campaigns. This method of raising money involves the students in a very real way in the forthcoming author-visit and further helps to raise awareness and interest throughout the school. The local library will also be more than happy to notify schools of forthcoming author-visits and will usually be pleased to invite class groups, with their teacher, to attend storytelling and other free events.

While it is most regrettable that there is still no 'official' website of children's literature in Ireland, students should be encouraged, using the computers now available in every school, to access publishers' websites, which often provide author profiles, reviews and other information. Teachers and parents might also access the recently launched website **www.irishbooks4kids.com** which aims to provide a forum for discussion about award-winning titles with an Irish interest and up-to-date information on Irish authors and their books, including detailed summaries of many of those books. Such knowledge helps young readers to view the books they read in class in the context of the wider literary scene, and enables them to choose books and assess their worth in a country where little space is allocated in the national newspapers for literary discussion and book reviews.

It sometimes seems as if we expect young readers in schools to behave in a way few adult readers do – we ask them to read books, selected by adults for certain curricular objectives, which may not engage their interest or hold their attention and with whose characters they may have little or no empathy. Booksellers will

The Cinnamon Tree, illustration by Angela Clarke. ➡

agree that 'young adults' will often choose to buy books from the adult section, ignoring those books deemed suitable for their age and interest. Yet there is a wide range of novels and collections of short stories available that might be of considerable interest to teenagers in post-primary schools. *Out of Nowhere* is an extremely demanding and rewarding story that can be appreciated and understood on many different levels and which challenges commonly held perceptions about the nature of reality. *The Shakespeare Stealer* and its soon-to-be published sequel, *The Shakespeare Scribe,* both excellent stories in their own right, will stimulate an interest in and knowledge of the world of Elizabethan England. Collections published recently (*Flame Angels, One Grand Sweet Song, Ecstasy and Other Stories*) showcase the best of writing for young adults, and novels such as Jane Mitchell's *Different Lives* or Aubrey Flegg's *The Cinnamon Tree* deal with contemporary issues of interest to these readers.

It could be argued that if schools throughout the country were adequately stocked with, and actively using, relevant and well-written novels, we might see the increased interest in reading and literacy levels so desired by parents, teachers, librarians and by all those interested in both the future of reading and the future of young readers.

REFERENCES

→ Dombey, H. *Words And Worlds*. York: National Association For Teaching Of English, 1992.

RECOMMENDED TITLES

Ann Pilling
BLACK HARVEST
Collins Press

First published in 1983 by Armada, this is a reissue of the book which, we are told in the Postscript, was inspired by a reading of Cecil Woodham Smith's *The Great Hunger*. Three children and their dog, holidaying in Ireland with parents and baby sister, gradually unearth the cause of the mysterious illness that has been affecting them since they moved into a modern bungalow on the west coast of Ireland. Having learned that the strange apparitions they had seen were Famine victims whose bones lie unburied in a scalpeen near the bungalow, the three children realise that, in some strange way, they too had been experiencing the effects of malnutrition and starvation. Seen through the eyes of twentieth-century English children, this is a story of the Irish Famine that is accessible to young readers with a taste for horror or historical detail.

Siobhán Parkinson
CALL OF THE WHALES
O'Brien Press

Memories and dreams of childhood are stirred when Tyke, now a lecturer in history, meets Henry at an international conference in Geneva. This chance meeting prompts Tyke to recount his experiences and adventures of those summers, long ago, when he had visited the remote and fascinating

Call of the Whales,
illustration by
Finbarr O'Connor.

lands of the Arctic in the company of his anthropologist father. His lifelong enthusiasm for whales, and his respect for the small communities dependent on them, date back to those endless summer days when he first heard the call of the whale and witnessed, at close range, the magnificent beasts rolling in the icy waters. This is a haunting and lyrical adventure story set in the snowy lands of the Arctic Circle, but it is much, much more. It is a coming-of-age novel and, as Tyke's opinions and feelings grow and develop over the course of three summers, he begins to question his father's willingness to leave home and 'play whalers', ultimately realising that 'we get nothing for nothing in this world'.

Matthew Sweeney
THE SNOW VULTURE
Faber and Faber

Born not only in different years but in different decades, twins Carl and Clive may look identical but no one could ever mistake one for the other. Even a stranger might notice that in Clive's eyes was calmness, in Carl's was badness. Carl is a bully whose activities serve to make him popular with a certain element in school while making life miserable for his twin and his well-intentioned but ineffectual parents. After a heavy snowfall, the boys build snow creations which unwittingly represent aspects of themselves – Clive builds a traditional snowman while Carl chooses to make a snow vulture. The snowman and its successor, a snowbear, both melt in

The Snow Vulture,
illustration by
David Austen.

due course, but the vulture remains, white and apparently indestructible, on the roof-garden of their London flat. Secretly worried, Carl's behaviour is even worse than usual, influenced perhaps by the evil presence on the roof, and it is not until he finds himself haunted at home and at school by the presence of his sinister creation that he seeks help from his twin. This is much more than a story of good and evil, it is a superbly written and complex story of two sympathetically drawn and very credible boys whose thoughts and actions have a dramatic and chilling impact on the world around them.

Eddie Lenihan
A SPOOKY TALE FOR IRISH CHILDREN
Mercier Press

Ideal for reading aloud in class, this story tells how Fionn Mac Cumhaill and the Fianna foiled the evil Draointeoir's plan for world domination. After many setbacks, in which Fionn and his men are shown to be far more human and, in some instances, slightly less heroic than many tales would lead us to believe, they reach Thuringia. Having captured Draointeoir's apprentice, they force him to reveal the dark and terrible secret of his artist's pack. Eddie Lenihan's skills as a storyteller are immediately obvious in this rich, idiomatic and above all humorous addition to the Fianna stories.

Read also: Eddie Lenihan's vivid account of the events set in motion when Fionn Mac Cumhaill asks the wise druid Taoscán for help to make him dream in *Gruesome Irish Tales for Children*.

*Gruesome
Irish Tales for
Children,*
illustration by
Amy Berenz.

Bairbre McCarthy
THE ADVENTURES OF CÚCHULAINN
Mercier Press

A wonderful retelling of many of the best-loved adventures of Ireland's legendary hero, Cúchulainn, this book serves as an ideal introduction to the Ulster cycle. Fresh and lively, yet simply told, these stories bring to life epic battles, courageous deeds and the passionate (and often overlooked) love interests of this famous warrior.

Michael Morpurgo
THE GHOST OF GRANIA O'MALLEY
Mammoth

Jessie Parsons is determined that her 'lousy cerebral palsy' will not prevent her from reaching the summit of the Big Hill, but when she finally succeeds, with a little help from an unseen hand, she at first doubts her achievement. Then her visiting American cousin, Jack, accompanies her to the top and they meet the infamous sixteenth-century pirate Grania O'Malley, who needs their help if she is to prevent the despoliation of her beloved hill by those who wish to mine for gold on the tiny west-coast island. The Big Hill is eventually preserved with practical and ethically questionable help from Grania and her pirates, and the future seems secure when the islanders agree to a proposal to market the clear spring water. Universal themes of pragmatism versus idealism, of schoolyard enmity and intolerance for the disabled or different, of family illness and parental separation and concern (or the lack of it) and for the future of our environment are cleverly and sensitively handled by Morpurgo in this gripping adventure story that was deservedly shortlisted for the NASEN Special Educational Needs Award in 1996.

Gerard Whelan
OUT OF NOWHERE
O'Brien Press

Out of Nowhere is a highly original novel that operates on many levels. It may be read as a straightforward adventure mystery, but it also raises questions about intolerance, violence, belief, identity, gender and reality. Events and identities keep shifting, requiring reappraisal. Stephen wakes up in a monastery, knowing nothing about himself but his name. The only other inhabitants are four monks, four 'unfortunates' and a young girl, Kirsten, who, like himself, is suffering from total amnesia. Beyond the walls, all traces of human life have disappeared. But then who are the unseen killers who seem determined to destroy them all? Who are the bizarre 'agents' and what is their mission? This is a book in which appearances turn out to be almost always deceptive, set in a world where little is as it seems.
Read also: *Dream Invader,* a novel which again can be interpreted on many levels and which raises thought-provoking questions as it moves seamlessly between myth, fantasy and folklore and the real world of everyday life. Twelve-year-old Saskia is powerless to help her young cousin, Simon, who is being visited at night by the terrifying Pooshipaw. The family seeks advice from Birdie Murray, who has known the ancient forces over many lifetimes, and together they confront the latest appearance of this timeless evil.

Louise Lawrence
THE CROWLINGS
Collins

Deservedly shortlisted for the Bisto Awards, *The Crowlings* is a compelling and disturbing story that tells of the challenges faced by different generations of the clan as they attempt to protect and maintain their heritage and culture in a world that has lost respect for traditional ways. Young Ben Crowling and the indomitable Cloud, advised and aided by Baxter and Kate, share a vision of how they must protect the clan in the inhospitable lands granted to them by the star-people. But their descendants refuse to see any merit in the old ways and long for the comfortable lifestyle they imagine would be theirs if they lived in the big cities. When the cities are threatened by the terrifying creatures from which her family took its name, Linni Crowling, who has previously rejected the old ways, is forced to make those difficult decisions which may ensure the safety and future of her clan. Challenging the reader to consider modern, individualistic society and to reassess the importance of traditional values, this novel is a gripping and powerful portrayal of changing philosophies across the generations.

Sam McBratney
FUNNY, HOW THE MAGIC STARTS
Mammoth

Teenagers who are, for the most part, content with their families, enjoy their school-life and even appreciate some of their teachers are quite unusual in books for young adults these days. And, while there is definitely a place for gritty realism, McBratney tells the other story. Monica lives with Mummy, Daddy and chess-obsessed younger brother Raymond 'in a superior semi-detached villa after the style of Swiss Chalets'. Into this ordered new housing development comes Seymour Brolly, an apparently eccentric young man who sports binoculars and who has not only read but enjoyed *Under the Greenwood Tree*. As he writes letters to his local MP, organises an anti-whaling petition to be sent to the Emperor of Japan and tries to save nesting sand-martins from encroaching development, Seymour gradually gains the respect of even the most philistine of his schoolmates. Monica, initially reluctant to side with the individualistic Seymour against her more worldly friend Debbie, finds herself drawn to his quixotic campaigns and discovers for herself how the magic starts. A perceptive, humorous and charming story and a most welcome reissue of a book that remains as fresh as when first published over a decade ago.

Read also: *One Grand Sweet Song,* Sam McBratney. Egmont, 1999.

Jane Mitchell
DIFFERENT LIVES
Poolbeg Press

At sixteen, Sarah feels like a stranger in her conservative, middle-class family with its emphasis on academic and other achievements. She herself believes 'avidly in the wider education of life experience, not the narrow education of books and school and college.' Leaving behind a brief note for her parents, she sets off, eager to stretch, expand and grow. London is huge, crowded and expensive, but Sarah eventually finds both accommodation and employment. When she witnesses a fight over drugs that ends in a knife-attack on her friend, she is  forced onto the streets – knowing that the assailant has seen her too. Her days are spent in tube stations, anxiously scanning the crowds for signs of the attacker. When she makes a friend in Turdy, she discovers in herself an ability to communicate with other outcasts from society. This is a dramatic and gripping account of the challenges faced by a teenager who wants to make her own decisions and live life on her own terms.

Different Lives,
cover photography by
Mark Nixon.

Aubrey Flegg
THE CINNAMON TREE
O'Brien Press

The author's note at the end of this book separates for us the fact from the fiction. Inspired by Princess Diana's campaign to highlight the evils of landmines, the author travelled to Angola, where he met the Norwegian People's Aid who work to defuse the mines, and to Kenya, where he met the people on whom Yola, Gabbin and other characters are based.

The heroine, Yola Abonda, is seriously injured by an exploding mine, and when her leg is amputated from just above the knee she can no longer make the journey to and from school. She seems doomed to spend life in the compound, until approached by Mr Hans of Northern People's Aid and offered a position as a mines awareness teacher. Her command of English, her status as the daughter of a wise and respected local chief and her own disability make her the ideal candidate for such a role. She is sent to Ireland, where she is fitted with a good artificial leg and where she meets Fintan, who is to play a very important role in her life when she returns to work for the NPA. This is a complex story that demands we seriously consider the long-term effects of the arms trade, 'legal' and illegal, on children and their families in the developing world.

Brian Keaney
FAMILY SECRETS
Orchard Books

Brought up in London, Kate has learned to accept brief and unsatisfactory replies to questions about the father she has never known and about the secret that led her mother, Anne, to abandon her home and family. Fiercely independent, Anne protects her past and lives in the present, enjoying the success she has struggled hard to achieve. Forced by her own mother's serious illness to return to western Ireland, Anne is quite unprepared for Kate's enthusiastic adoption of the rural lifestyle and her friendliness with the neighbours who help out on the small farm. Kate has inherited the family trait of determination and persists with her questions until, in 'a moment of complete understanding', the three generations of women forgive one another for hurts caused by prejudices and half-truths. In her six weeks in Ireland, Kate finds her father, gets to know the grandmother she had never met and, in the process, discovers much about herself.

Polly Nolan (ed.)
FLAME ANGELS,
AN ANTHOLOGY OF IRISH WRITING

Mammoth

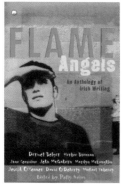

All of the stories in *Flame Angels* have an Irish setting, but the characters and events will be recognisable to readers anywhere. Defining moments in the lives of eight young characters are captured, and may be summed up in the words of the youth in John McGahern's 'Christmas': 'I felt a new life had already started to grow out of the ashes, out of the stupidity of human wishes'. With the exception of the seven-year-old narrator in 'True Believers' by Joseph O'Connor, all of the protagonists are on the cusp between childhood and adulthood. But the world of older generations is not necessarily appealing, and one has the impression that at least some of the young protagonists will endeavour to do things differently.

The settings for the eight stories range from Dublin to Derry to rural Ireland, and span issues such as teenage runaways, a bullying teacher, the fifteen-year-old footballer sent home from England – 'the boy with the golden touch and the brilliant future already behind him'. In several cases the interplay between youth and old age is at the kernel of the matter, as in the stories by June Considine and Marilyn McLaughlin.

Only two stories, 'Christmas' and 'True Believers', have previously been published.

Flame Angels,
illustration by Jo Hassall.

TITLES REFERRED TO IN ARTICLE AND IN RECOMMENDED LIST

→ Blackwood, Gary. *The Shakespeare Stealer.* Dublin: O'Brien Press, 1999. 0-86278-634-7
→ Carroll, Ann. *Rosie's Troubles.* Dublin: Poolbeg Press, 1996. 1-85371-681-2
→ Conlon-McKenna, Marita. *Under the Hawthorn Tree.* Dublin: O'Brien Press, 1990. 0-86278-206-6
→ Flegg, Aubrey. *The Cinnamon Tree.* Dublin: O'Brien Press, 2000. 0-86278-657-6
→ Keaney, Brian. *Family Secrets.* London: Orchard Books, 1997. 1-86039-540-6
→ Lawrence, Louise. *The Crowlings.* London: Collins Press, 2000. 0-00-675464-3
→ Lenihan, Eddie. *A Spooky Irish Tale for Children.* Dublin: Mercier Press, 1996. 1-85635-150-5
→ Lenihan, Eddie. *Gruesome Irish Tales for Children.* Dublin: Mercier Press, 1997. 1-85635-197-1
→ McBratney, Sam. *Funny, How the Magic Starts ...* London: Mammoth/Egmont, 1999. 0-7497-0313-X
→ McBratney, Sam. *One grand sweet song.* London: Mammoth/Egmont, 1999. 0-7497-3835-9
→ McCarthy, Bairbre. *The Adventures of Cúchulainn.* Dublin: Mercier Press, 2000. 1-85635-312-5
→ Mitchell, Jane. *Different Lives.* Dublin: Poolbeg Press, 1996. 1-85371-507-7
→ Morpurgo, Michael. *The Ghost of Grania O'Malley.* London: Mammoth/Egmont, 1997. 0-7497-2582-6
→ Nolan, Polly (ed.). *Flame Angels.* London: Mammoth/Egmont, 2000. 0-7497-3958-4
→ Ó Laighléis, Ré. *Ecstasy and Other Stories.* Dublin: Poolbeg Press (Beacon Books), 1996. 1-85371-611-1
→ Parkinson, Siobhán. *Call of the Whales.* Dublin: O'Brien Press, 2000. 0-86278-691-6
→ Pilling, Ann. *Black Harvest.* London: Collins Modern Classics, 1999. 0-00-675426-0
→ Quinn, John. *The Summer of Lily and Esmé.* Dublin: Poolbeg Press, 1999. 1-85371-208-6
→ Sweeney, Matthew. *The Snow Vulture.* London: Faber and Faber, 1994. 0-571-17168-0
→ Trevor, William. *Juliet's Story.* Dublin: O'Brien Press, 1995. 0-86278-457-3
→ Whelan, Gerard. *The Guns of Easter.* Dublin: O'Brien Press, 1996. 0-86278-449-2
→ Whelan, Gerard. *Dream Invader.* Dublin: O'Brien Press, 1997. 0-86278-516-2
→ Whelan, Gerard. *Out of Nowhere.* Dublin: O'Brien Press, 1999. 0-86278-637-1

One grand sweet song,
cover by Blacksheep.

ENCOURAGING THE RELUCTANT
READER — POST-PRIMARY

It is not too difficult to identify reluctant teenage readers: they're the ones whose eyes glaze over, who look bored and become fidgety whenever the word 'book' is mentioned. They're not illiterate. In fact, there's nothing wrong with them that might explain their not reading. For these teenagers, books are boring and reading a chore that must be endured, usually for the sake of educational success.

What happened to these teenagers who are well able to read but choose not to? I asked that very question in a survey I conducted of almost eight hundred second-level pupils in Dublin in the autumn of 1999. Their ages ranged from twelve to seventeen; they were an equal mix of male and female; they were from all socio-economic groups. The results weren't all that surprising. Life in general tends to become more demanding around this time. Socially, things begin to move up a notch or two. Sport, music, television and computers all become more important. For the older teenager, part-time jobs provide the money necessary to feed their social life. Finally, the demands of school and study are not to be underestimated.

So where does reading come in all this activity? 'Nowhere' would seem to be the answer for a lot of teenagers. This can lead to problems for them in many ways. The guidelines for the new Leaving Certificate English syllabus state:

> In a culture that emphasises visual and oral texts and reduces
> and abbreviates written texts, it is no mean challenge to develop
> advanced reading and writing skills in students. Many read
> little, write less and consequently have lost respect for language
> and the way they use it.

Quite apart from the academic problems that reluctant readers may experience in trying to cope with courses where so much emphasis is put on evaluating reading assignments independent of their teacher, there is the real fear that students may leave school without the advanced reading skills necessary to enter into adult life.

The more we read, the more we learn to respect language and, as the guidelines state, 'the way we use it'. Apart from the obvious academic advantages, students who learn to express themselves clearly and to use language with respect possess something of great personal value that will serve them well for the rest of their lives.

Emotionally, books often provide teenagers with the safety net necessary to deal with their own pain and fears, reflected in the lives of others. One of the best ways to get reluctant readers reading is to point them in the direction of things that they find interesting, and many of them seem to have a close affinity with teenage angst. This can be difficult for adults to take at the best of times and it takes a certain balance in writing not to trivialise their pain on the one hand or overindulge it on the other. Good writers are able to go beyond the hackneyed angst we all know, and deal with some of the more serious issues confronting many teenagers. Difficulties associated with relationships abound – family, friends, love, infatuation, coming to terms with sexuality, feelings of alienation, of being different, an outsider, not being accepted for what you are, difficulties in just being yourself and accepting others for what they are.

All of these problems can be dealt with in a variety of ways, but a good book will often create situations which change the characters so fundamentally that the reader can now see the world in a different way. Both Chris Lynch and Martina

Murphy have written some excellent books for teenagers, more of them later. Over the last few years, many reluctant readers have been drawn to Marilyn Taylor's books about young love: *Could this be Love? I Wondered, Could I Love a Stranger? Call Yourself a Friend?* Margrit Cruickshank's *Circling the Triangle* has also proved popular, as has Sam McBratney's *You Just Don't Listen*, originally published as *Put a Saddle on the Pig* (winner of the teenage section of the Irish Children's Book Trust Bisto Book of the Year Award for 1992–1993).

For many reluctant readers, their only experience of reading is as part of their English class in school. Most junior classes enjoy reading Michelle Magorian's *Goodnight, Mr Tom*, and this can serve as an introduction to other books with similar themes by Irish authors. Joan O'Neill's *Daisy Chain War*, *Daisy Chain Wedding* and *Bread and Sugar* have proved very popular in the past, as has *Katie's War* by Aubrey Flegg, *Melody for Nora* by Mark O'Sullivan,

Call Yourself a Friend?, cover by Angela Clarke.

The Guns of Easter by Gerard Whelan, *The Good Liar* by Gregory Maguire, *Faraway Home* by Marilyn Taylor, *Safe Harbour* by Marita Conlon-McKenna and *Amelia* and *No Peace for Amelia* by Siobhán Parkinson.

Books set in Northern Ireland (often with the Troubles as their background), have also proved extremely popular, for example, Joan Lingard's *Kevin and Sadie* series, which includes *Twelfth Day of July* and *Across the Barricades*; Peter Carter's *Under Goliath*; Bernard MacLaverty's *Cal*; and Brian Moore's *Lies of Silence* (now an option on the new Leaving Certificate English syllabus).

Every one of us has certain criteria which we apply to any book we deem a good read, and this is doubly so for the reluctant reader. In fact, reluctant readers often don't get as far as the first page. Something as simple as the cover, the size of the type used or even the number of pages will be enough to put them off a book. Sometimes these non-readers find the diary format more accessible, with its short, snappy, easily read entries. Two such books published comparatively recently were Bernadette Leach's *4 Ever Friends* and Claire Hennessy's *Dear Diary*. On the other hand, perhaps the unusual 'flipper' format of Siobhán Parkinson's *Sisters ... No Way!* would be enough to lure a reluctant reader into starting this book and then enjoying it for the good read that it is.

4 Ever Friends, cover by Kunnert + Tierney

If regular readers would like a book to be interesting, reluctant readers need it to be compelling. A well-paced book for general readers could be too slow for the reluctant reader. 'Readers' will often make allowances if a book isn't quite what it should be, but a reluctant reader is totally unforgiving.

There is nothing to forgive in the novels of Chris Lynch and Martina Murphy, and the fact that they make you laugh leads to another important point. A common thread in many successful books for teenagers is humour. As any parent or teacher will know, teenagers dislike didacticism of any kind and messages conveyed in 'meaningful' ways are rightly dismissed for the propaganda they are. However, in the right hands, humour can be used to convey darker, more serious subjects in a way that teenagers find acceptable. Chris Lynch's books, *Mick*, *Blood Relations* and *Dog Eat Dog* (reviewed here), are well-written, fast-paced books. The world they depict is a tough one, but then many fifteen or sixteen year olds have grown out of the idealised world of childhood fiction and may prefer to identify with a character who is trying desperately to gain some measure of respect for himself. The humour through which the more unpalatable side of life is conveyed will make many a reluctant reader, and particularly the older teenage boy, read each one with interest and then ask for more.

Martina Murphy, too, is an Irish author whose books *Livewire*, *Fast Car* and *Free Fall* fit all the criteria for the reluctant reader. She obviously hasn't been remotely intimidated by the likes of Roddy Doyle in communicating her personal brand of Dublin wit.

Cirque du Freak.

Sometimes a particular genre may appeal to a reluctant reader and many have already been drawn to the fantasy world of Cormac MacRaois's *Giltspur* trilogy and more recently Michael Carroll's *She Fades Away*. Many boys, in particular, will be attracted to the darker world of Darren Shan's unsettling *Cirque du Freak* and its sequel, *The Vampire's Assistant*. His ability to weave credible stories from the strands of darkness makes these books excellent introductions to the genre.

Of course, many reluctant readers have no interest in fiction whatsoever and will remain totally unmoved by your best efforts. If this is the case, the younger teens may well enjoy books on drawing, music, film quizzes, sport and Guinness Records-type books of all sorts. The older teen, as revealed in the survey I did, is often drawn to biography, autobiography and factual accounts of social issues, such as *Lisa: The Story of an Irish Drug Addict* or Christina Noble's *Bridge Across my Sorrows*.

With a little help and direction from teachers, and a little effort and commitment from the teenager, we may eventually witness the magic of seeing a reluctant reader take out a book and read solely for pleasure; maybe then, everything will seem worthwhile and we can all live happily ever after.

RECOMMENDED TITLES

Chris Lynch
MICK
Poolbeg Press

Chris Lynch
BLOOD RELATIONS
Poolbeg Press

Chris Lynch
DOG EAT DOG
Poolbeg Press

Martina Murphy
LIVEWIRE
Poolbeg Press

Martina Murphy
FAST CAR
Poolbeg Press

Martina Murphy
FREE FALL
Poolbeg Press

Mick is a teenager in a tough Irish neighbourhood. The bigoted ghetto mentality prevalent there finds its personification in Mick's brother, Terry – the brother from hell. Mick is drawn to others who are outsiders like himself and struggles to free himself from the old ways that he has now come to despise.

In *Blood Relations*, Mick continues with his attempts to make an independent life for himself, while Terry, in particular, makes this difficult for him. Mick's friendship with the super-cool Toy and his long-desired-for Evelyn sustain him. He even rekindles his friendship with Sully, who had got left behind in Mick's search for all that was new.

By the time we read *Dog Eat Dog*, Mick has attained a measure of freedom by moving in with Sully and by getting a part-time job in his parents' dingy bar. Emotionally, however, Mick is still chained to the brutality of Terry's world and is sucked into the horror of dog-fighting.

These are strong, honest, powerfully written books, which provide a credible working-class hero (or anti-hero) and can make readers out of the most reluctant of teenagers.

Blood Relations,
illustration by Vince LaCava.

Livewire: Joey sees his future in playing music with his cool band, but unfortunately his father has a somewhat more conventional view of what his son should do. The conflict that ensues will be familiar to teenagers and parents alike and provides some wonderfully funny, angst-ridden entertainment.

In *Fast Car*, April's overly ambitious parents go abroad for nine months and leave her with the ultra laid-back Walsh family. April grows in confidence and even the Walshs are taken aback when she starts going out with the wild, truculent Luke and her school grades fall. Things really hot up when April's parents return to deal with the situation.

Free Fall is a slightly darker book. Hannah's anger when her father leaves home affects her relationships with everyone she knows and cares for. However, all of this pales when she thinks of what happened to Alice.

These books are hugely entertaining, with quick-fire dialogue and keenly observed characters. Great for the reluctant reader.

Fast Car,
illustration by
Leonard O'Grady.

Ann Carroll
AMAZING GRACE
Poolbeg Press

Staying with a great-aunt in a big old house doesn't hold much promise of fun for young Grace, but she couldn't have been more wrong. After she discovers a magic comb in the attic, the most amazing things begin to happen. Ann Carroll's fun-loving Grace and her unusual exploits provide endless amusement. The simple style, larger print and funny illustrations will hold a special appeal for the younger reluctant reader.

Sam McBratney
YOU JUST DON'T LISTEN
Mammoth

When Laura's young, widowed mother reveals that she has accepted a proposal to re-marry and move to the country, Laura refuses to leave her old home, school and friends. The real human dilemmas which result from this impasse are fairly and honestly dealt with by Sam McBratney. He creates convincing characters who have the ability to amuse without losing sight of the emotional truth of their predicament.

Darren Shan
CIRQUE DU FREAK
Harper Collins

Darren and his friend, Steve, find themselves in the audience of a mysterious freak show. Slowly they become enmeshed in a web of horror until finally Darren is forced to make a bargain with one of the entertainers if he wishes to save Steve. The somewhat unusual consequences of this bargain may bother some adults, but will hardly be noticed by most teenagers, particularly of the male variety. Shan is adept at creating murky, shadowy scenes that will keep the pages turning.

Bernadette Leach
4 EVER FRIENDS
Attic Press

Anna is sixteen and decides to reveal 'the real me' in her new diary. Her desire to become a writer, her latest love interest, her friends, family, neighbours and relations all get a mention. Trying to follow the multiplicity of characters and problems can sometimes be distracting (as can some of the grammar

mistakes!). However, Leach deals with some of the more serious aspects of family life in a direct, well-observed way. The diary format will certainly appeal to teenage girls.

Claire Hennessy
DEAR DIARY
Poolbeg Press

Five school friends, all around thirteen, and their revealing diary entries will ensure that this book will appeal to an audience of the same age. The usual teenage preoccupations are certainly dealt with at length. Claire Hennessy is a most assured young writer and deals with adolescent angst in a light, humorous way.

Marita Conlon-McKenna
IN DEEP DARK WOOD
O'Brien Press

Mia Murphy and her brother, Rory, watch as an old lady moves in next door one dark, stormy night. '"She's like a witch, Rory!" said Mia.' When Mia disappears, Rory travels to a land full of dragons and danger in a desperate attempt to bring his sister home safely. All those who loved and enjoyed Marita Conlon-McKenna's other books will not be disappointed by this one.

Mary Arrigan
LANDSCAPE WITH CRACKED SHEEP
The Children's Press

Fourteen-year-old Maeve Morris and her eleven-year-old know-all cousin Leo are spending some of their summer holidays with their grandparents in a quiet Galway village. The pace quickens when some unusual characters begin to show an unhealthy interest in the paintings which their friend, Lady Gowan, has for sale in her large, rambling house. Jamie (who also features in Mary Arrigan's *Dead Monks and Shady Deals*) helps the two cousins to solve the mystery and provides some romantic interest for Maeve. Mary Arrigan knows how to tell a good story, with just the right amount of suspense and humour to keep the younger, post-primary student interested.

Landscape with Cracked Sheep,
illustrated by Terry Myler.

TITLES REFERRED TO IN ARTICLE AND IN RECOMMENDED LIST

→ Anon. *Lisa*. Dublin: Poolbeg Press. 1-85371-011-3

→ Arrigan, Mary. *Dead Monks and Shady Deals*. Dublin: The Children's Press, 1995. 0-94796-2913

→ Arrigan, Mary. *Landscape with Cracked Sheep*. Dublin: The Children's Press, 1996. 0-94796-297-2

→ Carroll, Ann. *Amazing Grace*. Dublin: Poolbeg Press, 1999. 1-85371-980-3

→ Carroll, Michael. *She Fades Away*. Dublin: Poolbeg Press. 1-85371-621-9

→ Carter, Peter. *Under Goliath*. Oxford: Oxford University Press, 1977. London: Puffin, 1980. 0-14-031132-7

→ Conlon-McKenna, Marita. *In Deep Dark Wood*. Dublin: O'Brien Press, 1999. 0-86278-615-0

→ Conlon-McKenna, Marita. *Safe Harbour*. Dublin: O'Brien Press. 0-86278422-0

→ Cruickshank, Margrit. *Circling the Triangle*. Dublin: Poolbeg Press. 1-85371-1373

→ Flegg, Aubrey. *Katie's War*. Dublin: O'Brien Press. 0-86278-525-1

→ Hennessy, Claire. *Dear Diary*. Dublin: Poolbeg Press, 2000. 1-85371-917-X

→ Leach, Bernadette. *4 Ever Friends*. Cork: Attic Press, 1998. 1-85594-189-9

→ Lingard, Joan. *Twelfth Day of July*. London: Hamish Hamilton, 1970. 0241019842. Puffin Books. 0-14-037236-9

→ Lynch, Chris. *Mick*. Dublin: Poolbeg Press, 1996. 1-85371-781-9

→ Lynch, Chris. *Blood Relations*. Dublin: Poolbeg Press, 1996. 1-85371-781-9

→ Lynch, Chris. *Dog Eat Dog*. Dublin: Poolbeg Press, 1996. 1-85371-786-X

→ MacLaverty, Bernard. *Cal*. Vintage Press. 0-09-976711-2

→ MacRaois, Cormac. *The Battle Below Giltspur*. Dublin: Wolfhound Press, 1989. 0-86327-356-4

→ MacRaois, Cormac. *Lightning over Giltspur*. Dublin: Wolfhound Press, 1991. 0-83627-361-0

→ McBratney, Sam. *You Just Don't Listen*. London: Mammoth, 1994. 0-7497-1699-1

→ Maguire, Gregory. *The Good Liar*. Dublin: O'Brien Press. 0-86278-395-X

→ Moore, Brian. *Lies of Silence*. Vintage Press. 0-09-999810-6

→ Murphy, Martina. *Livewire*. Dublin: Poolbeg Press, 1997. 1-85371-757-6

→ Murphy, Martina. *Fast Car*. Dublin: Poolbeg Press. 1-85371-848-3

→ Murphy, Martina. *Free Fall*. Dublin: Poolbeg Press. 1-85371-970-6

→ Noble, Christina. *Bridge Across my Sorrows*. London: Corgi. 0-552-14288-3

→ O'Neill, Joan. *Daisy Chain War*. Cork: Attic Press, 1990. 1-85594-004-3

→ O'Neill, Joan. *Daisy Chain Wedding*. Dublin: Poolbeg Press. 1-85371-419-4

→ O'Neill, Joan. *Bread and Sugar*. Dublin: Poolbeg Press. 1-85371-313-9

→ O'Sullivan, Mark. *Melody for Nora*. Dublin: Wolfhound Press, 1994. 0-86327-425-0

→ Parkinson, Siobhán. *Amelia*. Dublin: O'Brien Press, 1993. 0-86278-352-6

→ Parkinson, Siobhán. *No Peace for Amelia*. Dublin: O'Brien Press, 1994. 0-86278-378-X

→ Parkinson, Siobhán. *Sisters ... No Way!* Dublin: O'Brien Press, 1996. 0-86278-495-6

→ Shan, Darren. *Cirque Du Freak*. London: Harper Collins, 2000. 0-00-675416-3

→ Shan, Darren. *The Vampire's Assistant*. London: Harper Collins, 2000. 0-00-675513-5

→ Taylor, Marilyn. *Could this be Love? I Wondered*. Dublin: O'Brien Press, 1994. 0-86278-377-1

→ Taylor, Marilyn. *Could I Love a Stranger?* Dublin: O'Brien Press, 1995. 0-86278-442-5

→ Taylor, Marilyn. *Call Yourself a Friend?* Dublin: O'Brien Press, 1996. 0-86278-500-6

→ Taylor, Marilyn. *Faraway Home*. Dublin: O'Brien Press, 1999. 0-86278-643-6

'The Past is
A foreign country ...'
Writing About History

CHILDREN'S BOOKS IN NINETEENTH-CENTURY IRELAND

This essay is a study of the socio-cultural and political forces that influenced children's literary culture in the essentially, if ambiguously, colonial world of nineteenth-century Ireland. It argues that the development of a juvenile literature, in English, for young nineteenth-century Irish 'subjects' is best understood in relation to imperialist ideas of social control and reform. The assimilationist ideology and discursive benevolence constituted by the Act of Union (1800) directed the narrative impulses of many imperialist juvenile writers. There was a significant interest in children's culture from nationalist critics and writers concerned about the 'Anglicisation' of Irish life. Throughout the nineteenth century, Irish children's education and literature became a critical site of textual and historical contestation as authors and critics competed to control juvenile cultural allegiances.

The Act of Union frames the political landscape of nineteenth-century Ireland. While the legislation was mainly the result of economic and strategic concerns to strengthen the power and prestige of the British Empire, many contemporary political arguments portrayed it as a symbol of a new, liberal, imperial consciousness and of an enlightened, more tolerant mode of government between 'Crown and colony' in the new century. In the wake of the Union, there was a proliferation of political pamphlets, essays, letters and even novels, which sought to delineate the new political configuration between the imperial motherland and Ireland. The authors were mainly Anglo-Irish and English MPs, landowners, philanthropists and clergymen. Though written for diverse reasons, many of these writers shared an ideological vision of the Union, in which the empire appeared as a 'family' and Ireland as a newly adopted 'errant child' in need of a civilising 'English' education. Typical is the analysis by an anonymous Officer of the Customs of Ireland in a pamphlet in 1820 entitled *The Absentee: or, A Brief Examination into the Habits and Conditions of the People of Ireland, and the Causes of the Discontent and the Disorganised State of the Lower Classes*. The author believed that the Irish had been left too long to their 'own rude ways'. Scant regard had been paid to the 'culture of their minds, or the improvement of their morals' and neither did 'anyone recommend and enforce habits of order, cleanliness, obedience and industry' on 'the brawny, active, quick-feeling son of Erin', who 'lived on his mountains, or in his unreclaimed bogs, almost as uncouth as the meagre, stinted cattle that grazed on them; ignorant of the language, laws, customs, comforts, and regulations of civilised society' (p.10). The author recommended that educational reforms be introduced, which, given time, would produce 'a visible and permanent effect on the habits, manners and morals' of the 'rising and subsequent generations' (p.12). Thus the project of re*generating* Ireland relied intimately on the project of educating the new *generations* of Irish children.

Central to this discourse of tutoring 'young Ireland' is the nineteenth-century concept of the child's mind as a *tabula rasa* onto which adults could write their social values and political ideals: youth was 'the season for fixing habits'. There was unprecedented interest in the education and socialisation of the new young subjects of Queen Victoria's empire. The cultural imperialism of the administrators of the National School system, set up in 1831, is typical of the faith vested in education as a means to promote political stability in the unruly colony. Numerous reports on education in Ireland were commissioned in the post-Union period, and all recommended that a new 'systematic and uniform plan of instruction' should be introduced to not only 'gratify the desire of information which manifest[ed] itself among the lower classes of the people', but also to 'form those habits of regularity and discipline' which would be 'yet more valuable than mere learning' (*Fifth Report*, p.29). Archbishop Whately, in his capacity as Commissioner of National Education, was a central figure in this social drama. The textbooks which he produced for the system are thinly veiled 'sermons' of empire. Whately believed Ireland had been badly 'brought up' and he frowned upon the irrational strife caused by land wars. He envisioned bringing order out of Irish chaos by colonising young Irish minds. Allusions to the glories of England feature prominently in books written for Irish boys. In the *Second Reading Book* boys are informed that 'On the east of Ireland is England, where the Queen lives, many people who live in Ireland were born in England, and we speak the same language and are called one nation' (1858, p.135). This was reinforced in the *Third Reading Book* as children were taught that 'the people of these islands have one and the same language (at least all who are educated), one and the same Queen, and the same laws' (1843, p.159). Geography lessons in the more advanced readers taught the boys about the glories of empire and Ireland's contribution to the great imperial machine. In a lesson on the 'Coast Scenery of Ireland' in the *Fourth Book*, the harbour of Cobh in Cork is applauded for its value to the imperial mission: 'the harbour is one of the most secure, capacious, and beautiful of the Kingdom, and is large enough to contain the whole navy of the British empire' (p.60). An alluring expression of cultural imperialism is 'A Child's Hymn of Praise' by Ann Taylor, included in *Hullah's Manual*, the songbook sanctioned for use by the Commissioners:

> Thank the goodness and the grace,
> Which on my birth had smiled,
> And made me in these Christian days
> *A Happy English Child.*

> (emphasis mine)

The Board's aim of creating 'happy English children' in Ireland was not, however, allowed to proceed without challenge from prominent nationalists of the day. Thomas Davis condemned the national school system in an essay entitled

'Schools and Study', and pledged his allegiance to the schools controlled by Christian Brothers. The Brothers had initially joined the National Board's system in the early 1830s but had severed the relationship within four years, feeling it was the 'lion's den' for Irish Catholic nationalists. They tried to instil in their pupils the sense that they had a country of their own and a separate cultural identity different and apart from England. The Brothers rejected the 'family romance' imperialism of Whately and his co-administrators in the national schools, and instead created a romanticised nationalist history to set alight the spirits of their boys and make them 'racy of the soil'. The Brothers wrote or edited their own textbooks, drawing on nationalist sources. The *Nation*, newspaper of the Young Ireland movement, praised the Brothers' 'silent patriotism', and one editorial suggested that 'a race reared up on such intellectual food, so strong and healthy, should be good men and good citizens' (16 March 1844). Thus the mindscape of 'young Ireland' was a contested territory in post-Union Ireland. The lines drawn between imperialism and nationalism over the formal education of Irish youth remained visible in juvenile periodicals and fiction throughout the rest of the century.

Maria Edgeworth was the most prolific writer of children's literature in Ireland in the early nineteenth century. She produced, with her father, R.L. Edgeworth, a prodigious body of educational tracts and didactic 'moral' literature, and was primarily interested in using fiction to regulate 'character formation' in children. The theories expounded in *Practical Education* suggest that the goal should be 'the general improvement of the understanding and formation of moral character' (II, p.501). Maria Edgeworth's fiction is, to a large extent, consciously didactic in the sense that its purpose was to promote this philosophy of education, which she and her father believed to be a necessary foundation for national reform after the Union. Many of her juvenile tales are specifically set in Ireland, or make reference to Irish character, and can be interpreted as pedagogical allegories for the kind of society that both she and her father envisioned Ireland could be after the Union. Tales such as 'The Orphans' and 'The White Pigeon' from *The Parent's Assistant*, 'Rosanna' and 'The Limerick Gloves' from *Popular Tales* and the later *Orlandino* present 'family romance' configurations of union and benevolent ascendancy rule. The tales were produced, it seems, to provide role-models for their child readers. They seek to naturalise the relations between landlord and tenant, who are seen to live in harmonious mutual cooperation. Colonial subordination is represented as promoting 'security for all'. Her lessons of duty and submission to different forms of authority reinforced the imperial curriculum of the national schools. The Commissioners of the Board of National Education considered her a suitable writer for inclusion in their textbooks. Extracts from her tales and from *Practical Education* appear throughout all revisions of the school textbooks. When the Great Famine and the subsequent repeal movement radically altered political and social Ireland, Edgeworth's idealisation of the Irish peasant's happy subservience to benevolent colonial government remained a fiction. Few of their fellow landlord class adopted the Edgeworths's exemplary methods of governance by 'reason' – the education question became a ground for sectarian quarrel and the scourge of absenteeism continued despite her appeals. Edgeworth's ideal of post-Union Ireland had never quite appreciated the grievances or desires of Irish nationalism.

Young Ireland, Christmas edition, 1890.

The newly charged climate is recorded in much of the mid- to late-century juvenile literature, and while 'Edgeworthian' fictions of the Union continued to be produced for Irish youth, there is a decidedly more resistant response from nationalist writers who increasingly sought to 'de-Anglicise' Irish life. Two specifically juvenile Irish periodicals, *Young Ireland* (1875–1891) and *Our Boys* (1914–1918 initially), revealed the growing interest in children as an audience for nationalist ideas in post-Famine Ireland. These magazines were established as self-consciously defensive manoeuvres to help provide a bulwark against the perceived 'floods' of English periodicals 'invading' Ireland. The Union had opened up Ireland as a new market for English consumer goods and Ireland was more intensely exposed to English culture, including much juvenile literature produced in London. These magazines relied on the imperial adventure for tales of 'dash and daring', and there was a significant anxiety amongst many nationalists that their tales might encourage Irish boys to become west-British 'empire boys'. *Young Ireland* was not only a late manifestation of the 'spirit' of the earlier nationalist movement, it may be argued that it developed from the teachings of 'Young Ireland'. It was, indeed, for its first editor, A.M. Sullivan, a juvenile form of the *Nation*, which he also owned and edited. The magazine's counteractive tendency is evident in its fiction, historical-biographical sketches, poems, ballads and editorials. Sullivan used the journal to teach lessons in Irish history, for he believed it would provide many instances of heroism to match, if not surpass, those of the English nation. Resistance to English rule formed the essence of 'adventure' in *Young Ireland*, and he catalogued heroes from Cúchulainn to Sarsfield to the men of 1798 and 1848. In 1914 the Christian Brothers introduced *Our Boys*, a nationalist boys' journal. The magazine is remarkably similar in ethos to *Young Ireland*, although it espoused a more militant, sacrificial patriotism among its readers, in a period of heightened political tensions.

The gender politics which marked the Victorian era provided another instance of conflict between the coloniser and the colonised. These gender distinctions were reproduced in children's literature. While most fiction was directed at the male child, much was also written for girls to set out the rules governing proper 'feminine' behaviour for the 'domestic' sphere. Many Anglo-Irish women writers adopted the socially acceptable feminine role of 'educator' in the later nineteenth century and wrote 'Edgeworthian' tales of the civilising influence of English culture and education in Ireland. They gave their stories an Irish interest by including 'wild Irish girls' who were inevitably civilised and tamed when they became accustomed to the improving ways of an English relative or school. The authors were often quite prolific but their work has generally been neglected. They include Josephine M. Callwell, Violet Finny, Flora Shaw and L.T. Meade. Meade has fared better than most, and has been seen as a major figure in the British tradition of 'school-stories'. Her Irish birth and Anglo-Irish identity has been ignored by successive critics however, despite the fact that several of her juvenile novels deal with issues of Irishness and Ireland's place in the united empire. Her titles include *Wild Kitty* (1897), *The Rebel of the School* (n.d.), *Light o' the Morning: The Story of an Irish Girl* (1899) and *A Wild Irish Girl* (1910). Nationalist writers also contrib-

uted to the 'girl's library'. One of the more politically motivated writers was Helena Concannon. Works such as *Daughters of Banba, Defenders of the Ford, Defence of our Gaelic Civilisation* and *Women of '98* were all recommended by the critic and bibliographer Stephen J. Brown for the girls of Ireland. These books sought to revive a sense of nationalist pride in Ireland's past by reviewing all major and minor characters in a history of the long struggle of Irish resistance against colonial rule.

Irish boys' literature was an even more pressing concern for nationalist critics and writers, for it was understood that the future of the nation lay in their hands. The most popular form of English boys' fiction in the late nineteenth century was the historical adventure tale. The main authors included Captain Marryat, J.G. Ballantyne, Gordon Stables, Herbert Strang, Manville Fenn, and G.A. Henty. In an article on 'Juvenile Literature' in 1904 in the *United Irishman*, a nationalist critic, 'Sarsfield', advised readers against Henty's fiction:

Wild Kitty,
illustration by
J. Ayton Symington.

> In all climes and in all ages his hero is English ... and all his books tend to foster pride of race and the plausible delusion that 'God first made his Englishman' ... The Englishman is always held up as a model, references are constantly made to his patriotism, his 'glorious heritage, civilising mission ... and is it any wonder if so many of our boys become Empire-worshippers when subjected to the insidious attacks of literature of this description.

'Sarsfield' argued that the Irish juvenile imagination was still colonised by the 'alien' medium of English cultural images, and suggested that it was a matter of national concern that efforts be made to introduce Irish children to Irish historical literature and tales of Irish heroes. Henty did feature Irish themes and characters in his own fiction, but subscribed to the 'fiction of the Union', which held Ireland as a part of the empire. In *Orange and Green, In the Irish Brigade, With Moore at Corunna* and *Under Wellington's Command*, Henty detailed the complex involvement of Irishmen in the empire by representing the 'Irishness' of the imperial army in many of the overseas colonies. Nationalist critics such as Brown and 'Sarsfield' rejected these narratives. They were unwilling to acknowledge any element of Irish complicity in the empire – their imperative was to 'recruit' children to the nationalist ideal. Brown was aggrieved that although the Irish sagas held a wealth of cultural history that was 'truly' Irish, heroic figures such as Cúchulainn and Finn were virtually 'strangers' to most Irish children. It was in this climate that Cúchulainn was popularised and made especially available to young Ireland. Standish O'Grady produced *The Coming of Cuchulain, Finn and his Companions, In the Gates of the North* and *The Triumph and Passing of Cuchulain*, while Lady Gregory produced *Cuculain of Muirthemne* (1902) and *Gods and Fighting Men* (1904). Eleanor Hull published *Cuchulain, the Hound of Ulster*, while William Lorcan O'Brien wrote *A Land of Heroes, Kings and Vikings* and *Children of Kings*. It was the beginning of a cultural awakening and a fascination with the old legends which remain popular in children's literature to the present day.

In 1997 the critic Robert Dunbar contributed an essay to the journal *The Lion and the Unicorn* on the subject of 'The World of Irish Children's Literature', which remains one the few critical assessments of this largely neglected 'world'. Dunbar observed that although there was an Irish tradition of children's writing encompassing nearly three hundred years, 'the authoritative history of the subject remained to be compiled', but he felt that when and if it were produced it ought to be a 'very lengthy and wide-ranging work' (p.309). There has certainly been a dearth of research in the history of Irish children's literature. However, I hope this essay has illuminated the wealth of cultural and social history to be recovered, and detailed how children's literary culture, an area generally neglected by historians and cultural critics alike, is a valuable window through which to view the particular status of Ireland in both imperialist and nationalist discourse in the nineteenth century.

REFERENCES

→ Anonymous (An Officer of the Customs of Ireland). *The Absentee: or, a Brief Examination Into the Habits and Conditions of the People of Ireland, and the Causes of the Discontent and the Disorganised State of the Lower Classes*, p.556. Joly Pamphlet, National Library of Ireland, 1820.
→ Anonymous ('Sarsfield'). 'Juvenile Literature'. In *United Irishman*, p. 3. March 26 1904.
→ Brown, Reverend Stephen J. 'Irish Fiction for Boys'. In *Studies*, Vol.7, pp.665–70. 1918; Vol.8, pp.469–72, pp.658–63. 1918.

→ *Catholic Juvenile Literature: A Classified List.* Catholic Bibliographical Series, No. 5. London: Burns and Oates, 1935.

→ Davis, Thomas. *Essays and Poems.* Dublin: M.H. Gill and Son, 1945.

→ Dunbar, Robert. 'Rarely Pure and Never Simple: The World of Irish Children's Literature'. In *The Lion and the Unicorn, Special Issue on Irish Children's Literature,* Vol.21, pp.309–321. 1997.

→ Edgeworth, Maria and Edgeworth, R.L. *Practical Education.* London: Joseph Johnson, 1798.

TITLES REFERRED TO IN ARTICLE

→ Callwell, Josephine Martin. *Timothy Tatters: A Story for the Young.* London: T. Nelson & Sons, 1896.

→ Callwell, Josephine Martin. *A Little Irish Girl.* London, Glasgow and Dublin: Blackie & Son, 1902.

→ Concannon, Mrs Thomas. *Women of '98.* Dublin: M.H. Gill & Son, 1919.

→ Callwell, Josephine Martin. *Daughters of Banba.* Dublin: M.H. Gill & Son, 1922.

→ Edgeworth, Maria. *The Parent's Assistant: or, Stories for Children.* Six volumes. London: J. Johnson, 1804.

→ Edgeworth, Maria. *Popular Tales.* London: C. Mercier, 1804.

→ Edgeworth, Maria. *Orlandino.* Edinburgh: Chambers, 1848, 1883.

→ Finny, Violet. *A Daughter of Erin.* London, Glasgow and Dublin: Blackie & Son, 1898.

→ Henty, George Alfred. *Orange and Green: A Tale of the Boyne and Limerick.* Glasgow, Edinburgh and Dublin: Blackie & Son, 1888.

→ Henty, George Alfred. *With Moore at Corunna: A Tale of the Peninsular War.* London, Glasgow and Dublin: Blackie & Son, 1898.

→ Henty, George Alfred. *Under Wellington's Command: A Tale of the Peninsular War.* Glasgow and Dublin: Blackie & Son, 1899.

→ Hull, Eleanor. *Cuchulain the Hound of Ulster.* London: George C. Harrap, 1909.

→ Meade, L.T. (Elizabeth Thomasina Toulmin Smith). *Wild Kitty.* London: Chambers, 1897.

→ Meade, L.T. *Light o' the Morning: The Story of an Irish Girl.* London: Chambers, 1899.

→ Meade, L.T. *Rebel of the School.* London: Chambers, n.d.

→ Meade, L.T. *A Wild Irish Girl.* London: Chambers, 1910.

→ O'Byrne, William Lorcan. *A Land of Heroes: Stories from Early Irish History.* London: Blackie & Son, 1899.

→ O'Byrne, William Lorcan. *Kings and Vikings.* London: Blackie & Son, 1901.

→ O'Byrne, William Lorcan. *Children of Kings.* London: Blackie & Son, 1904.

→ O'Grady, Standish. *Finn and His Companions.* London: T. Fisher Unwin, 1892.

→ O'Grady, Standish. *The Coming of Cuchulain.* London: Methuen, 1894.

→ O'Grady, Standish. *In the Gates of the North.* Kilkenny: Standish O'Grady, 1901.

→ O'Grady, Standish. *The Triumph and Passing of Cuchulain.* Dublin: Talbot Press, 1920.

Classic Irish Children's Books

Mention the word 'classics' in the context of English children's literature and almost immediately we find ourselves discussing the *Alice* books or *Treasure Island* or *The Wind in the Willows*. Change the focus to America and we are soon contemplating *Little Women* or *The Adventures of Tom Sawyer* or *The Wonderful Wizard of Oz*. But when we turn to Irish children's literature no similar list of titles readily suggests itself. Those children's books from the late nineteenth and early twentieth century which can, with varying degrees of legitimacy, be considered 'Irish' books and which would have appeared more or less contemporaneously with the English and American titles mentioned above, today have only an antiquarian or academic interest. They may be fascinating in what they reveal of the social, cultural, political and literary conditions in which they were produced, but, with only a few exceptions, they have not outlived those conditions to speak to later readers. They have failed, in effect, to attain the status defined by Italo Calvino in one of his claims for 'classics', namely that they 'are books which exercise a particular influence, both when they imprint themselves on our imagination as unforgettable, and when they hide in the layers of memory disguised as the individual's or the collective unconscious.'

Before considering some of the exceptions to this general scarcity of the indigenous Irish children's 'classic', it is fair to point out that prior to the nineteenth century there were at least two significant contributors to our native literature for the young: Jonathan Swift and Maria Edgeworth. Jonathan Swift's *Gulliver's Travels* (1726), remains a central text in arguments as to what constitutes or does not constitute writing for children. Swift's most recent biographer, Victoria Glendinning, after commenting that there is much in Swift's 'lavatory humour' and 'love of wordplay' that can appeal to children, nevertheless concludes: 'But it is a book for adults.' In its original, full-length form, endowed with its blistering satirical intent, this is undoubtedly true. But the fact remains that within a few years of its first publication, retellings and abridgements with a young audience specifically in mind had begun to appear – and have continued to do so. Today, in most cases, these retellings and abridgements concentrate on the first two of Gulliver's voyages, to Lilliput and Brobdingnag. The timeless appeal of these voyages lies in the traveller's succession of extraordinary encounters and in the graphic detail that makes the extraordinary credible. These are also the qualities which have long made *Gulliver's Travels* a popular subject for illustration, a dimension of many of the modern versions that has enhanced their appeal.

Gulliver's Travels,
illustrated by Martin Hargreaves.

It was Maria Edgeworth, another early writer with some claim to inclusion in a survey of Irish children's 'classics', who, in an essay co-written with her father, conceded that *Gulliver's Travels* could be enjoyed by children, but then went on to propose that children's taste for adventure 'is absolutely incompatible with the sober perseverance necessary to success.' The utilitarian, didactic note in this statement goes some way towards explaining the central concerns in her own stories, in collections such as *The Parent's Assistant* (1796) and *Moral Tales* (1801), and why these would generally be seen to be out of tune with modern tastes. It would, however, be possible, by choosing judiciously from them, to edit a selection reflecting Edgeworth's sense of humour, her skilful handling of dialogue and her occasional understanding of the real child beneath the being especially created to expound an educational philosophy.

Historians of children's literature in its written form usually trace its origins to a country's store of traditional stories, myths, legends and folk tales. This is an area in which the Irish are particularly rich and the one that, more than any other, has dictated the course of development for our children's writers, especially when they engage in the writing of fantasy. Our ancient narratives, initially transmitted orally, have served as the starting point for numerous retellings, adaptations and novelisations for both child and adult readers (and sometimes for both simultaneously). This tendency, which reached its fullest expression during the Irish Literary Revival, between, approximately, the 1890s and the 1920s, continues today in the multicoloured 'Irish Myths and Legends' collections which pour from our publishers' presses. While in most cases these modern collections have replaced the more overtly ideological output of the Revivalists, some of the earlier manifestations of the genre have survived – though, interestingly, not always those with an immediately obvious Irish thematic link.

In *Granny's Wonderful Chair* (1856), Donegal-born Frances Browne, produced a set of seven 'tales of fairy times', clearly influenced more by the work of Hans Christian Andersen and the Grimm brothers than by Irish tradition, in which the magic chair of the title is gifted with the power of speech; it is a tribute to the freshness of her style and content that the book has rarely gone out of print. Similarly, the two volumes of fairy tales by Oscar Wilde, *The Happy Prince* (1888) and *A House of Pomegranates* (1891), owe more to influences from continental Europe than from Ireland, though these influences were adroitly adopted by Wilde for his own purposes, which can range from the sentimental to the socialist, the sombre to the cynical. Written, according to one of his own letters, 'partly for children and partly for those who have kept the childlike faculties of wonder and joy', Wilde's fairy tales, which are usually amalgamated into a single volume in modern versions, may have an ambivalent status as 'children's literature', yet it is for a young readership that most new editions are

Oscar Wilde, Stories for Children, illustrated by P.J. Lynch.

published: these, whether in the form of individual stories or selections or all nine originals, are often luxuriously illustrated.

While numerous references to fairy worlds are to be found in W.B. Yeats's poetry from his first collection onwards, it was in his role as anthologist that he brought his fascination with the Irish supernatural to a wide audience. His two principal compilations, *Fairy and Folk Tales of the Irish Peasantry* (1888) and *Irish Fairy Tales* (1892), embody the Revivalists' desire to restore Ireland's cultural heritage through a rediscovery of its ancient sagas and a recognition of the strength and colour of its folklore. In total, the anthologies comprise some seventy stories. Nineteen of these, selected by Neil Philip and assembled as *W.B. Yeats: Fairy Tales of Ireland*, were published in 1990 'with young readers in mind' in a handsome edition illustrated in black and white by P.J. Lynch. The prose of many of the stories is now rather dated, but still likely to appeal in its sheer spookiness is the story called 'The Man Who Never Knew Fear', specially translated for Yeats from the Irish by Douglas Hyde. Some of the stories from Yeats's anthologies, together with others from such Revivalist names as Standish O'Grady and Eleanor Hull, can be found in Gordon Jarvie's collection, *Irish Folk and Fairy Tales* (1992).

Ella Young, whose County Antrim upbringing provided a first acquaintance with ancient Irish stories, recalls how she travelled throughout 'Gaelic Ireland' hearing 'the poems of the Fianna recited by folk who had heard the faery music and had danced in faery circles.' There may be suggestions in the vocabulary of a sort of 'Oirish' whimsy, but her own retellings, in collections such as *Celtic Wonder Tales* (1910), *The Wonder Smith and his Son* (1927) and *The Tangle-Coated Horse* (1929), are noticeably free from such excesses. Instead, they are typified by an almost childlike sense of wonder in the face of the world's marvellous strangeness: they remain among the highest achievements of their kind. 'She speaks of Celtic times,' wrote Padraic Colum, 'as though she were recalling them.'

Colum himself, in, for example, *The King of Ireland's Son*, is much more convoluted, but a story such as this impresses by its dignity and its refusal to sacrifice authenticity of tone for easy effect. It is widely accepted that his children's versions of myths from such disparate sources as the Welsh, Greek, Hawaiian and Norse traditions are models of the genre, though only one, *The Children of Odin* (1920), is currently available. These and his collection of eight folk tales about horses, *The Forge in the Forest* (1925), stunningly illustrated by Boris Artzybasheff, deserve early reissue.

The King of Ireland's Son, illustrated by Willy Pogány.

First published in 1920, James Stephens's *Irish Fairy Tales* was described by Stephens himself as 'not a book for children at all'. Whatever their primary audience, these tales are historically significant in that they offer elemental themes and forms which, at a time when Irish identity was in a state of flux, are themselves change and changing. Two years later, Mícheál Mac Liammóir provided a more homely touch in his *Faery Nights* (*Oícheanta Sí*), a sequence of four bilingual stories celebrating some of the ancient Celtic festivals and featuring some likeably realistic young people caught up in those seasonal mysteries. Where realistic young fictional people are concerned, however, the most immediately likeable of the period was unquestionably Jimeen, the eponymous hero of the Irish-language novel (1921) by Pádraig Ó Siochfhradha. Some sixty years were to pass before the escapades of this mischievous scamp were available in an English translation.

Faery Nights, illustrated by Mícheál Mac Liammóir.

The word 'classic', as applied to books, is used loosely in everyday conversation to imply notions of merit or excellence, irrespective of the age of the material concerned. However, its more precise use generally suggests books which have demonstrated over a period of time (perhaps we could use fifty years as a minimum?) their enduring significance. If we relate this interpretation to Irish children's literature, then in an essay such as this we automatically dismiss consideration of the work of a number of writers who first came to prominence in the 1940s, 1950s and 1960s. In many cases, their work has fared little better than that of most of their predecessors and is already out of print. Some of our publishers, however, have made a commendable effort to revive what they perceive as the best of it, thus providing today's readers with an opportunity to encounter such writers as Eilís Dillon, Patricia Lynch, Walter Macken, Janet McNeill, Eileen O'Faoláin and Meta Mayne Reid. The fact that most of these were prolific writers means that not everything they wrote is necessarily of the highest attainment, but, as the annotations below suggest, at least some of their work has been worth preserving. To these names must be added that of Belfast-born C.S. Lewis, whose seven *Narnia* novels remain Ireland's most widely known contribution to children's literature – at least outside his own country. Most of the writers mentioned here, together with some from the succeeding generation, are represented in Robert Dunbar's *Enchanted Journeys* (1997), an anthology of seventeen excerpts which take the reader backwards from contemporary Irish children's writing to what was first available in the 1940s.

When Eilís Dillon and her co-editors produced an anthology called *The Lucky Bag* (1984), subtitled *Classic Irish Stories*, she wrote in her introduction: 'One thing they (the stories) all have in common is that they are Irish, and that means they are good stories in the sense that you will never be bored by them.' Later, she concedes that 'A good many of our stories were not written for children at all but, like *Gulliver's Travels*, can be read by everyone.' Sixteen years on, the uncertainty voiced by Dillon as to what the 'classics' of Irish children's literature might be still remains, though it is clear enough that they are not in very plentiful supply. Does any of this matter? The modern young reader, with so much printed material to choose from, is unlikely to be drawn to any kind of earlier writing which too heavily bears the traces of its time and, moreover, is likely to be deterred from approaching such books if they come recommended by well-meaning adults who perceive them as 'classic'. Perhaps the solution is to encourage the young to read everything *other* than whatever 'classics' there are, and to let this reading serve as an apprenticeship for the adult years when the 'classics' may be more happily encountered. To return again to Italo Calvino: 'The classics are those books which constitute a treasured experience for those who have read and loved them; but they remain just as rich an experience for those who reserve the chance to read them for when they are in the best condition to enjoy them.'

Jimeen,
illustrated by
Kieron Black.

REFERENCES

→ Calvino, Italo. *Why Read the Classics?* London: Vintage Press, 2000.
→ Colum, Padraic. *Ella Young, an Appreciation.* New York: Longman, Green, 1931.
→ Edgeworth, R.L. and Maria. *Practical Education.* London: Joseph Johnson, 1798.
→ Finneran, Richard J. *Letters of James Stephens.* London: Macmillan, 1974.
→ Glendinning, Victoria. *Jonathan Swift.* London: Hutchinson, 1998.
→ Hart-Davis, Rupert. *The Letters of Oscar Wilde.* London: Hart-Davis, 1962.

RECOMMENDED TITLES

Frances Browne
GRANNY'S WONDERFUL CHAIR
ACC Children's Classics

When Snowflower's grandmother, Dame Frostyface, goes away on a journey, the little girl is left alone in their cottage – except for an old wooden chair. This chair has a special, wonderful property: it has the power of speech. This ability is put to marvellous use as it entertains young Snowflower during Frostyface's absence with a succession of fairy stories. Additionally, it has the power to transport Snowflower anywhere she wishes to go, and their travels take them to the court of King Winwealth. At the nightly banquets the chair's storytelling talents are much in demand – an opportunity that it seizes to tell stories which highlight the moral inadequacies of corrupt court life. This edition has vividly coloured illustrations by Gisèle Rime and, as a bonus, part of an introduction written in 1904 by Frances Hodgson Burnett.

Granny's Wonderful Chair,
illustrated by Gisèle Rime.

Padraic Colum
THE KING OF IRELAND'S SON
Floris Books

'Conall was the name of the king who ruled over Ireland at that time.' From this straightforward opening sentence, Colum weaves a complex quest story of the travels of the eldest and wildest of Conall's three sons, resulting in a multi-layered book which, in effect, is a series of tales within a tale. For most young readers it may prove a challenging read, although there is plenty in the two contrasting hero-narratives – the son's search for the Enchanter's daughter and Gilly of the Goatskin's search for his parents – to maintain their interest. Published originally in the United States in 1916, the book had its beginnings in an English translation, by Colum, of an Irish language story. This translation was seen by the Hungarian illustrator Willy Pogány, and it is Pogány's original black-and-white illustrations which decorate this reissue.

Eilís Dillon
THE SINGING CAVE
Poolbeg Press

Like most of Eilís Dillon's adventure stories, *The Singing Cave* (1959) is set in the west of Ireland. The natural wildness of this terrain serves as an admirable background for this dramatic quest story, in which young Pat and his friend, Tom, embark on the trail of a missing Viking skeleton, originally encountered by Pat in the singing cave of the title. In addition to the author's usual skill in constructing a narrative of fluctuating tension and subtly conveyed atmosphere, she here shows a particular flair for the highly charged set-piece: the second chapter, in which Pat first discovers the skeleton and his ancient 'gaming board', is a triumph of disciplined writing. Also recommended: *The Coriander, The Cruise of the Santa Maria, The Island of Ghosts, The Lost Island, The San Sebastian.*

Eilís Dillon, Pat Donlon, et al (eds)
THE LUCKY BAG
O'Brien Press

As Eilís Dillon's introduction to this anthology indicates, definitions of 'classic Irish children's stories' (the subtitle of the book) are elusive. Settling for a comprehensive interpretation, she and her co-editors have assembled twenty prose excerpts, only a minority of which would originally have been written for children. Dillon's own contribution, a short story entitled 'Bad Blood', is a powerful variation on the 'bridging' theme of adolescence, showing, as she expresses it in her introduction, 'boys on the edge of being grown up and learning to handle the good and bad aspects of being a man.'

C.S. Lewis
THE NARNIA STORIES
Collins

The imaginary land of Narnia provides the setting for seven stories, listed on p.68, by C.S. Lewis. Although adult opinion about their merits is divided, it is undoubtedly the case that in the fifty years since their first publication they have remained popular with generations of children. Today, there may be some reservations about the extent to which Lewis's own prejudices and preferences distort the stories, but the young reader, happy to enjoy action, excitement and, unarguably, the workings of a rich imagination, is likely to respond favourably to their sheer narrative power. The centenary of Lewis's birth, in 1998, brought reissues with newly coloured versions of the original black-and-white illustrations by Pauline Baynes.

Patricia Lynch
THE BOOKSHOP ON THE QUAY
Poolbeg Press

Author of some fifty books for children, Patricia Lynch worked in a variety of genres, including fantasy, historical fiction and the adventure story. While her 1934 novel *The Turf-Cutter's Donkey* was to become one of the most loved children's books of its time, its 'magic' may seem too whimsical for today's young reader. Her lasting appeal is more likely to be with a book such as *The Bookshop on the Quay* (1956), where Shane Madden, an orphan, leaves his native village in County Cork to walk to Dublin. There, while hoping to find his uncle Tim, he is befriended by the O'Clery family, proprietors of the bookshop of the title. The themes of rejection, loneliness and loss, typical of Lynch's more serious novels, are handled with considerable poignancy. Also recommended: *Fiddler's Quest, The Dark Sailor of Youghal, The Grey Goose of Kilnevin* and *The Mad O'Haras*. Robert Dunbar's *Secret Lands: The World of Patricia Lynch* is an anthology of fifteen excerpts from Lynch's work, with an introduction setting it in its historical and literary context.

Walter Macken
FLIGHT OF THE DOVES
Pan Piper Books

Primarily known for his adult novels and for his plays, Macken's work for children amounts to two books. *Flight of the Doves* (1968) is an exciting variation on the 'runaway' story, in which Finn Dove and his younger sister, Derval, escape from England and their vindictive uncle Toby to Galway, where their Granny O'Flaherty lives. The narrative, lively and speedily paced, becomes a series of encounters, the diversity of which is one of the book's greatest strengths. Dominating it all, however, is young Finn, against whose unwavering sense of purpose all other actions and motives are measured. Macken's other children's novel, *Island of the Great Yellow Ox*, is no longer in print.

Mícheál Mac Liammóir
FAERY NIGHTS: OÍCHEANTA SÍ
O'Brien Press

A minor rather than a major 'classic', this collection of stories (presented alternately in English and Irish) has nevertheless a number of claims on the young reader's attention. Subtitled *Stories of Ancient Celtic Festivals*, the book provides appropriate stories for St Brigid's Eve, May Day Eve, St John's Eve and Hallowe'en. These are thematically linked not merely by the seasonal cycle but also by their epigraph, which reminds us that 'the darkness is the best time for adventure'. But the child characters at the centre of the stories can, in their quick-wittedness and sense of fun, more than hold their own against whatever forces temporarily threaten their well-being.

Janet McNeill
MY FRIEND SPECS McCANN
Poolbeg Press

Born in Dublin and resident for most of her life in Belfast, Janet McNeill wrote some forty children's books. Although highly regarded at the time of their publication, her books have been allowed to go out of print; it is to be hoped that the best of them, such as the excellent *The Battle of St George Without*, *Goodbye, Dove Square* and *We Three Kings*, might be reissued. *My Friend Specs McCann* (1955) introduces the irrepressibly optimistic Ulster schoolboy Specs, who good-humouredly lives with and learns to exploit the frustrations of being merely a boy in an apparently bizarre adult world. Unlikely though the details of the plot may be, and hard though it may be for today's young readers to accept that Specs is thirteen, it remains true that the stories have their own weird logic.

My Friend Specs McCann, illustrated by Jon Berkeley.

Eileen O'Faoláin
THE LITTLE BLACK HEN
Poolbeg Press

This is a charming little story (1940) of how two children, Julie and Garret, take on the forces of fairyland when their best friend's little black hen is snatched away and forced into the role of Queen Cliona's servant. There is an impressive cast of picturesque characters – human, fairy and animal – with Seana Thady, the leprechaun, easily stealing the show.

Pádraig Ó Siochfhradha
JIMEEN
O'Brien Press

'But that's the way with me. I never think first.' The high-spirited antics of the young hero of *Jimeen* (1921), newly illustrated by Kieron Black, retain all their original fun. The sprightly first-person narrative of the translation carries the reader along at a good pace. Thirteen years of age, Jimeen has the knack of invariably finding mischief wherever it is to be found. The final chapter, taking Jimeen to a very unexpected calling, can still come as a bit of a shock.

Meta Mayne Reid
THE TWO REBELS
Poolbeg Press

Born in Yorkshire, Meta Mayne Reid was of Irish descent and spent most of her adult life in Northern Ireland. Her twenty-three children's books include historical fiction, time-slip fantasy and contemporary stories; nearly all of them are set in Ulster. Well regarded critically at their time of publication, they are now almost entirely out of print, though her historical fiction has a strong claim to be read and remembered, not least because its Ulster setting gives much of it an incidental contemporary relevance. Dealing with the Antrim town uprising of 1798, *The Two Rebels* convincingly presents for a young readership the conflicting ideologies and loyalties of the time. Also recommended: *Beyond the Wide World's End*.

Jonathan Swift
GULLIVER'S TRAVELS
Dorling Kindersley

Unlike most versions produced for a young readership, this adaptation, by James Dunbar, does not concentrate exclusively on Gulliver's voyages to Lilliput and Brobdingnag. It offers retellings of the additional journeys to Laputa and to the country of the Houyhnhnms, and also provides, in its borders and fact panels, a fascinating range of information about Swift and the eighteenth-century literary and political circumstances which gave rise to his satire (first published in 1726). In the desire to make the original so accessible some losses are inevitable, but Dunbar still manages to convey the Swiftian spirit, including some of its savagery and candour. The full-colour artwork, by Martin Hargreaves, is in the pictorial narrative style and captures Swift's play with scale and dimension – one of the aspects of the original that appeals to the young reader. The use of photography in the supporting background material enhances a volume in which text, illustration, layout and design combine most attractively.

Oscar Wilde
THE FAIRY TALES OF OSCAR WILDE
Little, Brown & Company

This edition comprises the nine 'fairy tales' from Wilde's two original collections (1888 and 1891) and comes with an introduction by Neil Philip, who reminds us that Wilde himself described them as having 'many secrets and many answers'. While Wildean scholars may devote their energies to disinterring these secrets and to speculating about their own answers, young readers will respond more to the stories' haunting combination of the beautiful and the tragic, and to the picture which emerges of the essential fragility of worldly happiness and success. The ornateness of the prose may be an occasional obstacle to full enjoyment, but this does not diminish the poignancy of 'The Happy Prince' or 'The Selfish Giant'. The full-page illustrations in this edition are by Isabelle Brent, whose richly bordered and highly coloured pictures, complete with a touch of gold leaf, accentuate the opulence of Wilde's language. Also recommended: *Oscar Wilde: Stories for Children*, illustrated by P.J. Lynch; *Oscar Wilde: Stories for Children*, illustrated by Jenny Thorne.

Ella Young
THE WONDER SMITH AND HIS SON
Floris Books

First published in 1927, this volume provides a version of the Gubbaun Saor story which remains extremely vivid and fresh. While dealing with larger-than-life characters and events, Young invests her stories with the sights, sounds and colours of everyday existence. In a brief foreword she recalls how the stories, which she first encountered on Achill Island, became mixed in her head 'with sunshine and sweet air and wide empty spaces' – a facet of their origins which is invigoratingly transferred to her prose. This edition includes the black-and-white art deco artwork which Boris Artzybasheff provided for the original publication; its sharp angles and pristine linear precision are strongly evocative of the book's subtitle, *A Tale from the Golden Childhood of the World*. Also recommended: *Celtic Wonder Tales*; *The Tangle-Coated Horse*.

The Tangle-Coated Horse, illustrated by Vera Bock.

TITLES REFERRED TO IN ARTICLE AND IN RECOMMENDED LIST

→ Browne, Frances/Rime, Gisèle (illus.). *Granny's Wonderful Chair*. Suffolk: ACC Children's Classics, 1990. 1-85149-706-4

→ Colum, Padraic/Pogány, Willy (illus.). *The Children of Odin*. Edinburgh: Floris Books,1993. 0-86315-522-7

→ Colum, Padraic/Pogány, Willy (illus.). *The King of Ireland's Son*. Edinburgh: Floris Books, 1986. 0-86315-512-X

→ Dillon, Eilís. *The Coriander*. Dublin: Poolbeg Press, 1992. 1-85371-214-0

→ Dillon, Eilís. *The Cruise of the Santa Maria*. Dublin: O'Brien Press, 1991. 0-86278-263-5

→ Dillon, Eilís. *The Island of Ghosts*. London: Faber and Faber, 1990. 0-571-14267-2

→ Dillon, Eilís. *The Lost Island*. Dublin: O'Brien Press, 1986. 0-86278-118-3

→ Dillon, Eilís. *The San Sebastian*. Dublin: Poolbeg Press, 1996. 1-85371-666-9

→ Dillon, Eilís. *The Singing Cave*. Dublin: Poolbeg Press, 1991.1-85371-153-5

→ Dillon, Eilís, Donlon, Pat, et al (eds)/Galel, Martin (illus.). *The Lucky Bag*. Dublin: O'Brien Press, 1984. 0-86278-064-0

→ Dunbar, Robert (ed.)/Johnston, Aileen (illus.). *Enchanted Journeys*. Dublin: O'Brien Press, 1997. 0-86278-518-9

→ Dunbar, Robert (ed.)/Johnston, Aileen (illus.). *Secret Lands: The World of Patricia Lynch*. Dublin: O'Brien Press, 1998. 0-86278-575-8

→ Jarvie, Gordon (ed.). *Irish Folk and Fairy Tales*. London: Puffin Books, 1992. 0-14-035141-8

→ Lewis, C.S./Baynes, Pauline (illus.). *Prince Caspian*. London: Collins Press, 1998. 0-00-671679-2

→ Lewis, C.S./Baynes, Pauline (illus.). *The Horse and his Boy*. London: Collins Press, 1998. 0-00-671678-4

→ Lewis, C.S./Baynes, Pauline (illus.). *The Last Battle*. London: Collins Press, 1998. 0-00-671682-2

→ Lewis, C.S./Baynes, Pauline (illus.). *The Lion, the Witch and the Wardrobe*. London: Collins Press, 1998. 0-00-671677-6

→ Lewis, C.S./Baynes, Pauline (illus.). *The Silver Chair*. London: Collins Press, 1998. 0-00-671681-4

→ Lewis, C.S./Baynes, Pauline (illus.). *The Voyage of the Dawn Treader*. London: Collins Press, 1998. 0-00-671680-6

→ Lewis, C.S./Baynes, Pauline (illus.). *The Complete Chronicles of Narnia*. London: Collins Press, 1998. 0-00-185713-4

→ Lynch, Patricia. *Fiddler's Quest*. Dublin: Poolbeg Press, 1994. 1-85371-333-3

→ Lynch, Patricia. *The Bookshop on the Quay*. Dublin: Poolbeg Press, 1995. 1-85371-443-7

→ Lynch, Patricia. *The Dark Sailor of Youghal*. Dublin: Poolbeg Press, 1995. 1-85371-517-4

→ Lynch, Patricia. *The Grey Goose of Kilnevin*. Dublin: Poolbeg Press, 1994. 1-85371-406-2

→ Lynch, Patricia. *The Mad O'Haras*. Dublin: Poolbeg Press, 1997. 1-85371-721-5

→ Macken, Walter/Keeping, Charles (illus.). *Flight of the Doves*. London: Pan Piper Books, 1988. 0-330-02655-0

→ Mac Liammóir, Mícheál. *Faery Nights: Oícheanta Sí*. Dublin: O'Brien Press, 2000. 0-86278-681-9

→ McNeill, Janet. *My Friend Specs McCann*. Dublin: Poolbeg Press, 1995. 1-85371-537-9

→ O'Faoláin, Eileen. *The Little Black Hen*. Dublin: Poolbeg Press, 1989. 1-85371-049-0

→ Ó Siochfhradha, Pádraig/Black, Kieron (illus.). *Jimeen*. Dublin: O'Brien Press, 2000. 0-86278-680-0

→ Reid, Meta Mayne. *Beyond the Wide World's End*. Dublin: Poolbeg Press, 1995. 1-85371-509-3

→ Reid, Meta Mayne. *The Two Rebels*. Dublin: Poolbeg Press, 1994. 1-85371-443-7

→ Stephens, James/Rackham, Arthur (illus.). *Irish Fairy Tales*. Dublin: Gill & Macmillan,1995. 0-717-12298-0

→ Swift, Jonathan/Hargreaves, Martin (illus.). *Gulliver's Travels*. London: Dorling Kindersley, 2000. 0-75137-245-5

→ Wilde, Oscar/Lynch, P.J. (illus.). *Stories for Children*. Hemel Hampstead: Simon & Schuster, 1990. 0-75000-302-3

→ Wilde, Oscar/Thorne, Jenny (illus.). *Stories for Children*. Leicester: Armadillo, 1999. 1-90046-582-5

→ Wilde, Oscar/Brent, Isabelle (illus.). *The Fairy Tales of Oscar Wilde*. London: Little, Brown & Co., 1994. 0-316-90987-4

→ Yeats, W.B./Lynch, P.J. (illus.). *Fairy Tales of Ireland*. London: Collins Press, 1990. 0-00-184437-7

→ Young, Ella/Gonne, Maud (illus.). *Celtic Wonder Tales*. Edinburgh: Floris Books, 1988. 0-86315-510-3

→ Young, Ella/Bock, Vera (illus.). *The Tangle-Coated Horse*. Edinburgh: Floris Books, 1991. 0-86315-517-0

→ Young, Ella/Artzybasheff, Boris (illus.). *The Wonder Smith and his Son*. Edinburgh: Floris Books, 1992. 0-86315-521-9

THE FAMINE TOLD TO THE CHILDREN

Although the story of the Great Irish Famine of the 1840s and its aftermath is complex and emotive, it has been the subject of some seventeen novels for children in the last ten years. This is no bad thing in view of the fact that famine still threatens many people in today's world, and that refugees come to Ireland to escape the threat. It is important that Irish children learn that we once shared their plight.

However, it is not surprising that efforts to tell the story to children should prove difficult for British and Irish writers alike. The subject is intrinsically difficult to shape into a narrative for child readers. It lacks many of the ingredients of a good children's story, the most important of which is the potential for action. The Great Famine is a story of mass suffering. The children's writer must do justice to that without the relief that adventure or conflict can provide, and without indulging in suffering and despair in the manner of a horror story. The second and related missing ingredient is that of an agreed villain. Only in the most extreme nationalist history can it be suggested that the Famine was deliberate genocide by the British. Only in the most extreme unionist version of the story can the lazy Irish peasants or the greedy Irish landlords be solely blamed. Children's writers like to use strong plots, clear characterisation and simple explanations of events. Even characterisation becomes difficult in Famine narratives – there is a tendency for the hungry to become indistinguishable from each other, to become mere objects of pity and horror.

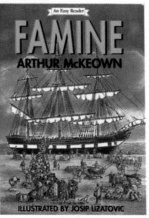

Writers resort to a variety of expedients to make the Famine in some way tellable to children. One device used by several novelists is to abandon the Famine quite early in the novel so that the narrative becomes an emigration story, usually to North America. This transforms a tale of suffering into one of adventure, of travel to exciting places, of chance encounters and the opportunity to make fortunes. This is the pattern in Michael Morpurgo's *Twist of Gold*, Arthur McKeown's *Famine*, Michael Smith's *Boston! Boston!* and Colette McCormack's *Mary Anne's Famine*. In a number of novels with this pattern a family survives intact, or is reunited in North America. This is the structure most likely to offer a happy ending, which often includes love, marriage and prosperity. The most explicit expression of this comes at the end of Arthur McKeown's story, *Famine*, when the elderly father says:

Famine, illustrated by Josip Lizatovic.

> 'It's a long way from Ballymore, Maggie. I'm glad we made the decision to come here all those years ago'.

> 'Yes, I'm glad we came too,' Maggie replied. 'It was a hard journey but we have a good life here [in West Virginia].'

Another related device is the promise of a sequel set in America, as happens at the end of Elizabeth Lutzeier's *The Coldest Winter*. One novel, Soinbhe Lally's *The Hungry Wind*, uses the emigration plot in an unusual way. The destination is Australia, not North America, and the long journey comes quite late in the novel. The bulk of the novel is an account of the experiences of two sisters in the workhouse, a setting avoided by most writers for children. (Yvonne MacGrory is another of the very few writers who treat the workhouse realistically in *The Quest for the Ruby Ring*.) Issues of pubertal sexuality and sexual exploitation by the master of the workhouse are confronted by Lally. There is a note of hope in the end, but not a happy ending.

A feature of Famine novels by Irish writers is that not a single one gives an account of emigration to Britain, and yet during the period of the Great Famine, Britain was the destination of the vast majority of refugees. Between 1841 and 1851 the number of people born in Ireland but taking up residence in Britain doubled. These emigrants provided a sizeable proportion of the workforce in the industrial towns of Yorkshire and Lancashire, and had a profound effect on the culture of those towns where they found refuge, as Frank Neal shows in his book *Sectarian Violence, The Liverpool Experience 1819–1914: an Aspect of Anglo-Irish History*. My suspicion is that these English stories are not being told because they do not conform to the national myth of freedom. Freedom can be found in America or in Australia, but not in the bosom of the ancient oppressor. The Irish relationship with Britain has been too problematic to tell this story yet. Until very recently there was a particular sense of failure or shame surrounding Irish emigration to Britain.

If there are omissions in the stories that Irish writers tell about the Famine, there are difficulties for British writers, too. A particular difficulty seems to be created by the role of British soldiers in Ireland during the Famine. Soldiers would have been the most obvious manifestation of British power in Ireland; they were English, not Irish. In Irish accounts they figure in two ways: assisting at evictions and protecting stocks of food from hordes of starving people. In two novels by British writers, Michael Morpurgo's *Twist of Gold* and Elizabeth Lutzeier's *The Coldest Winter*, an individual soldier behaves in a way that, frankly, would be unthinkable in a novel by an Irish writer. In both novels a kind soldier is appalled at the role he is forced to play in Ireland and gives food, money, in the form of a gold coin, and physical protection to starving children. In both cases his intervention is pivotal to the narrative. Morpurgo's soldier even includes fishing lessons in his benevolence.

> One day I'll not be here to feed you, and you must learn to live
> from the land. There's people dying in this country because they
> don't know where to look for their food. They've dug the pota-
> toes for so long they've forgotten. Eels are there in plenty if you
> can only catch them, and I shall teach you.

Here, an unconscious colonial condescension assumes that the natives need to be taught how to exploit their own land by a representative of the colonising power. The assumption that country boys wouldn't know how to fish is absurd and the historical fact that fishing rights belonged to landlords is ignored. Elizabeth Lutzeier's novel is much more nuanced, but her soldier gives a gold coin to the hero, Eamonn, saying, 'Here, buy yourself something to eat'. The soldier doesn't seem to have much of an idea of the value of the coin; we later discover it's enough to pay rent for almost a year. Lutzeier is aware that the device of the soldier giving the boy so much money is an unusual one. Later in the novel another character is surprised at the soldier's altruistic gesture: 'the baker's wife had never heard of a soldier giving away money before'.

The Coldest Winter is a very fine novel; Lutzeier's focus is initially on peasant boy Eamonn's family, who are poor, hungry and have been evicted from their home. She succeeds where many other Famine novelists fail. She gives an intelligent consciousness to her characters so that we can identify with them. They are not mere victims and objects. Hence, it is a cause of real disappointment that although she avoids using emigration as a way of escaping from the implications of Famine, she resorts to a related device. In chapter five, she shifts the centre of interest from hungry, Catholic, peasant Eamonn, to middle-class, Protestant, altruistic Kate, to look at Kate's and her family's efforts to alleviate Famine misery. So, in a sense, Lutzeier retreats from her central story to tell another story of how the Irish were saved by charity, and Eamonn Kennedy and his family, who are so well-drawn in the novel up to this point, now become victims and objects of charity. Of course, what is really happening is that the political implications of the Famine are avoided. In Lutzeier's sequel, *Bound for America*, Eamonn is restored as the hero of the novel and his efforts to survive and save his family form the main plot. However, difficulties are again resolved by middle-class intervention, this time by Kate's father, now a wealthy but humanitarian mill-owner in Boston.

Bound for America, illustration by Peter Gibson.

One novel which is explicitly political in its intentions is Eve Bunting's Famine adventure novel *The Haunting of Kildoran Abbey*, which was published in the USA in 1978. The perspective is distinctly northern unionist. In the beginning, the hungry children blame England for their misery and threaten revenge. However, they are proved wrong. England is Ireland's saviour in the form of an English boy, Christopher, and the all-benevolent Lord Lieutenant of Ireland, Lord Bessborough, who says, 'I have always found the Irish to be a simple people but not stupid. It's difficult to believe that if you have been a good landlord all these years they would turn against you for no reason'. In this novel the villains are unscrupulous Irish landlords whom England would punish, if only she knew. 'It's hard for him [the Lord Lieutenant] to know when something needs remedying when it looks alright on the surface', one of the characters says and Colum, the reformed rebel, remarks, 'It's hard for us to understand that there can be justice if we look for it'. The problem here is that the simple adventure story sits a little uneasily alongside the colonial polemics.

There is a number of points to be made about the treatment of religion in almost all of these novels. The most striking point is that they all avoid the most common motif of traditional Famine folklore, that is the proselytising dimension of the soup kitchens, or 'soupers' as they were known. If people converted from Catholicism to Protestantism, it was said that 'they took the soup'. The charity of the Quakers was the one strong exception in this myth, as their charity was seen as disinterested. In none of the contemporary novels with an Irish setting is any hint of this sectarian tension to be found, nor is there any depiction of the heroic efforts made by clergymen, Catholic and Protestant alike and often in cooperation with each other, to alleviate suffering in a disinterested way. Another point about the depiction of religion in contemporary Famine novels for children is the unflattering way that Catholic priests are frequently depicted. They are shown eating cheese and fried bacon, plump with smooth hands, taking money from desperate people, refusing to attend the sick and giving cliché-ridden sermons about sin and self-indulgence to starving people. This may be a reflection of modern Irish anticlericalism. There is little hint of it in Famine folklore, where the priest is often as poor as the people and is their only comfort. W.B. Yeats's poem 'The Ballad of Father Gilligan' comes closer to the traditional image of the Famine priest.

It is only in very recent books that the depiction of Protestant victims of the Famine occurs. In Arthur McKeown's *Famine,* Joe and his daughter are Protestant County Antrim farmers, living in comfort on the fruits of their farming and linen-weaving until the Famine strikes. They leave their farm, sell their loom and emigrate to America with their savings and their Bible, and are able to buy a farm in West Virginia. They hear stories about the Famine from other, less fortunate people on their journey to America, an example of a very obvious distancing device. In a sense, they conform to stereotypes of Protestant prosperity and the unionist myth that the Famine spared Ulster – a myth recently challenged by Christine Kinealy in *The Famine in Ulster: the Regional Impact.* Only in Soinbhe Lally's *The Hungry Wind* do we find Hannah and Rachel in the workhouse, Protestant victims of destitution and exploitation, who can speak Irish and who find comfort in their Bible, particularly in the story of Jonah in the belly of the whale.

Perhaps the greatest cultural effect of the Great Famine was the near destruction of the Irish language – many of the writers are aware of this and it occasionally causes problems in their narratives. Sometimes we are told that families speak only Irish, but we find that they have learned very good English in a matter of months. Sometimes they tell each other to speak quietly so that soldiers won't hear what they are saying. Soinbhe Lally, in *The Hungry Wind,* is the only writer who integrates the language issue into her plot and characterisation in a creative way. When her Irish-speaking heroine wants to explain about the sexual abuse of another girl by the workhouse master, she is overwhelmed by the fluency of her interrogator's English and loses her confidence in her own ability to speak English, and so justice fails.

One of the strangest references to the Irish language occurs in Ann Pilling's novel *Black Harvest*, in which three modern English children holidaying in Ireland are possessed by the ghosts of a family which died in the Famine. When the English children hear an old man talking, we are told '... the voice was shrill and harsh. They couldn't tell whether he was speaking Irish or just making horrible noises ... he was letting out a stream of foul Irish ... spitting the words out, slavering.' The English family suffers all the pangs of hunger – the baby almost dies, the dog pines away – until the Famine grave is found and the original victims are given a proper burial. It is a ghost story, a horror story that is redolent of a post-colonial sense of guilt and a desire to atone for past wrongs. The suffering is internalised and, in a sense, becomes 'ours' rather than 'theirs'. Pilling finds an interesting solution to a narrative problem by setting her story in the contemporary world.

The Hungry Wind, illustration by Alison Gault.

Marita Conlon-McKenna's *Under The Hawthorn Tree* is the best-known Irish Famine story for children and it too finds ways around some of the problems of this kind of narrative. Her narrative is simple, third person and stays with the Famine from beginning to end. It has no unbelievable adventures, no great gifts, no magic, no soldiers with money. Three children set out in search of their grandaunts after they are evicted from their home. In order to make their suffering tolerable, Conlon-McKenna emphasises the beauty of nature, the changes of the seasons, the colours of the sky, gorse, hawthorn, bluebells. Famine narratives usually assume that all nature, not just the potato, had failed. Women's storytelling is a device used to relieve suffering. The mother tells tales of her grandmother and aunts, and her daughter, Eily, repeats these tales to comfort her younger siblings. Women's domestic skills function as emblems of hope. The tragedy of the baby's death is framed by the fact that she is buried in a little white robe, which had been made by her grandmother for her mother's christening, and that she is buried under the hawthorn tree, which protected the living children at play as it will now protect the dead child. The hawthorn is where people often buried infants who died before they were christened, it is a fairy burial place, a sacred place where memories are kept. Conlon-McKenna uses myth, legend, storytelling and religious tradition to humanise a nightmarish world. Her characters are always allowed to speak for themselves. Loyalty and resourcefulness are what save them. This is a deceptively simple narrative in which the courage of ordinary people triumphs.

The Long March, by Marie-Louise Fitzpatrick, extends the parameters of Famine literature for children. Starkly beautiful black-and-white illustrations and a simple, elegiac text bring the suffering of the Choctaw and Irish nations together. The effect is to universalise pain without diminishing it. The fact that both nations are called 'Potato People' highlights their common humanity.

The Long March, Illustrated by Marie-Louise Fitzpatrick.

Irish Famine stories for children reverse a tendency that is prevalent in other forms of Irish fiction for children, which frequently reject urban life and its values in favour of a romantic, rural ideal. Famine narratives end with rural children finding refuge in the comfort of large towns and cities, whether in Ireland or in America. The horrors of the Irish Famine are an antidote to the fashionable notion that most human problems are caused by urban living.

In summary, the challenge of writing stories for children about the Famine has created some difficulties common to all writers who choose this theme. These difficulties are related to the nature of the material, i.e., the lack of conflict, the lack of action and the passivity of the victims. As a subject it also poses problems specific to writers from particular cultures or traditions. In the largely post-colonial culture of Ireland and post-imperial culture of Britain in the late twentieth century, it is not surprising that a process of revision should continue. Post-colonial angst is not experienced solely by the colonised nation; British writers need to re-examine their colonial history in the light of their dramatically changed relationships with the larger world. Children's writers feel the burden of the past in a particularly acute way because they believe that their books may influence the values and even the actions of young people. It is, therefore, not surprising that the truth is sometimes a little fudged. For a British writer it is difficult to depict a world in which a British soldier is merely an oppressor. For an Irish writer it is difficult to depict Britain as a refuge for many victims of the Irish Famine. In both cases cherished national narratives are challenged.

REFERENCES

Books

→ Hayden, Tom (ed.). *Irish Hunger, Personal Reflections on the Legacy of the Famine.* Dublin: Wolfhound Press, 1997.

→ Kelleher, Margaret. *The Feminisation of Famine, Expressions of the Inexpressible?* Cork: Cork University Press, 1997.

→ Kinealy, Christine. *This Great Calamity, The Irish Famine 1845–52.* Dublin: Gill and Macmillan, 1994.

→ Kinealy, Christine and Parkhill, Trevor (eds). *The Famine In Ulster: the Regional Impact.* Belfast: Ulster Historical Foundation, 1997.

→ Neal, Frank. *Sectarian Violence, The Liverpool Experience 1819–1914: an Aspect of Anglo-Irish History.* Manchester: Manchester University Press, 1988.

→ Póirtéir, Cathal (ed.). *The Great Irish Famine.* Dublin: RTÉ/Mercier Press, 1995.

Articles

→ Lake, Wendy. 'A Question of Identity: Some Aspects of Historical Fiction for Children Set in Ireland'. In *Children's Literature in Education*, pp.13–19. Vol.18, 1. 1987.
→ Lysaght, Patricia. 'Perspectives on women during the Great Irish Famine from the oral tradition'. *Béaloideas* Iml., pp.64–5. 1996–1997.

RECOMMENDED TITLES

Soinbhe Lally
THE HUNGRY WIND
Poolbeg Press

This book, which has been discussed at some length in the article, must be strongly recommended for the way in which it deals with issues like sexuality, religion and language, which would be of particular interest to the young adult reader. It is carefully researched, well written and deserves to be better known. In particular, it conveys a strong sense of the importance of communal bonds in harsh times.

Elizabeth Lutzeier
BOUND FOR AMERICA
Wolfhound Press

This is a sequel to *The Coldest Winter*. Eamonn Kennedy, his two brothers, Shaun and Dermot, and their mother have survived the worst of the famine fever and set sail for America. The horrors of life on board a coffin ship and at Grosse Isle in Canada are described in perhaps excessive detail. In spite of the efforts of a good and conscientious captain and a heroic doctor, great numbers of people die. Eamonn's family is broken up, his mother dies and his brothers are fostered to different families. The mainspring of the action now becomes Eamonn's determination to reach Boston, make money and try to reunite his family. He finds himself in a harsh and brutal world of exploited children and sectarian hatred. This is a salutary corrective to the rather sanitised image of nineteenth-century America depicted in much Irish children's fiction. Catholic churches and workplaces are burned down by members of a secret society called the K.N. (Know Nothings) – a group rather like the Ku Klux Klan – inspired by anti-Irish and anti-Catholic prejudice. The horrible dangers of work in the Massachusetts mills are described in great detail. The story examines the early efforts of workers to organise their labour and get better working conditions. The hardship of strike action is well described.

Eamonn triumphs in the end with the help of a humanitarian mill-owner who treats his workers well. He happens to be the father of Kate, Eamonn's rescuer in *The Coldest Winter*. Lutzeier's strength is in her faithful eye for historical detail and her vivid characterisation. However, her plot is problematic. The novel is divided into three parts: the sea voyage, the Canadian experience and the Boston section. It has material for two novels and should have been severely pruned.

Kevin McDermott
A MASTER OF THE SULTAN
Poolbeg Press

Manus O'Rourke, the young hero, loses his mother in the opening pages of this novel, set in the fifteenth century. The author enters imaginatively into a child's experience. He conveys the terror, excitement, freshness and colour of childhood. The novel moves from Kilkenny to Paris, to Toledo and to Istanbul as Manus learns to illuminate manuscripts. Terrible thunderstorms are a metaphor for the arbitrary nature of life: 'Life is change,' Manus reminds himself. Horror and beauty, magic and ghosts coexist. A world in which intolerance is largely associated with Christianity and liberal values with Judaism and Islam is a salutary reminder that no religion has a monopoly on fundamentalism. The horrors here are those of the Spanish Inquisition. But the

A *Master of the Sultan,*
illustration by Finbarr O'Connor.

art of the illuminator transcends those horrors. 'In his mind Manus saw himself as a great magician, controlling and shaping the natural world.' Characterisation is subtle and varied and stereotyping is rigorously avoided. The plot is fast-moving and well controlled.

Josephine Feeney
TRUTH, LIES & HOMEWORK
Puffin Books

This novel has a lot to say about the relationship between the individual and history, and about how the truth is often more difficult for adults than for children. History can be dangerous. For the young heroine, Claire, a first generation child of Irish parents growing up in the English midlands, what begins as an exciting school project ends in a deeper understanding of herself, adults and the difficulty of distinguishing between courage and cowardice. Claire's teacher sets a project on the experience of the children's grandparents' during the Second World War. While other children discover tales of endurance and heroism, Claire is shocked to find that her beloved grandad spent part of the war in prison because he ran away to avoid being drafted.

There is a funny moment when Claire's teacher thinks that Grandad was a conscientious objector and exclaims, 'How interesting'. She is less impressed when it becomes clear that he was simply a young Irish navvy who saw no reason to fight in 'someone else's war', although subsequently he bravely saved the life of a comrade in a mining accident. Family tensions emerge when Claire's mother prevents her from displaying her project in the local war museum because it would bring shame on the family. In spite of this, Claire feels proud of her grandad and displays similar honesty and courage to his. This book doesn't flinch from the politically incorrect, for example, Grandad drinks Guinness, smokes Woodbines and displays an appalling lack of respect for religions other than his own. But he is also a warm, caring and comforting man, Claire's principal support in a busy and cold world where

Truth, Lies & Homework,
cover images © Hulton Getty; Hannah Goodchild.

parents are preoccupied with their own concerns. The complexity of the Irish reaction to the Second World War is treated with more understanding and truthfulness than many of the books published in Ireland on the same topic.

Mark O'Sullivan
ANGELS WITHOUT WINGS
Wolfhound Press

This novel offers the young reader another experience of the necessity for truthfulness – artistic truthfulness in the face of the lies that Nazism depended on to seduce the German people. The central figure of the book is a children's writer who writes Blyton-like adventure stories set in an idyllic Bavarian world. The crisis arises when the Nazi regime insists that he change his characters in line with current propaganda. He must demonise a popular Jewish character and a disabled character. In order to try to prevent this from happening, the characters in his books actually come to life and become the 'angels without wings' of the title. This is the most complex of O'Sullivan's books to date, but children who are accustomed to the complexity of computer games and science fiction should easily rise to its challenge. The importance of its theme, the magic of its images and the strange, sad attraction of its characters are what make it memorable.

Michael Smith
AFTER THE DARKNESS
Scholastic Children's Books

Set in France, largely during the Second World War, this is a kind of time-slip or ghost story in which a late twentieth-century boy is burdened with the need to find out what happened to Jean Pierre and Lucie, the ghosts of two Jewish children who haunt the gardens of the house where he is living. The story of their foiled escape from persecution is poignantly told in a story rich in fairy-tale elements. Because of the degree of terror aroused, this compelling and moving story is suitable for the older reader.

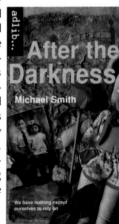

After the Darkness,
illustration by Nina Davis.

Marilyn Taylor
FARAWAY HOME
O'Brien Press

This novel is very carefully researched and brings to our attention a little-known story about the fate of Jewish children who escaped death in the Nazi genocide of their people. Many found refuge at Millisle Farm in County Down, in Northern Ireland. They had lost their families, their homes and their country, but they had survived. This book does not minimise their loss or their pain, and yet it is not devoid of hope. The children care for each other and find kindness in County Down. For a brief moment the two parts of Ireland reach out to each other as Dublin fire-brigades race to Belfast to help put out the fires of the blitz. 'Help was asked of a neighbour and help was given,' a warden explains.

Apart from the historical truthfulness of this book, there is a particular psychological truthfulness in the portrait of the young hero, Karl, who at times feels very angry that he has had to grow up and be responsible so prematurely.

Bill Wall
THE BOY WHO MET HITLER
Mercier Press

THE POWDER MONKEY
Mercier Press

The Boy Who Met Hitler is an unusual and interesting book about the impact of 'The Emergency' on a small community in County Cork. The relationships between the children are well-drawn and there is something hauntingly sad about the boy of the title. Divisions about the war are depicted as some fami-

lies have relatives fighting in the war as members of the British Navy. The teacher in the local primary school, an ardent nationalist who sides with Hitler against the British, is abusive, insensitive and cruel. He has none of the complexity of the other characters. The only excuse given for his behaviour is that

his brother had been killed by the Black and Tans. This caricature detracts from the overall balance of the novel. What is remembered is the monstrous teacher and not the children. The ideology here is clear, as it was in Wall's earlier hymn to the British Navy, set in the period of the 1798 rebellion, *The Powder Monkey*. However, in spite of its political oversimplifications (can the French or the Americans never be trusted? Are the British always on the side of right? Must little rebels invariably see the error of their ways?), *The Powder Monkey* has tension and excitement, a strong plot, interesting characterisation, a love and knowledge of the sea and sailing, a relish in the violence of battle and a real sense of adventure. It is a book that boys especially would enjoy.

Tom McCaughren
RIDE A PALE HORSE
Anvil Press

This book will also appeal strongly to boys. Based on the journals of Joseph Holt, one of the leaders of the 1798 rebellion in Wicklow, it has a very strong, simple third-person narrative, but the author uses the device of boy-hero Tom Howlett's diary to let us come close to his feelings at times of stress. In this way the horror of battle is conveyed but there is no indulgence in violence for its own sake. Though the plot is fast-moving and exciting and the rebel camp is the centre of most of the action, the politics of the period are not oversimplified. In particular, McCaughren shows the danger of irrational sectarian reactions in times of stress. Joseph Holt, a Protestant republican, remarks that when things go wrong for the rebels, they are quite likely to turn on him by saying that his relatives are Orangemen and therefore that he must be a spy. The Bible is used well here to give the title of the story, the flavour of the period and also as a clever device in the plot.

The Boy Who Met Hitler,
illustration by Caroline Hyland.

Ride A Pale Horse,
illustrated by Terry Myler.

Eithne Loughrey
ANNIE MOORE, FIRST IN LINE FOR AMERICA
Mercier Press

This novel traces the journey of the first immigrant to land at the newly constructed Ellis Island in New York in 1882. The author creates a fictional tale around the event, filling in Annie's family background and exploring her first year in New York. Annie is not a victim of famine or oppression, but goes to America to join her parents in search of a better life.

The harsh realities of working people's lives at that time, in particular their dangerous working conditions, are balanced with optimism about their ability to organise themselves in unions and political parties to ensure a better future.

The older members of Annie's family are very convincingly drawn. The younger people are somewhat more stereotyped. Annie is individualistic, independent and somewhat selfish. Mike Tierney, a handsome, reliable, streetwise, smiling Irish boy, provides potential love interest as well as coming to the rescue when needed, and is something of a stock figure in this kind of story. Annie's attractive older brother, Tom, succumbs briefly to the lure of gambling, but is rescued and diverted into the less risky world of Tammany Hall politics.

The novel is strong on social and historical detail. However, there is a twentieth-century flavour in its concern with multicultural harmony. Annie's best friend is a Jewish girl, Sophie. Annie enjoys a warm welcome in Sophie's home. Neither anti-Semitism nor anti-Irish racism is allowed to surface.

See also the sequel: *Annie Moore, The Golden Dollar Girl.*

Gerard Whelan
A WINTER OF SPIES
O'Brien Press

This sequel to *The Guns of Easter* treats the murky world of spying and counter-espionage during the War of Independence in Dublin. The heroine this time is eleven-year-old Sarah Conway, sister of Jimmy from the earlier novel. The challenge here lies in the very complex plot and the fact that Sarah is a more passive observer of the terrible things adults do than Jimmy was. Unspeakable violence is witnessed. The sense of evil is almost all-pervasive, relieved only by moments of ordinary gentleness and affection. The tenderness between father and daughter is effectively conveyed in the simplicity of the image of an umbrella 'its stretched black cloth, frail yet strong, covered both of them, protecting both of them from the angry night.'

Aubrey Flegg
KATIE'S WAR
O'Brien Press

Katie's War takes us into the most troubling episode in Irish history: the Civil War. As with so many of the books set between 1916 and 1924, the First World War is both an emotional and a moral background to the action. Particularly effective is the depiction of Katie's shell-shocked father. Katie is a lively, individualistic character who finds her loyalties torn, as do so many of the characters in novels set in this period. This is how the modern writer chooses to tell children about the complexity of the past. However, the perhaps unfortunate reality is that at the time most people knew exactly where they stood and which side was right in any given conflict. Katie is well-drawn as an adolescent girl, with all her desires and fears. The lovely rural landscape is memorable. The plot, which moves at an attractive, leisurely pace for most of the novel, rushes somewhat towards the end.

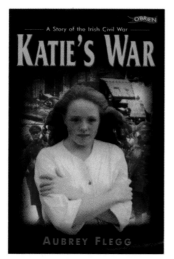

Katie's War,
illustration by Angela Clarke.

TITLES REFERRED TO IN ARTICLE AND IN RECOMMENDED LIST

The Famine
→ Bunting, Eve. *The Haunting of Kildoran Abbey*. New York: Frederick Warne, 1978. 0-72326-152-0
→ Conlon-McKenna, Marita. *Under The Hawthorn Tree*. Dublin: O'Brien Press, 1990. 0-86278-206-6
→ Fitzpatrick, Marie-Louise. *The Long March*. Dublin: Wolfhound Press, 1998. 0-86327-664-X
→ Lally, Soinbhe. *The Hungry Wind*. Dublin: Poolbeg Press, 1997. 1-85371-717-7
→ Lutzeier, Elizabeth. *The Coldest Winter*. Dublin: Wolfhound Press, 1996. 0-86327-557-5
→ Lutzeier, Elizabeth. *Bound for America*. Dublin: Wolfhound Press, 2000. 0-86327-843-4
→ MacGrory, Yvonne. *The Quest for the Ruby Ring*. Dublin: The Children's Press, 1999.
→ McCormack, Colette. *Mary-Anne's Famine*. Dublin: Attic Press, 1995. 1-85594-185-6
→ McKeown, Arthur. *Famine*. Dublin: Poolbeg Press, 1997. 1-85371-505-0
→ Morpurgo, Michael. *Twist of Gold*. London: Kaye and Ward, 1983.
→ Pilling, Anne. *Black Harvest*. London: Collins Press, 1983. 00-06-92603-7
→ Smith, Michael. *Boston! Boston*. Dublin: Poolbeg Press, 1997. 1-85371-885-8

The Fifteenth Century
→ McDermott, Kevin. *A Master of the Sultan*. Dublin: Poolbeg Press, 1997. 1-85371-706-1

The Second World War
→ Feeney, Josephine. *Truth, Lies & Homework*. London: Puffin Books, 1996. 0-14-03770-7
→ O'Sullivan, Mark. *Angels Without Wings*. Dublin: Wolfhound Press, 1997. 0-86327-591-5
→ Smith, Michael. *After the Darkness*. London: Scholastic Children's Books, 1996. 0-590-54260-5
→ Taylor, Marilyn. *Faraway Home*. Dublin: O'Brien Press, 1999. 0-86278-643-6
→ Wall, Bill. *The Boy Who Met Hitler*. Dublin: Mercier Press, 1999. 1-85635-269-2

The Rebellion of 1798.
→ Wall, Bill. *The Powder Monkey*. Cork: Mercier Press, 1996. 1-85635-154-8
→ McCaughren, Tom. *Ride a Pale Horse*. Dublin: Anvil Press, 1998. 1-90173-708-X

Irish Diaspora
→ Loughrey, Eithne. *Annie Moore, First in Line for America*. Dublin: Mercier Press, 1999.
→ 1-85635-245-5
→ Loughrey, Eithne. *Annie Moore, The Golden Dollar Girl*. Dublin: Mercier Press, 2000.

War of Independence, Civil War
→ Whelan, Gerard. *A Winter of Spies*. Dublin: O'Brien Press, 1998. 0-86278-566-9
→ Flegg, Aubrey. *Katie's War*. Dublin: O'Brien Press, 1997. 0-86278-525-1

CULTURE, IDENTITY AND IMAGE

DOES EVERY PICTURE TELL AN IRISH STORY?

The shillelaghs, shebeens and leprechauns image of Ireland is no longer acceptable, if it ever was. In picture books, where the words of text frequently are few, visual images, as well as helping to tell a story, provide a backdrop against which it unfolds. Conventional iconography, however oversimplified, may at times be a useful way of providing a readily identifiable setting. While no one regrets that stereotypical images, such as those listed above, are no longer acceptable, a more modern image of Ireland has not emerged in Irish-produced picture books. What then might, or should, take the place of broadly drawn symbols to convey a sense of a particular country or place in a picture book? Or, *is* it desirable to portray people or events in a manner that identifies them with any particular ethnic group or location? It can be argued that it is not necessary to convey any particular notion of local identity through text or image in a book, and in the picture book market, which relies heavily on translations and co-editions, that it is better not to have anything which might limit a book's appeal overseas. It would, however, seem a pity if young readers were to lose all sense of finding themselves in the pages of a picture book, in addition to gaining opportunities to learn about other countries and cultures, often at a subliminal level. Talking at the 1994 IBBY Congress about children's books as a means of understanding cultural diversity, Carmen Diane Dearden of IBBY Venezuela remarked that:

> … we can, through books, become used to being in another's place from an early age. And because we can be many characters, in a pleasing and playful space, we will be on the way to accepting diversity with joy.

Jamie O'Rourke and the Big Potato, illustration by Tomie dePaola.

Fewer than two hundred children's books are published in Ireland each year, and on average approximately an eighth of these are picture books. Of what might be termed 'original' picture books those in the Irish language predominate. In contrast, an increasing number of picture books with a relevance to Ireland, whether in content or by virtue of having an Irish author or illustrator, are published outside Ireland. The reasons for the small number of what might be termed 'indigenous' picture books published in Ireland are various. Usually the cost of originating art work and the relatively small home market are quoted as the main factors inhibiting the production of more original work. It makes sound economic sense for Irish publishers to market books which are likely to be successful, and equally Irish authors/illustrators want to make their name internationally as well as at home. Of the picture books published in Ireland or by Irish authors or illustrators, few have any noticeably Irish reference points, apart from a number of retellings of Irish myths, legends and folk tales. These highly dramatic stories lend themselves to visual interpretation, and there is a demand for books like this from the tourist market as well as from schools and parents.

Until recently, Irish artists have worked in the area of children's books as illustrators rather than producing picture books, although a number of Irish authors have written text for picture books. Eilís Dillon wrote a number of picture books which were illustrated by artists such as Gaynor Chapman and Alan Howard. Mary Lavin's *The Second-Best Children in the World* was illustrated by Edward Ardizzone, and works by Swift, Wilde, Yeats and Joyce have all been published in picture book format.

It may be argued that the 'Irish' picture book is now at the stage of the 'Irish' novel for young people some fifteen to twenty years ago. That is, struggling for a place in the market at home and for recognition as a quality product which could take a place beside publications from anywhere else in the world. In the past twenty years the novel has come a long way, not only in content but also in terms of presentation. While novels with an Irish setting had been available for many years, what might be termed the 'new wave' of Irish writing, which attempted to address the lives of young people in Ireland in the last quarter of the twentieth century, was greeted with considerable enthusiasm by young readers as literature that reflected their daily lives, their homes, their families, their history. These novels range widely in genre and content. Teen concerns, environmental issues, historical fiction, fantasy drawing on Irish mythology were and still are popular with readers, and the scope of what is appropriate to address in a book for young readers has expanded.

Definition of what is an 'Irish' picture book is problematic. Is it a book published in Ireland, a book by an Irish author or illustrator, or a book with a theme related to Ireland? While there are reasons for the relatively low number of picture books published in Ireland, it is somewhat perplexing that few Irish artists have chosen to reflect any aspect of modern Ireland, or indeed, Ireland's more recent history. At a time when there has been debate about cultural identity in Ireland, it might be reasonable to suppose that one of the manifestations of this would be discernible in picture books. Like the United States of America and Australia, Ireland is a former British colony and shares the legacy of the English language, but unlike those countries, Ireland does not have a body of picture books set in the local landscape. On the other hand, Irish authors and illustrators working abroad have used the landscape of their adopted country for their tales. Eve Bunting, from Northern Ireland, has written text for a number of picture books with an American background, including *Smoky Night*, which has been justly acclaimed for its treatment of riots in Los Angeles, and *Train to Somewhere*, which tells the story of a Japanese–American family's move from a war relocation camp in California to Boston. The themes of difference and understanding in these books have much to say to Irish readers, but Bunting's excursions into writing text for books with an Irish setting has none of their depth or sensitivity. The idiosyncratic *Saint Patrick's Day in the Morning* is an effort to accommodate two traditions in Northern Ireland as wee Jamie plans his celebration of 'St Pat's' – a term unlikely to be used by anyone in Ireland. *Barney the Beard* is set in County Cork, but reflects Bunting's Northern Irish background more than the southern county.

Irish artists whose work is set in a non-specific locality include Adrienne Geoghegan, Anita Jeram and Lucinda Jacob. Jacob's books are published in Dublin and are dual-language (Irish and English), but the characters and setting are not readily identifiable as Irish. P.J. Lynch has captured Ireland in ancient times, but it is America that is portrayed in his books set in more recent times. Sam McBratney, Martin Waddell, Una Leavy, Margrit Cruickshank and, more recently, Malachy Doyle have all written picture books. Most of these also have a non-specific locality, although Wales, where Doyle now lives, is represented in some of his work and, while no location is specified, the speech pattern of the characters in *The Great Castle of Marshmangle* is definitely Irish. Waddell's *John Joe and the Big Hen* has echoes of a rural Ireland in past times even though the location is not specified.

Irish themes have, however, inspired a number of non-Irish artists, for example, Tomie dePaola with his *Jamie O'Rourke* tales and *Patrick: Patron Saint of Ireland*, and Gary D. Schmidt's and Todd Doney's *Saint Ciaran: the Tale of a Saint of Ireland*. Caroline Binch's *Christy's Dream* is one of the very few picture books to have a contemporary Irish setting.

Christy's Dream, illustrated by Caroline Binch.

A number of Irish publishers have taken the plunge and produced original picture books, in co-editions in some cases. Some of these do reflect Ireland, while the settings of others are indeterminate, such as Wolfhound's *It's a Jungle Out There*, *Granny MacGinty* from the O'Brien Press, *There's a Wardrobe in my Monster* from Blackwater and Mentor's series by Annie West and Julie Shackman.

In *An Chanáil* and *The Sleeping Giant*, Irish artist and author Marie-Louise Fitzpatrick has given us picture books with a modern setting, Dublin and Kerry respectively. But *The Sleeping Giant*, in particular, looks to an Ireland of more traditional times in its rendition of a Kerry legend of an island giant who comes to life. *An Chanáil* uses the Grand Canal in Dublin as a device to link urban and rural. Ireland is still not far from a largely rural and agriculture-based society and both Fitzpatrick and Binch draw together these strands of Irish life. Binch's Christy lives in an urban wasteland, but it is the older more rural attraction of horse-riding that predominates in his life. Similarly, *A Day to Remember at the Giant's Causeway,* text by Declan Carville and illustrations by Brendan Ellis, features a modern-day young boy, but with its dreamscape setting of the Giant's Causeway in County Antrim has resonances of an older Ireland. *Róisín ar Strae* is an Irish language picture book featuring a little girl lost in the streets of Dublin, but it is to a rural home she returns when safely reunited with her mother.

This older Ireland seems more attractive when it comes to the production of picture books. In his introduction to *Tales from Old Ireland,* Malachy Doyle points out that 'Irish folk tales have a magic and a simplicity, a depth and a passion that appeal to people of all ages and nationalities'. These very qualities are apparent in a number of retellings of Irish tales published recently in picture book format, and the variety of visual approaches taken by artists shows the rich seam of imaginative stimuli that lies in

A Day to Remember at the Giant's Causeway, illustrated by Brendan Ellis.

these stories. These tales, in the hands of skilled storytellers such as those encountered in the books reviewed below, still have a power to thrill, to enthral and, even when the ending is well-known, to evoke afresh tears or laughter.

'Wonder tales' and stories of 'the little people', the *sidhe* (fairies), leprechauns and pookas are plentiful in Irish folk literature. While for many Irish people the 'squirm factor' can never be far from a mention of the word 'leprechaun', in the right hands the little people are invested with dignity, as Tomie dePaola shows in his *Jamie O'Rourke* stories. A tongue-in-cheek look at leprechauns is *Leprechaun* by Wayne Anderson and Niall MacNamara. Posing as an informational text, it offers an 'all you ever wanted to know' insight into the life and variety of leprechauns. This device has been used elsewhere to examine other forms of fabulous creatures, as in Robert Ingpen's *Australian Gnomes,* which includes a look at 'The Leprignome', an immigrant gnome who is 'subject to erratic behaviour'.

It is noticeable that there is a small number of stories from the huge store of Irish myths, legends and folk tales which crop up in most of the illustrated retellings. One of these is the Children of Lir. Expert opinions differ on the origins of this story, and in different retellings there are variations on the ending. In the best-known version the four children of King Lir, who have spent nine hundred years as swans, encounter a Christian monk (or hermit) in whose presence they are restored to their human form. They are now old people and are claimed by death, but it is implied that having accepted the Christian God, death is not the end for them; they join their long-dead father and mother. *The O'Brien Book of Irish Fairy Tales and Legends, Tales from Old Ireland* and *The Names Upon the Harp* have, in their retellings of 'Lir', chosen this ending, with some variations. Other versions of this story have the children restored to their youthful form, living, it is implied, happily ever after. This ending is favoured in *Favourite Irish Fairy Tales* and in the Sheila McGill-Callahan/ Ginnady Spirrin version, which introduces a whale and gives ancient Ireland a decidedly medieval, middle-European look. Celia Catlett Anderson argues that this 'happier' conclusion may be closer to the spirit of the Tuatha de Danann, in whose time the tale is set. Possibly some storytellers feel it is kinder (and possibly safer) to soften the ending of the story for children, but it is the tragic dimension that makes these stories great. The Children of Lir is taken from the earliest of the cycles of Irish tales: the Mythological cycle. Stories of Cú Chulainn from the Ulster cycle and of Fionn MacCumhaill and the Fianna from the Fianna cycle also occur in most collections.

'The pleasing and playful space' of Carmen Diane Dearden is inhabited by kings, queens, heroes, rogues, saints and clowns in Irish picture books, but there is an absence – the child of today. And here it has to be remembered that Ireland is fast becoming a multicultural society. No argument can be made for a plethora of books set in modern Ireland just for the sake of it, or for books which superficially replace the old with the newer, shinier emblems of Riverdance, romantic ruins and Celtic tigers. Nevertheless, the words of artist Charles Keeping concerning *Joseph's Yard*, his book about a very ordinary boy in London, are pertinent:

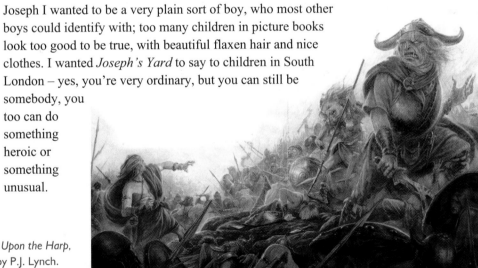

> Joseph I wanted to be a very plain sort of boy, who most other boys could identify with; too many children in picture books look too good to be true, with beautiful flaxen hair and nice clothes. I wanted *Joseph's Yard* to say to children in South London – yes, you're very ordinary, but you can still be somebody, you too can do something heroic or something unusual.

The Names Upon the Harp, illustrated by P.J. Lynch.

REFERENCES

→ Anderson, Celia Catlett. 'The further transformation of the Children of Lir'. In *Children's Books in Ireland*, pp.32–33. No.16. Summer 1997.

→ Dearden, Carmen Diane. *Children's Literature as a Means of Approaching and Understanding Cultural Diversity*, p.29. 24th International IBBY Congress on Books for Young People. Proceedings, 1994. Madrid: Organización Espanola para el Libro y Juvenil, n.d.

→ Keeping, Charles. *The Illustration of Children's Books*. In Frank Keyse (ed.), Loughborough '83. Proceedings of the 16th Loughborough International Seminar on Children's Literature, p.140. Aberystwyth: Welsh National Centre for Children's Literature, 1984.

RECOMMENDED TITLES

Malachy Doyle/Niamh Sharkey (illus.)
TALES FROM OLD IRELAND
Barefoot Books

Marie Heaney/P.J. Lynch (illus.)
THE NAMES UPON THE HARP
Faber and Faber

Soinbhe Lally/Finbarr O'Connor (illus.)
FAVOURITE IRISH FAIRY TALES
Poolbeg Press

These three books amply display the richness of Irish myth and folk tale, and the authors and artists have been well matched in each of the selections. They each have an appropriate sense of the intended audience and it is fascinating to see how different artists have interpreted the same stories.

The Poolbeg publication provides a useful introduction to the subject, with some of the best-known stories narrated in a straightforward, direct manner. O'Connor's illustrations are bright and highly cinematic in places, such as the battle between the two giant bulls on the plains of Connacht, although some of his human characters are more suited to advertisements for toothpaste or shampoo. He is undoubtedly at his best when he places animals, birds and fishes in a dramatic landscape, such as the clash of the bulls and the swan children of Lir as they are lashed by stormy waves on the Sea of Moyle.

Doyle's selection mainly consists of folk tales, and these he retells with gusto and humour. Sharkey's stylised figures are all curves and angles and points, and are wonderfully suited to Doyle's retellings. She remakes the traditional images in her own style, providing a sense of distance that commands attention for events which may have become over-familiar or stereotypical in interpretation.

These two presentations are aimed at younger readers than the Heaney/Lynch volume, which is more scholarly in approach and seems likely to become a classic work of Irish mythology. However, Heaney's language is highly accessible and eloquent, giving vividness to the tales she has selected from the Mythological, Ulster and Fianna cycles. Lynch's artwork is brutal and elemental in places: witness the scenes from the Battle of Moytura and the slaughter of Naoise and Fiacha.

Elsewhere, tragedy hovers broodingly, whether it attaches to old age, as in the death of the Children of Lir, or to separation, as in the agony of Finn Mac Cumhaill's mother when she parts with her infant son.

Favourite Irish Fairy illustrated by Finbarr O'Connor.

Each of the books carries a pronunciation guide to the names of the characters, and both the Doyle/Sharkey and Heaney/Lynch volumes carry useful source notes. The latter also contains a list for further reading.

Jude Daly
FAIR, BROWN AND TREMBLING: AN IRISH CINDERELLA STORY
Frances Lincoln

Jude Daly's account of this Irish Cinderella story is lively and attractive, both visually and verbally. (This tale is also contained in the Doyle/Sharkey collection above.) Daly's watercolours are vivid and strong, and the medieval landscape and figures are reminiscent of a Book of Hours.

Edna O'Brien/Michael Foreman (illus.)
TALES FOR THE TELLING: IRISH FOLK AND FAIRY STORIES
Pavilion

The twelve stories in this pocket-size collection are recounted with verve, though the language in a couple of them strays into stage 'Oirish', making them difficult to read to oneself or aloud. Otherwise, it is an excellent collection for reading quietly or out loud, with plenty of humour and dramatic moments, many of which are brilliantly captured by Michael Foreman's watercolours.

Dearborn, Sabrina/Olwyn Whelan (illus.)

A CHILD'S BOOK OF BLESSINGS

Evelyn Foster/Olwyn Whelan (illus.)

THE MERMAID OF CAFUR

Caitlín Matthews/Olwyn Whelan (illus.)

MY VERY FIRST BOOK OF PRINCESSES

Richard Walker/Olwyn Whelan (illus.)

MY VERY FIRST BOOK OF PIRATES

Barefoot Books

These three books of traditional stories and a book of blessings from around the world have all been illustrated by Olwyn Whelan. *The Mermaid of Cafur* is a Welsh story, and the other two are collections from different countries. Ireland is included in the pirates volume, which contains the story of Grace O'Malley and her dispute with the Lord of Howth. Each of the books is generously sized and lavishly illustrated by Whelan. Her pictures are richly detailed, and bear comparison with the work of Jane Ray.

*A Child's Book of Blessings,
illustrated by Olywn Whelan.*

Amy Hest/P.J. Lynch (illus.)

WHEN JESSIE CAME ACROSS THE SEA

Poolbeg Press and Walker Books

Douglas Wood/P.J. Lynch (illus.)

GRANDAD'S PRAYERS OF THE EARTH

Walker Books

There is a number of common themes in these two books illustrated by Lynch: love between a grandchild and grandparent, religion and spirituality, the 'American dream' and transition from childhood to adulthood.

Jessie epitomises the experience of many central-European Jews who sailed for America to find fortune and love. And if not fortune, she finds modest security as a lacemaker, an education as she learns to read and write English, and love in the form of Lou, a young shoemaker whom she initially meets on the boat to New York. Eventually, Jessie saves enough from her earnings to send for her grandmother. The book culminates with her grandmother's arrival on a quayside in New York and Jessie's reunion with the old woman, now much frailer than when Jessie last saw her.

Grandad's Prayers of the Earth is essentially a sylvan meditation, and the 'of', rather than 'for', is significant in the title. The boy narrator keenly feels the loss of his grandfather, his companion on rural walks, when the old man dies. But in remembering Grandad's belief in the inter-relatedness of all living things as he walks through the woodlands again, he evokes his presence and offers his own prayer *for* the old man and for the natural environment which they both loved. Lynch uses light to great effect, highlighting changing seasons and moods of the classic American scenery.

While the shape of *Grandad's Prayers* is square, emphasising the compact nature of the relationship between man and boy and nature, Jessie is in landscape format, giving Lynch space for scenes of land and sea. The scene where Grandmother stands on the quay, on the edge of the left-hand page, waving to Jessie's ship as it sails out of sight on the right-hand page, is broken by a block of text symbolising the parting of the two. This typifies Lynch's treatment of the story: atmospheric, deeply moving, but standing back from sentimentality. His attention to period detail is meticulous, as in the street scene Jessie looks down on from her window. Again, this scene is broken by a block of text, making Jessie one with but apart from the scene. If ever a picture book deserved the accolade 'classic', this is it!

*When Jessie Came Across the Sea,
illustrated by P.J. Lynch.*

Marie-Louise Fitzpatrick
THE SLEEPING GIANT
Wolfhound Press

Marie-Louise Fitzpatrick
THE LONG MARCH:
A FAMINE GIFT FOR IRELAND
Wolfhound Press

Both of these books link past and future. *The Sleeping Giant* brings to life, in late twentieth-century Ireland, a legendary giant who sleeps in the form of an island off the coast of County Kerry. *The Long March* recounts the story of money sent by the Choctaw Nation to relieve famine in Ireland in 1847. The Choctaw empathy with Irish famine victims was kindled by the memory of their own Long March, earlier in the nineteenth century. Emotional tension is focussed around young Choona and his growing understanding of the suffering of the Choctaw. His great-grandmother tells him how his people walked to New Lands in the west when dispossessed of their lands in Mississippi by the strangers who invaded their country.

Cheerful, lively watercolours and a straightforward text make *The Sleeping Giant* a delight for young readers. Black-and-white pencil drawings match the longer and more complex narrative of *The Long March* and serve to heighten the sense of realism of this powerful, true story for older readers, which displays Fitzpatrick's talents at their very best.

Ed Miliano
IT'S A JUNGLE OUT THERE
Wolfhound Press

Miliano's white cat stalks through the garden, the 'jungle', alert and aware of the danger that lurks everywhere: birds, beetles, ants, spiders are all there, but cat is vigilant. Cat is a white shape whose green eyes reflect back the lush, jungly greens which are the predominant hue on each page. We see the 'jungle' from the cat's perspective until the penultimate opening, where the garden is laid out in a panoramic view, leading us into the house with cat who retires for a bite to eat and a sleep.

It's a Jungle Out There, illustrated by Ed Miliano.

The book is distinguished by good design, and young listeners and readers will enjoy the spare, rhythmic text and stylish illustrations. They will also enjoy searching on each page for the small red ladybird among the foliage.

The Gigantic T illustrated by Niamh Sharke

Hugh Lupton/Niamh Sharkey (illus.)
TALES OF WISDOM AND WONDER
Barefoot Books

Alexsci Tolstoy/Niamh Sharkey (illus.)
THE GIGANTIC TURNIP
Barefoot Books

Richard Walker/Niamh Sharkey (illus.)
JACK AND THE BEANSTALK
Barefoot Books

These three books show how it is possible to make the old new and attractive, and also how the lasting truths in stories such as these can continue to entertain. Lupton and Walker interpret the stories with a light touch, which is amplified by Sharkey's witty and inventive style. Her familiar oil-on-gesso technique and lines of geometrical precision serve to point up moments of humour and drama in the plot. Her characters are caricatures, and in each she encapsulates some emotion essential to the plot, sometimes isolating them in white space or else enclosing them in rectilinear shapes for greater emphasis. Other scenes are spread across both pages of an opening, allowing for a sense of movement and adventure.

All of Sharkey's books are models of good design, but, in particular, the layout of the text of *The Gigantic Turnip* deserves special comment.

Ted Hughes/Flora McDonnell (illus.)
THE MERMAID'S PURSE
Faber and Faber

A single page opening is devoted to each poem in *The Mermaid's Purse*. Physically small and exquisitely designed, the book's shape and size heighten the dramatic intensity of the sweep of Hughes's and McDonnell's words and illustrations.

Each poem talks of a different creature or thing that lives on or in the sea or shoreline, with the exception of 'Wreck', which in time is also made the water's own: 'The sea's rare rust-flower'.

Whether it is the cormorant, ragworm, whale or any other creature, McDonnell's illustrations capture the mood of each poem in varying tones of browny grey against a white background. Nowhere is this better displayed than in 'Gulls', where 'wing--waltzing their shadows', the birds are creatures of water and air. This perspective is indicative of all of the illustrations where land, metaphorically and physically (when it is shown), is distant. This is a book to keep and to treasure.

Caroline Binch
CHRISTY'S DREAM
Mammoth

That dreams can come true is the essence of *Christy's Dream*. Christy lives with his large family in a crowded, high-rise flat in an urban wasteland, where, it is hinted visually, a local pastime might be burning out cars. All Christy wants is a pony of his own and a future as a jockey, but his Ma has other ideas. A visit to a local horse fair with Granda enables Christy to achieve the first part of his ambition, leaving him with the problem of breaking the news to Ma.

Christy's love of horses is typical of a body of young lads who keep horses in Dublin city. Binch's translucent watercolours and delicate pencil lines give character and fluidity to the participants, human and equine, and in particular to the scenes at the horse market. Urban and rural Ireland meet on the cobbled streets of Smithfield, in the faces and stances of the dealers and on the green space near the flats where Christy and his friends gallop exultantly – truly 'urban cowboys'.

**Marita Conlon-McKenna/
Leonie Shearing (illus.)**
GRANNY MacGINTY
O'Brien Press

The MacGinty family decide that Granny needs a pet to cheer her up. But what sort of pet would suit? Various creatures – a dog, a parrot, a rabbit, a snail – spend trial periods with Granny, but are all found to be unsuitable. At last, Granny solves the problem for herself and chooses her own pet, a little stray cat. Conlon-McKenna's text portrays Granny MacGinty as a lonely old lady in need of cheering up, but Shearing's colourful ink and watercolour illustrations show her to be lively and resourceful, providing a nice touch of tongue-in-cheek humour to a warm-hearted story.

Adrienne Geoghegan/Adrian Johnson (illus.)
THERE'S A WARDROBE IN MY MONSTER
Blackwater and Bloomsbury

Another story about a pet, but this time one with a difference, is recounted by Geoghegan. Both words and pictures show Martha to be a girl of some determination, but even she is daunted when the 'naughty, wicked great big ugly monster' she demands lives up to his description. Geoghegan's spare text and Johnson's *faux-naif* paintings blend to create a lively, entertaining story.

Margrit Cruickshank/Amanda Harvey (illus.)
DON'T DAWDLE, DOROTHY!
Frances Lincoln

The experience of going shopping with Mum and being overcome with weariness on the way home is a common childhood experience. Dorothy livens up the homeward journey with all sorts of fantastical experiences: a grumpy old bear precedes her up the hill, a tiger crouches in the bushes, a wicked witch appears out of the woods … Dorothy is urged past all of these diversions by her mother's exhortation, 'Don't dawdle, Dorothy!' An ultimately comforting tale with which many children will identify.

e Mermaid's Purse,
strated by Flora McDonnell.

Malachy Doyle/Paul Hess (illus.)
THE GREAT CASTLE OF MARSHMANGLE
Andersen Press

Malachy Doyle/Paul Hess (illus.)
HUNGRY! HUNGRY! HUNGRY!
Andersen Press

Both of theses books play with and challenge reality and what appears to be reality, and both offer reassurance when an unnamed boy protagonist confronts and deals with situations which seem to be strange or scary. A grisly, ghastly goblin pursues him around his house in *Hungry! Hungry! Hungry!*, but the situation is defused when the goblin displays a liking for jelly beans. In *The Great Castle of Marshmangle* the boy goes to stay with his grandfather who interprets everyday reality in his own way, but this becomes unimportant when there is a crisis to be dealt with. The location of Marshmangle is non-specific, but the protagonists' conversations display a gentle Irish cadence. Hess's outlandish perspectives contribute to the sense of distorted reality in both of these very enjoyable picture books.

Kieran Fanning
TRAPDOOR TO TREACHERY
Mentor Press

Books such as this, which encourage readers to participate in the story, have a role to play in encouraging reluctant readers (as well as providing good fun and mental stimulation for everyone). Here the two young protagonists try to solve a mystery and the reader is also involved in working out the puzzle clues (the answers are usefully supplied at the back of the book).

Trapdoor to Treachery, illustration by Jimmy Lawlor.

TITLES REFERRED TO IN ARTICLE AND IN RECOMMENDED LIST

→ Anderson, Wayne/MacNamara, Niall (illus.). *Leprechaun.* London: Pavilion, 1999. 0-8620-193-3

→ Binch, Caroline. *Christy's Dream.* London: Mammoth, 1999. 0-74974-092-2

→ Bunting, Eve/Gobbato, Imero (illus.). *Barney the Beard.* London: Frederick Warne, 1978. 0-72322-102-2

→ Bunting, Eve/Diaz, David (illus.). *Smoky Night.* San Diego: Harcourt Brace, 1994. 0-15269-954-6

→ Bunting, Eve/Brett, Hjan (illus.). *St Patrick's Day in the Morning.* New York: Clarion Books, 1980. 0-89919-162-2

→ Bunting, Eve/Soentpiet, Chris K. (illus.). *So Far From the Sea.* New York: Clarion Books, 1998. 0-39572-095-8

→ Carvill, Declan/Ellis, Brendan (illus.). *A Day to Remember at the Giant's Causeway.* Belfast: Discovery Publications, 2000. 0-95382-220-6

→ Conlon-McKenna, Marita/Shearing, Leonie (illus.). *Granny MacGinty.* Dublin: O'Brien Press, 1999. 0-86278-628-2

→ Daly, Jude. *Fair, Brown and Trembling: an Irish Cinderella Story.* London: Frances Lincoln, 2000. 0-71121-463-8 (hardcover)/2001. 0-71121-462-X (paperback)

→ Dearborn, Sabrina (comp.)/Whelan, Olwyn (illus.). *A Child's Book of Blessings.* Bath: Barefoot Books, 1999. 1-90228-372-4

→ dePaola, Tomie. *Jamie O'Rourke and the Big Potato.* New York: Penguin Putnam, 1992. 0-698-11603-8

→ dePaola, Tomie. *Jamie O'Rourke and the Pooka.* New York: G.P. Putnam's Sons, 2000. 0-39923-467-5

→ dePaola, Tomie. *Patrick: Patron Saint of Ireland.* New York: Holiday House, 1992. 0-82341-077-3

→ Dillon, Eilís/Chapman, Gaynor (illus.). *The Wise Man on the Mountain.* London: Hamish Hamilton, 1969. 0-24101-797-1

→ Dillon, Eilís/Howard, Alan (illus.). *The Voyage of the Mael Dúin*. London: Faber and Faber, 1969. 0-57108-811-2

→ Doyle, Malachy/Hess, Paul (illus.). *The Great Castle of Marshmangle*. London: Andersen Press, 1999. 0-86264-792-4

→ Doyle, Malachy/Hess, Paul (illus.). *Hungry! Hungry! Hungry!* London: Andersen Press, 2000. 0-8624-928-5

→ Doyle, Malachy/Sharkey, Niamh (illus.). *Tales from Old Ireland*. London: Barefoot Books, 2000. 1-90228-385-6

→ Fanning, Kieran. *Trapdoor to Treachery*. Dublin: Mentor, 2000. 1-84210-023-8

→ Fitzpatrick, Marie-Louise. *An Chanáil*. Dublin: An Gúm, 1988. 0-00207-225

→ Fitzpatrick, Marie-Louise. *The Long March*. Dublin: Wolfhound, 1998. 0-86327-644-X

→ Fitzpatrick, Marie-Louise. *The Sleeping Giant*. Dublin: Wolfhound Press, 1991. 0-86327-643-1

→ Foster, Evelyn/Whelan, Olwyn (illus). *The Mermaid of Cafur*. Bath: Barefoot Books, 1999. 1-90228-317-1

→ Geoghegan, Adrienne/Johnson, Adrian (illus.). *There's a Wardrobe in my Monster*. Dublin: Blackwater, 1999. 1841310263 and London: Bloomsbury, 1999. 0-74754-019-5

→ Heaney, Marie/Lynch, P.J. (illus.). *The Names Upon the Harp*. London: Faber and Faber, 2000. 0-57119-363-3

→ Hest, Amy/Lynch, P.J. (illus.). *When Jessie Came Across the Sea*. Dublin: Poolbeg Press,1997. 1-85371-787-8 and London: Walker Books. 0-74456-963-X

→ Hughes, Ted/McDonnell, Flora (illus.). *The Mermaid's Purse*. London: Faber and Faber, 1999. 0-57119-789-2 (hardback), 0-57119-621-7 (paperback)

→ Ingpen, Robert. *Australian Gnomes*. Sydney: Weldon, 1990. 1-86302-085-3

→ Keeping, Charles. *Joseph's Yard*. Oxford: Oxford University Press, 1969. 0-19279-651-8

→ Lally, Soinbhe/O'Connor, Finbarr (illus.). *Favourite Irish Fairy Tales*. Dublin: Poolbeg Press, 1998. 1-85371-777-0 (hardback) and 1-85371-829-7 (paperback)

→ Lavin, Mary/Ardizzone, Edward (illus.). *The Second-Best Children in the World*. London: Longman, 1972. 0-58215-179-1

→ Leavy, Una/Field, Susan (illus.). *The O'Brien Book of Irish Fairy Tales and Legends*. Dublin: O'Brien Press, 1996. 0-86278-482-4

→ Lupton, Hugh/Sharkey, Niamh (illus.). *Tales of Wisdom and Wonder*. Bath: Barefoot Books, 1998. 1-90122-315-9 (hardcover).1999. 1-84148-191-2 (paperback)

→ Matthews, Caitlín/Whelan, Olwyn (illus.). *My Very First Book of Princesses*. Bath: Barefoot Books, 1997. 1-90122-310-8

→ Miliano, Ed. *It's a Jungle Out There*. Dublin: Wolfhound Press, 1997. 0-83275-702

→ O'Brien, Edna/Foreman, Michael (illus.). *Tales for the Telling: Irish Folktales and Fairy Stories*. London: Pavilion, 1986, 1997 0-14032-293-0.

→ Ó Raghallaigh, Colmán/Ní Raghallaigh, Aoife (illus.). *Róisín ar Strae*. Dublin: An Gúm, 1996. 1-85791-163-6

→ Schmidt, Gary D./Doney, Todd (illus.). *Saint Ciaran: the Tale of a Saint of Ireland*. Michigan: Eerdmans Books, 2000. 0-80285-170-3

→ Shackman, Julie/West, Annie (illus.). *Olivia's Orchestra*. Dublin: Mentor Press, 2000. 1-84210-008-4

→ Shackman, Julie/West, Annie (illus.). *What's That Up There?* Dublin: Mentor Press, 1999. 1-90258-661-1

→ Tolstoy, Alexsci/Sharkey, Niamh (illus.). *The Gigantic Turnip*. Bath: Barefoot Books, 1998. 1-90228-311-2 (hardcover) and 1-90228-329-5 (paperback)

→ Walker, Richard/Sharkey, Niamh (illus.). *Jack and the Beanstalk*. Bath: Barefoot Books, 1999. 1-90122-361-2

→ Walker, Richard/Whelan, Olwyn (illus.). *My Very First Book of Pirates*. Bath: Barefoot Books, 1998. 1-90122-350-7

→ Waddell, Martin. *John Joe and the Big Hen*. London: Walker Books, 1995. 0-74455-243-5

→ West, Annie. *The Butterfly Who Wouldn't*. Dublin: Mentor Press, 1999. 1-90258-657-3

→ Wood, Douglas/Lynch, P.J. (illus.). *Grandad's Prayers of the Earth*. London: Walker Books, 1999. 0-74455-648-1

A SENSE OF PLACE IN IRISH CHILDREN'S BOOKS

What is most striking about representations of place in contemporary Irish children's and teenage literature is their variety and complexity. This is hardly surprising given that landscape and environment have provided both the theme and the backdrop of much Irish literature since the early Middle Ages. Although there are exceptions, such as Colfer's *Benny and Omar* and Hest's and Lynch's *When Jessie Came Across the Sea*, a good deal of recent children's fiction is sited primarily in Ireland, but it is a multifaceted Ireland of bleak urban streetscapes, of timeless pastoral pleasure and of small-town communities.

A recurring image is that of an Ireland in the throes of change, in which housing estates are as much a feature of west Mayo as they are of large urban centres. Past and present vie for supremacy in, for example, Mark O'Sullivan's *Silent Stones*, woven around New Age travellers and a prehistoric stone circle. The clash of the old and the new creates pressures and strains. Alienated adolescents collide with family and community, progress with poverty, booming modern self-confidence with elemental energy and ancient spirituality. The traditional constraints of class codes battle with a transglobal, affluent youth culture, often with the central characters torn between them. The Ireland of recent fiction is a place geographically and often imaginatively self-contained, yet linked to the global economic and cultural network. This emphasis on the rapidly changing face of Ireland serves a useful additional function within the narrative economy of the stories cited in this essay. For the most part, they depict older children edging painfully towards self-realisation and adulthood, enduring or enjoying rapid evolutions and transitions in their own lives. The changing face of Ireland serves as both a parallel and a foil to that change.

Mobility is integral to flux, and is a feature of many storylines. Several writers use the familiar strategy of placing their protagonists in an alien environment: Gébler's Phoebe and her family move from London to Northern Ireland (*Frozen Out, A Tale of Betrayal and Survival*); Lyons's Emma from Tallaght to Clare (*Call of Friendship*); Colgan's Luke from the northside of Dublin to Dun Laoghaire *(The Stretford Enders);* Colfer's Benny from town to country (*Benny and Babe*); Mark O'Sullivan's Mayfly and her New Age family from England to the midlands of Ireland (*Silent Stones);* and Patrick O'Sullivan's Rebecca to Kerry (*The Horses of Dereenard*). These plots could be summarised in terms of the characters' shift from resistance to their new environment to an enthusiastic acceptance of and commitment to it. In addition, the reader is conscious that secondary characters are constantly crossing

boundaries. The Moravian background of Lida's father in *More than a Match*, for example, plays an important role in Lida's life. Willie Cormack's (*Sea Dance*) brothers work in Cambridge and New York respectively, testament to the tradition of emigration that is inherent to the west of Ireland. At the other end of the spectrum, Mayfly's father served his musical apprenticeship in swinging California, and in *White Lies*, by Mark O'Sullivan, Nance's mother became pregnant with her by a young black teacher while working in Africa in the 1970s.

Irish space and culture are no longer insulated, and stories often draw on a wide hinterland. Teenage Nance, for example, effortlessly crosses and recrosses the southern counties in her efforts to trace her roots. In most cases, however, the characters eventually offer their allegiance to their homeplace. Morpurgo's *The Ghost of Grania O'Malley* stresses human beings' short tenure on this earth and their responsibility to conserve the landscape they inhabit. But there are notable exceptions, however, to the traditional rule of an Irish sense of rootedness. For Mark O'Sullivan's characters, locations lack colour because they are so caught up in their personal problems. Parkinson's homeless squatters (*Breaking the Wishbone*) are without roots when the story ends. It seems that for Irish writers, rootedness and family ties are still closely allied.

Sea Dance,
illustration by
Sam Hadley.

Stories set in urban Ireland challenge presumptions about stability and community. The disease of urbanised poverty abounds. Parkinson's squats are reminiscent of O'Casey's tenements, all the more deplorable nearly a century later. Waddell's evocation of hopeless existence in a nameless city (*Tango's Baby*) is a swingeing indictment of an uncaring society and its neglect and abandonment of its vulnerable young. The fact that the location is unidentified adds to its anonymity and its dystopian universality. This may not be your town, Waddell implies, but it could be. Binch's *Christy's Dream*, set in the Ballymun complex of north Dublin, imparts visually the sense of clutter, disorder and grime that are emblematic of poverty. However, this high-rise locality is not without its attractions, which include strong family bonds and a healthy youth culture evolving incongruously around horses. Quality of life is possible, even in an alien urban environment, the story suggests, if a boy is determined to avoid the pitfalls.

In contrast to the critical realism of the urban tales, many novels employ the tried-and-tested narrative manoeuvre of separating youngsters from adults and placing them in a negative, uncharted space in which they pit themselves against powerful forces. The fluid, inscrutable sea, mighty and wilful, becomes more than the mere context of adventure and adopts multiple roles in *Benny and Babe, Call of Friendship, Sea Dance, The Ghost of Grania O'Malley* and *Four Kids, Three Cats, Two Cows, One Witch (maybe)*. It is the supreme antagonist

Benny and Babe,
cover by
Angela Clarke.

against which the young characters pit themselves. These stories rehearse the ageless conflict between humans and the elements, acknowledging the sublime, seductive magnificence, munificence and capriciousness of the natural world. With few of the resources of civilisation, for these characters faith in personal ability, belief in a future and in friendship are vital.

An aspect of sea stories is the magic of islands, self-contained – and therefore the grounding for Crusoesque feats – but also beyond reach. For Gatti's Willie Cormack, the island that is his inheritance and his father's childhood home is the repository of tradition and enduring bonds, in sharp contrast to the degenerating and debilitating mainland. In *Four Kids, Three Cats, Two Cows, One Witch (maybe)* an island is home to a lone woman, ostracised by her more integrated neighbours. Her sensitivity and vulnerability stand in sharp contrast to the robustness and callousness required for survival in the modern world. Morpurgo's misty island in *The Ghost of Grania O'Malley* is a fantasy island inhabited by the pirate Grania O'Malley, a ghostly crone who embodies the resolute lawlessness necessary to curb those individuals who have law, but not right, on their side.

The sea, however, is not the only exemplum of uncharted space. The action of Lyons's *Call of Friendship* takes place in underground caves, which become a metaphor for the unconscious, for those dark and stormy passions that prey on the adolescent mind. The disturbing *Switchers* series by Kate Thompson, as the term suggests, moves between the ordinariness of daily living and nights filled with dark and often repulsive adventures. Ostensibly set in recognisable Dublin and Clare, the novels' main protagonists, Tess and her switcher friends, can elect to adopt any form they please, and most often become rats. In rodent form they speed through sewers and communicate in rat ideograms. As they rummage through trash and take pleasure in gobbling humans' leftovers and detritus, it is not difficult to read the stories as an exploration of the psyche, of what happens when the veneer of civilisation heaves and cracks to reveal darker appetites. The second book in the series, *Midnight's Choice*, in which Tess is tempted to adopt the form of a vampire for all eternity, deploys this theme most effectively. Through her exploration of a negative space, Thompson successfully casts light on the limits of superficial civilisation, and offers alternative, estranging perspectives on familiar reality. One factor in the trilogy's success is that the novels are not limited by the conventions of realism and they knit together meticulous details of everyday reality with a powerful evocation of the fantastic.

Other writers depict psychic conflicts played out in gloomy, cold or disorderly homes. The claustrophobic, disorienting interiors are correlatives to the anxieties and self-absorption that are invariably adolescent traits. So wrapped up in their own personal miseries are Mark O'Sullivan's protagonists that the topography of their place is reduced to a scattering of local points – the pub, the school and, in the case of Lida in *More than a Match*, the tennis court. *White Lies* has two narrators, Nance and her friend OD, the former living in 'a nice detached house in the best part of town', the latter in an unkempt, spartan bachelor hovel. What the domestic interiors have in common is an absence of warmth, of a hearth. As the plot of *White Lies* unravels, order replaces chaos and the arctic atmosphere begins to thaw. Nance helps to clean and tidy OD's home, and the story ends with OD entering the fraught space of a hospital ward to support his ill father. As Nance comes to terms with the painful facts of her parentage, the radiators noisily swing into action and the room gradually, and metaphorically, warms up.

Trevor Colgan's interiors in *The Stretford Enders* suggest the acute loneliness of Luke Farrell, only son of an upwardly mobile single mother who has uprooted the family from their familiar north Dublin city home on a housing estate. Now living in rented rooms in the faded glory of a shabby Regency house, the cold comfort of Luke's solitary pizza stands in sharp contrast to the camaraderie that can be achieved on the football field. Parkinson's *Breaking the Wishbone* graphically presents homelessness coupled with an intense desire for rootedness. Her description of the cosy fire and candles twinkling 'like Christmas' in the squat runs perilously close to bathos. The evocation of hearth and home ends, however, with an explicit description of a vicious drunken assault on a pregnant teenager. The young narrator, Johnner tells us he is 'awfully disappointed' because he wanted 'us all to be happy, I mean like a family'.

Physical rootedness may have its psychic compensations, but it also has its limitations: it constrains and limits. This is a sub-theme that permeates much teenage fiction, and many authors, such as Mark O'Sullivan, resolve that tension between rootedness and change by having their characters accommodate themselves to a shared reality. Nance in *White Lies* comes to the realisation that there would be 'New worlds, old worlds … – not a perfect world but nonetheless part of what I am'. Nance speaks for conservative values, for the virtue of adapting to hearth and home. The driving force of other stories, such as that of the squatting community in *Breaking the Wishbone*, is a shared sense of purpose – a burning desire for a place of their own that they might call home. Their dream of a conventional family life is almost realised and that is the resolution of their conflict.

For others, however, such conservatism and compromise is harder won. Adaptation to the mores of the community makes too great a demand on their emerging sense of selfhood, and so sovereignty over the imaginative space is essential to their understanding of the world. Their allegiance is greatest to the fantastical places conjured by the imagination. Among the books that successfully integrate fantasy into predominantly realistic stories are Thompson's *Switchers* series, Gatti's *Sea Dance* and Parkinson's *Four Kids, Three Cats, Two Cows, One Witch (maybe)*. Their achievement works in a variety of ways. *Four Kids* draws on the reader's previous knowledge of the conventions of storytelling, taking them beyond the here and now to the kingdom of the imagination. Kevin borrows – or rather steals – Hans Christian Andersen's tale of the mermaids and tells of a merman who abandons his

Four Kids, Three Cats, Two Cows, One Witch (maybe), illustration by Laura Cronin.

merwife and merchildren for a life on land, where earthly treasures are valued more than they are in the deep. Elizabeth transports her listeners to a world familiar from the brothers Grimm, replete with gingerbread houses, wolves in sheep's clothing and children transformed into animals, but it is a world that is uniquely hers, a world constructed from her fantasy. Strangely, her story portends events that happen later on the island. But that, the book seems to suggest, is the power of the fantastical universe: to make sense of strange places. Beverley's tale liberates its princess from a slimy pit, and from the loving clutches of the ideal prince of traditional tales, into an uncharted future, a world replete with possibilities but with few points of reference. The fantasy world that parallels the reality evoked in the story draws on familiar images but shapes them afresh.

Finally, there are novels that draw the reader's attention to books' textual space. At one level, the place where every written story is set is on paper, between the covers of the book. *Breaking the Wishbone* focusses attention on this, paradoxically, by presenting the tale in the form of a film script. What you are about to see, this device suggests, takes place not in the lived, real world, but in that parallel universe of the imagination, accessed in this case by celluloid. What we know about the world we know as much from the stories that we tell about it as we do from direct experience of it. Thompson's *Midnight's Choice* self-consciously draws on our knowledge of vampire lore, and on its televisual and cinematic representations, thereby enriching and extending our understanding. *The Ghost of Grania O'Malley* inserts itself into the world of story by seeing new problems – how to conserve a beautiful place in the teeth of progress – in the light of old stories.

Few stories for older children and young adults are content with the sepia-toned nostalgia for a cosy, traditional small farm to be found in a book such as Waddell's *John Joe and the Big Hen*. Indeed, Waddell himself elsewhere insists that his teenage readers confront the unpalatable reality that many of their peers inhabit. Place is an active agent in his and other recent fiction, playing multiple and often contradictory roles. In uninhabited spaces characters pit themselves against superhuman forces and in the process come to a heightened awareness of their place in the world. Place can be the locus of change, but also of enduring, constant values. It is variously presented as local and universal, accommodating outsiders as foils to individual protagonists and community prejudice. Place can evoke the idyll and the absence of community; it can take on the colour and tone of the characters' psychic state.   ◗

John Joe and the Big Hen,
illustrated by Paul Howard.

RECOMMENDED TITLES

Eoin Colfer
BENNY AND BABE
O'Brien Press

Benny Shaw is a cool dude. He's thirteen, a mean hurler and gifted with a lively imagination. What he (privately) lacks in terms of confidence he compensates for with public displays of bravado and heavy-handed adolescent wit. The book describes a seaside summer in which he navigates that treacherous passage between childhood and adolescence. Colfer's strength is in his humorous depiction of a credible character, combined with a tense adventure. The tale is all the more plausible because Benny is at once foolhardy, self-centred and blindly propelled by his competitive, combative streak: every inch the irritatingly cocky, wildly attractive teenager.

The events of the summer teach him a great deal: about the wages of selfishness (four months in hospital), and about apparent enemies who come to the rescue at the vital moment. He finds his match in fellow adventurers Babe Meara and her sidekick, the pesky mongrel Conger. By the end of the novel, Benny has awoken – to his own foolishness and brashness, and to the fact that Babe is not just a mate but, well, a girl. Doubtless we will encounter Benny in future tales. He still has miles to go and Colfer's real flair will speed him along his path. It is gratifying to read an adolescent yarn that is not cast in the typically black, angst-ridden mood.

Trevor J. Colgan
THE STRETFORD ENDERS
Praxis

Luke Farrell's confidence is badly shaken when he has to leave behind the camaraderie and status he enjoyed as a champion footballer in northside Dublin and put down roots in alien Dun Laoghaire. His problems multiply when he is bullied by the thug Swayne, whose girlfriend Cecilia takes a passing fancy to him. Then there's his mother's sadly uncool boyfriend, and the shadowy, lonely landlady, Mrs Hendy, whose husband was lost in the war. Luke runs the full gamut of adolescent frictions, but his prowess at football is his salvation, enabling him to contain and resolve conflict. He also encounters a pair of Romanian brothers and a black girl, all struggling in class-conscious Dun Laoghaire. The Romanian brothers' football expertise enables them to establish solidarity with the local youth community, paralleling Luke's own successful integration.

But Luke's victories are small and hard-won. To his disappointment, his team, the Stretford Enders, does not win the league and the fault lies with him. However, he and Ella, his feisty constant friend, create a moment of happiness for old Mrs Hendy and all three confidently face the future, reversing the pessimism of the opening pages. One notable attraction of this book is the ease and enthusiasm with which it recreates the electrifying charge of football culture. Another is the representation of the jungle of complex class codes and snobberies through which teenagers must steer a path. Colgan has an eye for detail of contemporary dress and idiom that is utterly persuasive, and which goes some way towards compensating for the many typographical errors in the text.

The Stretford Enders,
illustration by
Ian Cox.

Eilís Dillon
THE HOUSE ON THE SHORE
O'Brien Press

This tale by the doyenne of Irish children's literature is a rollicking, suspense-filled adventure that was first published in 1955. It contains all the ingredients of classic adventure: swarthy, menacing foreigners, hidden treasure, ever-present danger and a teenage hero who saves the day. To leave it at that, however, is to do Dillon's tale a disservice. With an acute eye for detail, she sketches convincingly the backdrop of an isolated rural community on the cusp of progress, moving from a traditional, unchanging lifestyle to accepting the merits of advancement. At the heart of the tale is the narrator's miserly uncle and his theft of the community's entire savings, intended to develop a factory. While the concept of progress is unequivocally accepted as a collective good, Dillon's probing pen exposes

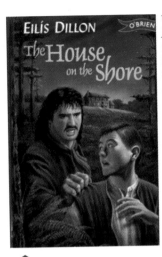

The House on the Shore,
illustration by
Finbarr O'Connor.

the community itself. John Faherty's domineering ways are noted but accepted, but Uncle Martin's crime unleashes a terrible lust for violence in the menfolk. It falls to Jim and Roddy to initiate practical action and to the women to contain the danger. Uncle Martin repents his greed but remains enigmatic and eccentric to the story's end. Jim inherits his land as his mother had hoped, and the young adventurer metamorphoses into a hard-working farmer.

Will Gatti
SEA DANCE
Oxford University Press

Gatti's haunting tale of Willie Cormack and his unlikely friend, the shipwrecked Algerian Malouf, is set in the isolated west Mayo community of Mullet, where bigotry and suspicion ferment in an atmosphere fetid with alcohol and greed. Willie's daring rescue of Malouf, who is brutally beaten after a local girl, Anna, is attacked, leads him to his father's uninhabited former island home. The story unravels Willie's complex relationship with his family, the island and Mullet, and the realisation dawns that he identifies with his island kin. In contrast to the wanderlust and greed of his brother, Ian, Willie emerges as a kind of visionary, a believer in the power of the godstone, which is venerated by the island folk but has been cast into the sea. This tale shies away from neat resolutions and happy endings. Willie's elder brother, John, remains disreputable to the end, and Anna, with whom Willie was infatuated, proves self-seeking and compromised. Despite the tale's bleak acceptance of human limitation, its hard-won optimism carries the reader along. Malouf manages to return home against all the odds. Willie hones his capacity to capture the spirit of the moment with a tune, and he comes to perceive his parents' fierce love for each other, which has led to unconscionable sacrifices on both parts. Finally, there is the godstone, still beneath the waves, but a guiding presence and a link between the dead and the living.

Nuala Lyons
CALL OF FRIENDSHIP
Attic Press

Imagine a family abandoning the bustle of Tallaght in favour of resettlement in rural County Clare. Imagine new schoolmates who take every opportunity to sneer at and belittle the new kid from the city, Emma. Imagine then what it's like for her, an only child with delicate health, when, in addition to all this, her parents are apparently lost in a boating accident. This story tells of Emma's heroic and unrelenting attempts to find them. Her quest leads her into a black underground labyrinth and to the realisation that Aran and Deirdre, her one-time torturers, have much to recommend them. Lyons does not flinch at the challenge of portraying a physically abusive father or of disposing of him violently. Neither does she wince at presenting Emma's mother's limitations and her lapses of concentration. This tale has more than a touch of Gothic intensity, conducted as it is in black holes, on cliff tops and in violent storms, with life-threatening illnesses and amputated limbs punctuating Emma's quiet, rhythmic narration. This wild, elemental landscape is a foil to her resilience and her unswerving belief in her capacity to rescue her parents. That conviction is captured in the image of the flask of soup she carries for them. A quest tale with a contemporary twist.

Call of Friendship,
cover by
Kunnert + Tierney.

Siobhán Parkinson
FOUR KIDS, THREE CATS, TWO COWS, ONE WITCH (MAYBE)
O'Brien Press

Parkinson adopts the Blytonesque formula of four children setting out for an uninhabited island in search of adventure, and they are as preoccupied with food, as far from adult influence and as prone to injury as their counterparts of two generations earlier. However, here the comparison with Blyton ends. The sensitivity and sophistication of the narrative technique means that the children's journey to the island becomes a rite of passage into independence and a discovery of selfhood. As the story starts, the island shimmers in the distance – testament to another reality beyond reach. Beverley, the eldest and the leader, sets out in a rather pedantic frame of mind: she will become acquainted with the terrain by recording, with scientific accuracy, the flora and fauna she observes. As the story progresses, however, the reader and the story's protagonists begin to discover that the world is knowable more through the medium of story. The adventurers – or pilgrims, as they begin to call themselves after Chaucer's taletellers – share stories. It becomes clear that they all simultaneously inhabit a tangible reality and a world of fantasy, and that each domain enriches and makes sense of the other. On the island we encounter a witch (maybe, but unlikely), and her isolated, lonely existence makes sense when we hear her story of the duckling who hated the rain and was happier with its life as a cement-covered statue.

Kate Thompson
SWITCHERS
Red Fox

MIDNIGHT'S CHOICE
Red Fox

WILD BLOOD, SWITCHERS 3: THE CONCLUSION …
Red Fox

The character who dominates Thompson's *Switchers* trilogy is Tess, an unhappy teenager who has never adapted to life in Dublin, but who has the capacity to change – to switch into any form she chooses. With Tess and her fellow switchers we share the exhilaration of being dragons, the fun of confusing the police by taking the form of a goat and

*Wild Blood,
Switchers 3:
The Conclusion …,*
illustration by
Darren Lock.

the power over death possessed by the phoenix. Tess and Kevin, however, mostly favour adopting the form of the most reviled animals: rats. They use their powers to fight evil. In the first book it is the relatively contained and distant evil of the Krools. In the second, the sinister rat-bat-wolf-boy, a vampire who feeds off his own emaciated mother and is the embodiment of malignancy. In the final story of the series it is Uncle Maurice's brother, Declan, a switcher who chose to become a member of the Tuatha de Danann and who remained forever a boy of fifteen, but who is a trickster – a spirit who will stop at nothing to achieve his aims. Declan is the evil presence in this re-enactment of the Pied Piper of Hamlin, tortured and unhappy. The power of this book is its ability to convey both the attractiveness and the accelerating nature of evil. This is a deeply disturbing trilogy that confronts the nature of evil, the limitations of human existence and the terror of many children when confronted with the inevitability of adulthood. Thompson's penchant for Gothic images and references, the pervasive atmosphere of anxiety and pain, the suppressed sexuality and absence of neat, affirming endings, raise more questions than they answer. Will Tess choose to remain a human being, or will she, like some of the other switchers we encounter, escape from the constraints of human form? Will readers interpret these stories as parables on the need for flexibility or depictions of adolescents' growing need for independence, as Thompson sometimes suggests they are? Or will they be arrested by the uncompromising, shape-changing and pervasive representations of evil? To reveal the ending of the final story of the trilogy is not permissible, but it does go some way towards answering these questions.

Martin Waddell
THE KIDNAPPING OF SUZIE Q
Walker Books

This tale oscillates between the familiarity of a small town near Belfast and an uncharted, mountainous region nearby where Suzie's hapless kidnappers find themselves. Their aborted robbery of a super-market led to their Bonnie and Clyde-style flight. Suzie, a model of sound sense and practical judge-ment (except in her weakness for fattening food), combines attempts to escape with mentoring her mindless captors. Waddell achieves a gloriously sur-real scene near the novel's end when Dodie, the pregnant teenage kidnapper, has been helped away from the mayhem by Suzie and awaits the arrival of the police in Mrs McKibben's front room. There they are regaled with endless details of her grown family in Boston. At the ensuing trial, Suzie pleads mitigating circumstances in an attempt to reduce teenage Dodie's sentence, but to little avail. Like Suzie, one shudders to think of the future of her baby born in jail.

This is a pessimistic, downbeat thriller de-spite Suzie's *bonhomie*. There is an inevitability about the fate of Waddell's captors that makes them even more dangerous. They live – survive – in the violent arena of Northern Ireland, where it seems philanthropy is unequal to brute strength. The reader finds little consolation in Suzie's conclusion that 'what they did was wrong and I don't think any-one should try to excuse it'.

TITLES REFERRED TO IN ARTICLE AND IN RECOMMENDED LIST

→ Binch, Caroline. *Christy's Dream*. London: Mammoth, 1999. 0-7497-4092-2

→ Colfer, Eoin. *Benny and Babe*. Dublin: O'Brien Press, 1999. 0-86278-603-7

→ Colgan, Trevor J. *The Stretford Enders*. Dublin: Praxis, 1999. 0-9537531-0-7

→ Dillon, Eilís. *The House on the Shore*. Dublin: O'Brien Press, 2000. 0-86278-673-8

→ Gatti, Will. *Sea Dance*. Oxford: Oxford University Press, 1999. 0-19-271803-7

→ Gébler, Carlo. *Frozen Out: A Tale of Betrayal and Survival*. London: Mammoth, 1998. 0-7497-2874-4

→ Lynch, P.J. and Hest, Amy. *When Jessie Came Across the Sea*. London: Walker Books, 1997. 0-7445-6963-X

→ Lyons, Nuala. *Call of Friendship*. Cork: Attic Press, 1999. 1-85594-199-6

→ Morpurgo, Michael. *The Ghost of Grania O'Malley*. London: Mammoth, 1996. 0-7497-2582-6

→ O'Sullivan, Mark. *Silent Stones*. Dublin: Wolfhound Press, 1999. 0-86327-722-5

→ O'Sullivan, Mark. *More than a Match*. Dublin: Wolfhound Press, 1996, 1998. 0-86327-496-X

→ O'Sullivan, Mark. *White Lies*. Dublin: Wolfhound Press, 1998. 0-86327-592-3

→ O'Sullivan, Patrick. *The Horses of Dereenard*. Dublin: Wolfhound Press, 2000. 0-86327-790-X

→ Parkinson, Siobhán. *Four Kids, Three Cats, Two Cows, One Witch (maybe)*. Dublin: O'Brien Press, 1997. 0-86278-515-4

→ Parkinson, Siobhán. *Breaking the Wishbone*. Dublin: O'Brien Press, 1999. 0-86278-635-5

→ Thompson, Kate. *Switchers*. London: Red Fox, 1997. 00-99-25612-6

→ Thompson, Kate. *Midnight's Choice*. London: Red Fox, 1998. 0-09-925613-4

→ Thompson, Kate. *Wild Blood, Switchers 3: The Conclusion ...* London: Red Fox, 1999. 0-09-926628-8

→ Waddell, Martin. *The Kidnapping of Suzie Q*. London: Walker Books, 1994. 0-7445-6989-3

→ Waddell, Martin. *Tango's Baby*. London: Walker Books, 1995. 0-7445-4304-5

→ Waddell, Martin and Howard, Paul. *John Joe and the Big Hen*. London: Walker Books, 1995. 0-7445-5243-5

CHILDREN'S BOOKS IN IRISH

The good news is that there is now a wide range of books available for children and teenagers in Irish, at least compared with formerly. The less good news is that while some categories of reading material are plentiful, other categories are only thinly represented. Thus, while books for the very young are readily available and teenage material has much improved, it is more difficult to get suitable material for that middle range of children who would be expected to read independently.

Irish is no different from any other language in that the child will be introduced to reading through picture books and simple sentences, usually by a parent. A book such as Irene Ní Mhuireagáin's *Aoife agus an Chuil Ghorm* contains no more than a few short sentences or sometimes just a word on each page. It is funny, simple and direct. Similarly, Mary Arrigan's *Mamó ag an Sorcas* has a sense of the absurd that will appeal to all young children. Many books carry a guidance to the effect that it is suitable for children between the ages of 'four and seven' or whatever. While this is very helpful, it need not always be strictly adhered to. Parents or teachers know their children and are the best judges of their ability.

Despite the best will in the world, literacy in Irish has its own problems. A native speaker of the language, either from the traditional Gaeltacht or raised through Irish in town or city, will be exposed to more reading material in English than in her/his first language. It follows that to read a book in Irish is almost always an act of deliberate *choice* rather than just picking up a book that happens to be hanging around. Sometimes a book in Irish is read simply because it is in Irish, and this is not always the best reason for doing so. Also, books in Irish have to encompass all genres, all categories, all types, so that each individual book in Irish carries a greater burden, a greater responsibility than its corresponding book in English.

Thus, a book such as Christina Balit's *Atlantis: An Chathair a Bádh* is one of a very few dealing with Greek history/mythology. It is stunningly beautiful and rendered clearly and cleanly into Irish by Gabriel Rosenstock. It is all the more conspicuous because it is in Irish, and therefore has a visibility that it would not have amongst the vast riches of reading material in English. On the other hand, Maitiú Ó Murchú's *Colm na Cille* tells the story of St Colm Cille in simple Irish, and we feel that this is right and correct. There are books that seem eminently appropriate in Irish because the language of their stories was originally Irish and, whatever the gap between then and now, there is

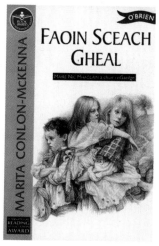

Faoin Sceach Gheal,
illustration by Anne Yvonne Gilbert.

a 'fit' that works for people with even a simple modicum of historical feeling. St Colm Cille was one of the most influential people in Irish and Scottish history as he brought both Christianity and the Gaelic language to Scotland. The book is historically accurate and brought brightly alive by Deirdre Ní Bhraonáin's broadly colourful illustrations. This appropriateness of language is also wonderfully apt in one of the really great successes of children's fiction in Ireland in the past few years. Marita Conlon-McKenna's *Under the Hawthorn Tree* is rightly regarded as a classic of our time. It has been beautifully translated by Máire Nic Mhaoláin as *Faoin Sceach Gheal*, and seems so appropriate as the language of the children who are searching for their salvation and their survival. This is a book that is superbly interesting in itself, but the Irish translation succeeds in drawing us back into the maw of time and recreating the conditions of talk and conversation and atmosphere which existed during the Famine in a way that the English version simply cannot do.

Those I have mentioned so far have been translations from the English. But one of the great paradoxes and successes of publishing in Irish has been the amount of translations from other languages which have been forthcoming. There has always been the conundrum that the bigger the language, the smaller the range of translations; and conversely, the less widespread the language, the broader its grasp of what is going on elsewhere. English does not need to translate; Irish must. So translations from the Swedish, or the French, or the Russian, or whatever figure largely in books available in Irish. Over the years translations of books by Marcel Marlier, Joos Ghislaine and Gunilla Wolde have become staples of the regular output of An Gúm. It would be wonderful to think that *Am Codlata i Lár na Coille* by Carole Lexa Schafer and Vanessa Cabban, a stunning book for children of four years old and upwards, could have been written originally in Irish with an Irish illustrator. But it is equally wonderful that it is available, translated from English, as a simple story and as a fabulous work of art. Therefore, Irish is on the one hand a resource for getting at what is going on in the greater world, and on the other a means of entering our own tradition.

Am Codlata i Lár na Coille, cover by Vanessa Cabban.

At the simplest level it is often said that Ireland has a great folk tradition. We have thousands and thousands of stories available to us, which were recently told by word of mouth and embellished and elaborated upon by *scéalaithe* and *seanchaithe* or storytellers. But story is no good unless it says something funny or wise or entertaining or different. Story is the building-block of knowledge and the seed from which we begin to feel the world. Story is the beginning and the end and the middle and the way and the life of all knowing. And Irish stories mediated the world for generations of Irish people. Gabriel Rosenstock's *An*

Phéist Mhór is a retelling of a folk tale about a great sea-beast who swallows an old woman. Echoes of Jonah and the whale abound, but it is both amusing and wise. Similarly, *An Rógaire agus a Scáil* concerns a joker who frightens the life out of all and everyone until his shadow is stolen by the devil and he begins to see the good in life. Both of these books are beautifully rendered into colour and wonder by Piet Sluis, who seems to see both Rosenstock's quirky imagination and the mind of a child in clear measure.

One of the great reworkings of the Irish and the European folk tradition is Peadar Ó Laoghaire's *Séanna*. As well as being an Irish version of the Faust legend, it was also a book that was often seen as the first novel in the Irish language and figured on syllabuses in schools in the Irish Republic for generations. Because it is a universal story about the triumph of good over evil and presents typical characters in an everyday setting, it continues to have a perennial appeal. The publishing house Cois Life have recently given us a simplified version, with a reading on CD by Liam Ó Muirthile. It is a work in which the oral tradition meets the literary tradition to produce something special.

This sense of the 'folk' – whatever we mean by it – appears to have a special place in books in Irish. One of the tensions felt is that of the language being both regional and national. Readers of a local dialect feel a certain estrangement from the national standard, and readers of the national standard feel put upon by the regional form. The national standard is essential and the dialects are an enrichment. It is not that there is a huge difference between them, but that the learner will spot the variables fairly quickly. Maidhc Dainín Ó Sé is a determinedly regional writer, even if his subject matter is broad and diverse. His tale of *Madraí na nOcht gCos* is Kerry through and through, although there is no reason why it should not be enjoyed from Cnoc Fola to Cahirciveen. Similarly, *Is Glas iad na Cnoic* gives us the tale of a cat who travels from West Kerry to New York and her adventures there and back. Part of the delight in any book in Irish must be the language itself, and the style which he employs is as clean as the wind that blows in from Inisvicillaun. His *Mair, a Chapaill* is a kind of Irish *Black Beauty* without a great deal of the slush and sentimentality. Meeting both dialect needs and the necessity for reissuing classics of an earlier generation is *Slán Leat, A Mhaicín*, Fionn Mac Cumhaill's short novel of goings-on in a Donegal Gaeltacht village. 'Quaint', 'evocative' or 'homely' are not the words we want to describe it, but it is in there somewhere between them.

One of the great riches of Irish storytelling is, of course, its mythology. For right or for wrong, reading our myths in Irish gives them a resonance and an echo which is missing from any translation. The tragic story of Deirdre and her brothers, *Bás Chlann Uisnigh*, has been told many times and bears retelling. Caoimhín Mac Giolla Léith's recent

Ruairí sa Zú,
illustrated by Anne Marie Carroll.

version attempts to mirror some of the language of the original and to make it accessible to a younger audience. A good level of Irish is required to get involved with the text, but the effort is well worth it. The big story of the western tradition is, of course, that of Christianity. The stories of the Bible have been central to our understanding of the world for centuries. They receive a very clear retelling in Caitríona Hasting's *Dea-Scéala,* in which forty-eight different events from the old and from the new testament are set before us. You might say that this is the Bible with the boring bits left out, and while the Bible might be the word of God, He was never a stickler for the minute detail of narrative. As the supreme storyteller, He realised that the Big Picture was all. This is the Big Picture in all its wonder and pleasantness and human failings and redemptions.

For all that, the great success of publishing in Irish has been for the youngest age groups. Picture books with bright illustrations and simple language, which can be used by parents or teachers and supplemented with talk and discussion, are the best that we have. Colmán Ó Raghallaigh and Anne Marie Carroll's *Drochlá Ruairí* and *Ruairí sa Zú* are exam-

ples of wonderfully gaudy, zanily illustrated and manically 'relevant' texts. Ruairí is one of those kids who just can't help screwing up, and his face and those of his colleagues tell us that this is just the way it is going to be. These books are funny and weird and an example of Irish humour at its best. Mary Arrigan writes for a somewhat older readership, but maintains some of that same slightly off-the-wall humour. *An Bhó Fhionn* concerns a stolen cow, which might seem very 'traditional' and rural, but the story is timeless and the illustrations guide us along with fun and with humour. Her *Siúlóid Bhreá* is a fable of all that can happen to anyone who goes out for a walk.

An Bhó Fhionn, illustrated by Mary Arrigan.

The best of these books try to break the association of Irish with school, although school is a necessary place for Irish to be. Children do not need to know every word of every book in order to appreciate a story. No adult knows the precise meaning and weight of every word in every newspaper article that he or she reads. We plough on because the context is clear, or clear enough. Children will enjoy reading in Irish if they get the meaning, there or thereabouts. Reading is an adventure, and reading in Irish is often an even bigger one. The pictures help to place the text more than the other way around. There is often, unfortunately, a gap between the language ability of the child and the suitability of the subject matter. Sometimes the child understands the language very well, but the matter is too easy; or conversely, the matter is within reach, but the language beyond his/her ken. Only guidance and help can bridge these gaps with sympathy and sense. But we shouldn't make too much of these difficulties either. Children will attack a text with courage and imagination and reading material in Irish has its own rewards.

When good habits have been established, independent readers can move on to more challenging material by Ré Ó Laighléis (his *Gafa* and other novels are as relevant as you require), or by Iarla Mac Aodha Bhuí (*An Lambourghini Buí* is great fun), or Cliodhna Cussen, whose beautiful *An Eala Dhubh* is based on a folk song from County Mayo. Beyond these is adulthood and the great unknown.

RECOMMENDED TITLES

Gwyneth Wynn
MICÍ AR AN BPORTACH
An Gúm

A story for six to nine year olds where the language is simple yet evocative. Whatever the attraction of Teddy Bears, they seem to fit into every situation. Big Teddy brings his son Micí to work on the bog, cutting turf. This is pleasantly romantic and lovingly illustrated with spare, colourful drawings. They work hard cutting and stacking until Micí hears a plaintive cry from underneath their bricks of turf. It is a mouse and its family building their home under the sods. Later, during the winter, Teddy and Micí hear a knock on the door. The mouse has come looking for protection against the cold. They take him in and feed him and warm him and look after him, and then free him when spring comes. It is not a fable with a lesson, but just a plain and good story about kindness and charity.

Gabriel Rosenstock
PÁIDÍN MHÁIRE MHUIGÍN
An Gúm

A witty rendering of a folk tale, which shows how a mixture of innocence and cuteness wins the day. Páidín seems to be an ordinary kind of a slob living with his mother until, at the age of thirty, he decides to get married. He is one of life's great innocents who tells the truth and sees no guile in anyone. When he marries the beautiful Nora, he wishes to give her a boomerang as a present. It might be just the sound of the word! She, being a woman, and therefore far more sensible and less romantic, can think of many more practical things than a boomerang! Their chance comes when the landlord passes by in his coach and drops a bag of gold by accident. Páidín picks it up and brings it home. He is delighted that he will now be able to buy his wife the boomerang. She tells him to do nothing, however, and sends him to school the next day, saying that he will eventually become a doctor! She orders the teacher to keep him in school until at least half-past three in the afternoon. Páidín's experiences in school are not very happy ones as he is jeered and mocked by the other pupils. He manages to escape when the postman comes, and goes back to working on the road. When the landlord arrives to question him about the bag of gold, he replies that he found it the day before he went to school! They laugh at his innocence and leave him alone. Nora knew all along that he would tell the truth, and the truth would help them to get the money.

The moral, if there is one, may be a bit skewed, but it is a tale of the less fortunate outwitting the more fortunate with fun and games. Piet Sluis's illustrations are hilarious, and suit the humour and temper of the book.

Colmán Ó Raghallaigh/Anne Marie Carroll
DROCHLÁ RUAIRÍ
Cló Mhaigh Eo

This is one of those stories that is so simple and so straightforward that it would seem prosaic in any retelling. It is everyday in that it recounts the unfortunate boy who has to get up in the morning and go to school and for whom disaster follows disaster, at least in that boyish way of breaking windows and forgetting lunch and getting punished and having paint spilled and getting chased by dogs. But it is the perfect matching of text and drawings which makes this book a treat. Everyone in the illustrations seems to be frightened or amused or scary or jeering or bored, and are utterly larger than life. It is all in the eyes. Anne Marie Carroll's depiction of eyes tells the story of the book, and Colmán Ó Raghallaigh's text matches them blow for blow. We feel sorry for Ruairí from beginning to end, and yet we feel this is exactly how it must be for a put-upon schoolboy in a big, bad world that he just can't understand.

Christina Balit
ATLANTIS: AN CHATHAIR A BÁDH
An Gúm

This is a truly beautiful book. It is a simple and direct retelling of the Atlantis legend, beginning with the creation of the world and how Poseidon built Atlantis and made it into a paradise on the sea. And then how the people of Atlantis became corrupt and vain, and how Poseidon had to destroy it all and bury it under the waves. The telling is straight and clear, but it is the illustrations that make this a work of art. Every picture can be lovingly ogled over. A kind of aquamarine blue is the dominant colour, with details of exotic animals on one page, or busy humans in great minutiae on another, or angry gods growling from the heavens on yet another. This is a book to fire the imagination of all ages. Linger over it and lovingly explore its folds and detail and language.

Maitiú Ó Murchú/Deirdre Ní Bhraonáin (illus.)
COLM NA CILLE
An Gúm

This is a fairly simple and direct retelling of the story of St Colm Cille from his youth in what is now Donegal to his death in Iona. It is a story that requires little embellishment as it is full of wonder and anecdote

Atlantis: An Chathair a Bádh,
illustrated by Christina Balit.

because it comes down to us from the oral tradition. It is told as a mixture of history and legend, which is probably the only way it can be told. We learn of his youth, of how he got his name changed from that of a Fox to that of a Dove because of his holiness, of his training to be a priest, of his travels around Ireland, of his founding of many monasteries, of his miracles, his involvement in dynastic battles, his voluntary exile to Scotland, his love of poetry and learning, his dissemination of the faith, his love of his community and his old age and death. It is a stirring tale that resonates throughout the ages. Deirdre Ní Bhraonáin's illustrations have a scope and breadth which draw us into the story without in any way replacing it. The book contains several simple maps which give the events their place and context.

Mary Arrigan
AN BHÓ FHIONN
An Gúm

This is one of those books that seems to call upon fairy-tales and folklore without the obvious lessons that they sometimes entail. There are echoes of 'Jack and the Beanstalk' and the 'Musicians of Bremen' and whatever else you wish to call upon without being in any way beholden to them. Mary Arrigan's drawings have a timelessness that harks back to Victorianism, and yet have the quirkiness and humour of all that is contemporary. We start with the comfortable setting of everything being alright with the world. Seán and his grandmother live in their comfortable house at the foot of a hill. They sing and play music and laugh. And then their white cow with big brown eyes is stolen. They travel the townlands and the countryside looking for their cow and having adventures. They come to a thieves' house, where the illustration shows us innocent gluttony and seemingly harmless blackguardism. They are sent to stay in the barn, where, lo and behold, they find their favourite white cow! After this, it is further adventures and success all the way. The humour is real, the characters are pleasant and the story belongs to us all.

Caitríona Hastings
DEA-SCÉALA
Cló Iar-Connachta

This retelling of the best of the Bible stories is clear and refreshing. Apart from any religious significance, the Bible is a compendium of great stories. It is also a basis for any understanding of western thought. It is our foundation of knowledge. Caitríona Hastings has rewritten the Bible in less than one hundred and fifty pages and has done so vividly. No story is more than two or three pages long and all that boring and irrelevant detail is excised. It is as good and as accurate a synopsis of the Judaeo-Christian tradition

Dea-Scéala,
illustrated by
Máire Keogh.

as you are likely to get in as many pages. Apart from being in Irish, it should be required reading in any religion class. The story of Abraham and Isaac is more scary in its spareness than in its more florid 'original'. Samson is not quite Cú Chulainn, but we see the similarities. The ten commandments are more charitable and understandable than in Exodus 20. The story of Jesus is pared to the best of the parables, the more significant of the miracles and His passion and death. Máire Keogh's illustrations are impressionistic and unobtrusive and allow us the space to think, reflect and imagine as we wish.

Michael Mullen
AN BÓTHAR FADA
Coiscéim

Although books in Irish may often inhabit a folklore, timeless world, it is less usual for them to be concerned with the big, bad world outside Ireland in a historical context. There is no reason for this, however, apart from a particular practice. Michael Mullen has always attempted to spread and widen this tradition, and this book deals with the adventures of

Pierre, a young French drummer boy who gets involved with Napoleon's Army on their rampage of conquest across Europe to the east. The story itself is, of course, hugely romantic and has captured the imaginations of people for nearly two centuries. The author taps into this, but does not shirk from the awfulness and savagery of war. He gives us vivid descriptions of the Battle of Borodino and of the Burning of Moscow. We learn how it was necessary to cut off the limbs of otherwise healthy men in order to save their lives, and how horseflesh became a delicacy in time of starvation. It is a book full of strange and weird, but all too human 'characters' – the Thief, the Giant, the Orphan, the Sniper, the Tailor – every one of them with their own recognisable traits. But it is a very human story, told in the midst of horror and destruction. That kind of mix of history, romance, adventure and realism appeals to many readers.

Caoimhín Mac Giolla Léith
BÁS CHLANN UISNIGH
Coiscéim

One of the biggest challenges facing writers in Irish is to present the old stories and sagas in a modern and readable form. It is a difficult task, not least because they were originally composed not for children or teenagers but for full-blooded adults, and because myth and legend has more recently been seen to be the preserve of a younger mind only. There is also the added difficulty that if they are rendered in any way in a more archaic language they become a turnoff, but if they are thoroughly modernised they are reduced to a story without atmosphere. But the story itself is great. A story of love and exile and betrayal that has been retold many times in prose, verse and drama. It would be a distinct help to have reasonably good Irish when approaching this version. Mac Giolla Léith's version is pacey and lively, but retains those verbal flourishes which flavour the telling. The rendering is poetic and is more of a verbal delight for those who can taste the words than any plain account could be.

An Bóthar Fada,
illustrated by Cormac Ó
Snodaigh.

Peadar Ó Laoghaire
SÉANNA
Cois Life

This is one of those original Irish classics which one feels should be read by everyone. It is the Irish folk version of the Faust legend as reinterpreted by Peadar Ó Laoghaire at the end of the nineteenth century, and  which has been abridged and adapted ever since. This is a simplified version with a lot of the stuffing left out. It is a gripping tale of an innocent shoemaker who unwittingly sells his soul to the devil in return for a purse of money that will never run out, on condition that he will 'go with him' after thirteen years. It is set in a kind of timeless Irish countryside with many shrewd and grotesque characters through which and among whom the innocent Séanna moves. There are bailiffs and landlords and dealers and merchants and farmers. Séanna himself gradually gains knowledge of the world as the end of his thirteen years approaches. His grappling with 'An Fear Dubh', the 'Black Man' or Devil towards the end of the story is a triumph of wit and horror. But before this we are treated to a huge slice of Irish life as it was, particularly as it was in the imagination, and we enter into it as innocently as Séanna himself. One of the triumphs of the book is that it is accompanied by a CD of the text, which is read by Liam Ó Muirthile in a clear and authoritative voice.

Séanna, illustrated by Marie-Louise Fitzpatrick.

TITLES REFERRED TO IN ARTICLE AND IN RECOMMENDED LIST

→ Arrigan, Mary. *An Bhó Fhionn*. Dublin: An Gúm, 1996. 1-85791-214-4

→ Arrigan, Mary. *Mamó ag an Sorcas*. Dublin: An Gúm, 1997. 1-85791-241-1

→ Arrigan, Mary. *Siúlóid Bhreá*. Dublin: An Gúm, 1999. 1-85791-280-2

→ Balit, Christina/Rosenstock, Gabriel (trans.). *Atlantis: An Chathair a Bádh*. Dublin: An Gúm, 1999. 1-85791-308-6

→ Conlon-McKenna, Marita/Nic Mhaoláin, Máire (trans.). *Faoin Sceach Gheal*. Dublin: O'Brien Press, 2000. 0-86278-653-3

→ Conlon-McKenna, Marita. *Under the Hawthorn Tree*. Dublin: O'Brien Press, 1990. 0-86278-206-6

→ Cussen, Cliodhna. *An Eala Dhubh*. Dublin: Coiscéim, 1996.

→ Fionn Mac Cumhaill. *Slán Leat, A Mhaicín*. Dublin: An Gúm, 1998. 1-85791-048-6

→ Hastings, Caitríona. *Dea-Scéala*. Connemara: Cló Iar-Connachta, 1998. 19-00-693389-5

→ Mac Aodha Bhuí, Iarla. *An Lambourghini Buí*. Dublin: An Gúm, 1998. 1-85791-261-6

→ Mac Giolla Léith, Caoimhín. *Bás Chlann Uisnigh*. Dublin: Coiscéim, 1996.

→ Mullen, Michael. *An Bóthar Fada*. Dublin: Coiscéim, 2000.

→ Ní Mhuireagáin, Irene. *Aoife agus an Chuil Ghorm*. Dublin: An Gúm, 1997. 1-85791-222-5

→ Ó Laighléis, Ré. *Gafa*. Dublin: Comhar, 1996.

→ Ó Laoghaire, Peadar. *Séanna*. Dublin: Cois Life Teoranta, 1996. 9-01171-600-2

→ Ó Murchú, Maitiú/Ní Bhraonáin, Deirdre (illus.). *Colm na Cille*. Dublin: An Gúm, 1998. 1-85791-256-X

→ Ó Raghallaigh, Colmán/Carroll, Anne Marie (illus.). *Drochlá Ruairí*. Mayo: Cló Mhaigh Eo, 1996. 1-89992-201-6 [available as interactive CD-ROM]

→ Ó Raghallaigh, Colmán/Carroll, Anne Marie (illus.). *Ruairí sa Zú*. Mayo: Cló Mhaigh Eo, 1997. 89922024.

→ Ó Sé, Maidhc Dainín. *Madraí na nOcht gCos*. Dublin: Coiscéim,1998.

→ Ó Sé, Maidhc Dainín. *Mair, a Chapaill*. Dublin: Coiscéim, 1999.

→ Ó Sé, Maidhc Dainín. *Is Glas iad na Cnoic*. Dublin: Coiscéim, 1997.

→ Rosenstock, Gabriel/Sluis, Piet (illus.). *An Phéist Mhór*. Dublin: An Gúm, 1996. 1-85791-152-0

→ Rosenstock, Gabriel/Sluis, Piet (illus.). *An Rógaire agus a Scáil*. Dublin: An Gúm, 1998. 1-85791-276-4

→ Rosenstock, Gabriel/Sluis, Piet (illus.). *Páidín Mháire Mhuigín*. Dublin: An Gúm, 1999. 1-85791-305-1

→ Schafer, Carole Lexa/Cabban, Vanessa (illus.). *Am Codlata i Lár na Coille*. Dublin: An Gúm, 2000. 1-85791-360-4

→ Wynn, Gwyneth. *Mící ar an bPortach*. Dublin: An Gúm, 1998. 1-85791-226-8

THE TROUBLED FICTION OF THE 'TROUBLES' IN NORTHERN IRELAND

PART I: A GENERAL VIEW

An Ulster Wean's A to Z, published in 1996, deserves mention in any article on the writing on offer to children emerging from the Northern Troubles. It was published by Blackstaff Press with the cultural traditions group, whose aim was to encourage an understanding of cultural diversity. It is described as a 'fun-packed new alphabet book'.

As the title suggests, it attempts to give expression to the language and culture of Ulster. This in itself was a laudable aim as the children of Northern Ireland won't find their culture reflected in many of the other books on offer to them. Where the book fails is the naively amusing way in which it tries to take the harm out of cultural and political difference by merrily juxtaposing icons of opposing traditions. 'P is for Pope' and 'Q is for Queen', for example. In a crowded text, with illustrations reminiscent of Richard Scarry's, rival pieces of graffiti nudge each other. The Red Hand of Ulster with '1690' underneath (associated with the Loyalist UVF) sits beside a harp on a green background and the barely discernible words 'Tiochfaid ár Lá' (a slogan associated with the Provisional IRA). The book was, of course, written during the first IRA cease-fire and its optimism is understandable, but it is in such efforts to be balanced that it stretches credulity. However, in its good-humoured way it is respectful of both traditions. It was one of very few books for children published in Northern Ireland. In my view, those two facts are related.

An Ulster Wean's A to Z, illustrated by Philip McIvor.

When a picture book to represent Northern Ireland was being chosen for the European Picture Book Project (Cotton, p.45), the book selected was Michael Foreman's *War and Peas* – a book by an English artist published in England in 1974. The reasons for this choice are very clear, but the fact that no representative book created and published in Northern Ireland could be found is very revealing.

There is no substantial publishing of children's books in Northern Ireland, in spite of the fact that there is a number of highly respected publishing houses there devoted to publishing books of quality for adults. This is doubly surprising in view of the success of children's publishing in the Republic of Ireland, where books for children are published in Cork, Galway and Mayo, as well as in Dublin.

This void in children's publishing in Northern Ireland has important reper-
cussions for Northern Irish writers of books for children. They must of necessity
look to London or Dublin for publication, and this has merely reinforced the cultural divisions in a deeply sensitive area. Broadly speaking, writers from the unionist
community publish in London and those from the nationalist community publish in
Dublin. This means that writers must be aware of the reception of their work outside their own communities rather than being conscious primarily of the children of
Northern Ireland.

A further constraint on writers seems to be an inordinate sense of moral responsibility in view of the serious nature of the northern conflict. They have expressed this sense in a variety of different ways. Mary Beckett, who has written so
superbly about the Troubles in her seriously neglected adult novel *Give Them Stones*,
has not written directly on the topic for children. She says: 'My adult stories had
frequently been described as "uncomfortable" and I have always thought that children's books should give them comfort and security ... in writing about Belfast it is
even more necessary to create a safe protected life for them'(Beckett, p.20).

Joan Lingard, writing in the same issue (Lingard, p.21), tells an anecdote
about a visit to her home by a friend who was an Orangeman and who regaled her
children with a bedtime entertainment in which the good man on a white horse is
King Billy, the bad man is the Pope. Lingard explains that she was inspired by this
incident to try to combat bigotry in her books for children. She says that her *Kevin
and Sadie* books are an appeal for tolerance, and that *The Twelfth Day of July* was constructed with balance in mind. This concern is reflected in the way that chapters
are alternatively devoted to Catholics and Protestants. The problem is that a great
deal is lost if the partisan storyteller, whose tale of good and bad men is reminiscent
of fairy and folk tales, must be silenced.

In his discussion of his novel *Rainbows of the Moon*, in an article

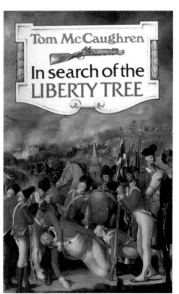

(McCaughren, p.8), Tom McCaughren discusses the constraints he felt when writing about modern Northern Ireland.
Violence and the use of strong language posed difficulties for
him, causing him to compromise by modifying the language
used by soldiers in stressful situations. Of violence he says: 'I
had also to be careful not to make violence in any way appealing to the young for that would have defeated the overall
theme of the story.' McCaughren elaborated on the moral intention of *Rainbows of the Moon* (McCaughren, p.12) '... having
been born in the North and lived much of my life in the
Republic ... I felt I could write a book that would help promote understanding, not only between the two communities
in the North but also between north and south and maybe
between the two islands.' *Rainbows of the Moon*, in which contemporary republican terrorists and the British Army are set

In Search of the Liberty Tree,
detail from 'The Battle of Ballynahinch' by Thomas Robinson.

against each other, is ultimately less successful than his historical novel *In Search of the Liberty Tree*, in which two boys, one from each side of the political divide in Ireland, become embroiled in dangerous and violent situations against the background of the 1798 Rebellion in Ulster. Here, McCaughren convincingly depicts the violence and confusion of the time.

Sam McBratney, another writer from Northern Ireland (McBratney, p.18), says, in explanation of his treatment of the Troubles, which is for the most part indirect or background (as is the case in his novel *You Just Don't Listen*, formerly *Put a Saddle on the Pig*): 'Writers should be careful of tackling the raw aspects of life here without being able to call on the complete range of adult concepts which help us make sense of what is happening. Themes involving violence, bigotry, sex, religion and death are bound to be tricky territory for writers of children's books'. Interestingly, in the same article McBratney says of his book *The Chieftain's Daughter:* 'This was written for the joy of writing'. *The Chieftain's Daughter* has all the themes listed by McBratney as difficult to handle – violence, bigotry, sex, religion and death. They are handled skilfully and forcefully. Is it the fact that the novel is set in the time when Christianity was in its infancy in Ireland and not in contemporary Northern Ireland that makes this possible? It is tempting to think so.

Maeve Friel in her time-slip novel *Distant Voices* locates much of the action in Derry, at the time of the Viking invasions of Christian Ireland. She makes subtle parallels with contemporary Northern Ireland by creating a heroine who is from the Protestant community in Derry and whose journeys across the border into Donegal are seen as incursions into alien territory. Like McBratney's, this is a very intense allegorical book. Its violence is graphic. It embodies adolescent desire. It says more about the Northern Troubles than many novels with a contemporary setting.

You Just Don't Listen, illustration by Daniel Faoro.

Even Martin Waddell, who, as Catherine Sefton, has written several highly successful books for young people explicitly about the Troubles, referred to the difficulties in doing so when he addressed the Children's Books Ireland Spring Seminar 2000. When asked how he felt about the fact that he is now best known as a writer of picture books, he replied that it had become impossible to write about the northern Troubles without falling into the Romeo-and-Juliet-type Catholic–Protestant narrative trap, and for this reason he had set his contemporary love story, *Tango's Baby*, not in Northern Ireland but in a kind of unidentifiable no-man's land.

Robert Dunbar, in his still very relevant paper 'Children's Fiction and The Ulster Troubles' (Dunbar, p.83), points to the fact that writers write better about the Troubles when they resort to metaphorical obliqueness rather than literal directness. He also points out that the insistence on impartiality at all costs can come very close to saying nothing at all.

One thing has changed in relation to the literature of Northern Ireland since Dunbar wrote his article, and that is the quality of writing for adults about its troubled world. There are now works which, if not quite 'Great' in the terms that Dunbar suggests, are certainly very fine, interesting and challenging. They manage to be at once realistic and metaphorical. Among them, novels such as *Give them Stones*, *Reading in the Dark*, *Hidden Symptoms*, *Burning Your Own* and the play 'In A little World of Our Own' are works which in their different ways speak out of their respective communities, and do so without apology, without the sense that they are mediating Catholic or Protestant, nationalist or loyalist experience for some wiser more rational 'Other' in London or Dublin. That they have managed to do this without causing hurt outside their respective communities is a tribute to their writers' skill.

There is, in my view, a lesson here for children's writers and indeed publishers. There is a need for less social and political morality and more artistic integrity. If they could take the risk of being attacked for being partisan because of writing out of and for their own communities, they might reap the rewards of truly reflecting the lives and experiences of the children of Northern Ireland. They might also aspire to universal significance in their work. At present, the lives and worlds of loyalist or republican children are simply not reflected in literature for children. In the most hurtful Anglo-centric stories, members of the Orange Order are stereotyped as boorish, harmless bigots. Catholics drink a lot and have inordinately large families. Protestants have no fun. Members of paramilitary organisations, usually the IRA, are stereotyped as psychopathic killers without affection or conscience. The British Army is depicted as a benevolent, neutral force caught in the crossfire of irrationally warring tribes. Some of these stereotypes can be found in the work of Peter Carter (*Under Goliath*), Joan Lingard (*The Twelfth Day of July*,) Gillian Cross (*Wolf*) and John Quinn (*One Fine Day*).

As argued by Bill Rolston (p.41), there is a tendency for many of those who write about the Troubles to find a resolution by having their characters escape from Northern Ireland, usually to Britain. It is most likely to be found in the work of writers from England and the Irish Republic (Lingard, Carter, Quinn). It does not reflect the reality for most people who continue to live and work there. It reflects a peculiar kind of despair not shared by most Northern people. It also fails to do justice to the fact that in spite of all their pain, it is the so-called ordinary people of Northern Ireland who have prevented the situation from descending to that of the former Yugoslavia. Is it right to imply that a child's homeland is unfit for human habitation?

One novel which reversed this pattern was *Frozen Out* by Carlo Gébler, in which a young English girl from London comes to live in Northern Ireland and manages to survive the trials of adolescence in much the same way as other young people. Bigotry is not avoided. The Orange band encountered on the ferry at the beginning is at once frightening and ordinary. At the same time other aspects of life are less sinister than in the London where the family formerly lived. This is most graphically illustrated when the heroine's little brother gets lost. His parents' worst fears are not realised and neighbours go out of their way to find him and bring him safely home.

Though it is my belief that writers and publishers need to be more courageous, I am not arguing for bad-mannered writing, an example of which can be found in *Horrible Histories: Ireland*, where words like Catholic and Protestant are used as terms of derision. Describing the execution of an IRA member in the 1940s, we are told: 'Catholics and Protestants squabbled out-side the ... jail. Catholics fell to their knees and prayed and Protestants sang 'God Save the King'...' It would be virtually unthinkable to offer this to, for ex-ample, the children who contributed to *I Am*, or indeed to any children.

I Am is a book in which children express their own feelings after the deaths of their friends and schoolmates in the Omagh bombing in 1998. Colours normally invested with political meanings – red, white, blue, green and orange – are reborn in the words of the children: 'Red looks like a ladybird ... blue looks like a summer's day ... orange ... smells like honey ... green tastes like seven-up.' At the same time their grief and anger is expressed:

> My worst day was when I woke up on Sunday morning to find that Shaun had died in the Omagh bomb. I thought it was cold and dark but bright. The place I was told he had died is gone now, like Shaun-at peace.

An Ulster Wean's A to Z, illustrated by Philip McIvor.

REFERENCES

→ Beckett, Mary. *Children's Books in Ireland*, p.20. May 1993.
→ Dunbar, Robert. 'Children's Fiction and The Ulster Troubles'. In *Proceedings of the 12th Annual Conference of the Reading Association of Ireland*, p.83. Dublin: RAI, 1987.
→ Cotton, Penni. *Picture Books sans Frontières*, p.45. London: Trentham Books, 2000.
→ Lingard, Joan. *Children's Books in Ireland*, p.21. May 1993.
→ McBratney, Sam. *Children's Books in Ireland*, p.18. May 1993.
→ McCaughren, Tom. *Children's Books in Ireland*, p.8. December 1989.
→ McCaughren, Tom. *Children's Books in Ireland*, p.12. No.20. Winter 1998.
→ Rolston, Bill. 'Escaping from Belfast: class, ideology and literature in Northern Ireland'. In *Race and Class XXI*, p.41. 1978.
Books Discussed in Article
→ Beckett, Mary. *Give them Stones*. London: Bloomsbury, 1987. 0-74750-216-1
→ Carter, Peter. *Under Goliath*. London: Puffin Books, 1980. 0-14031-132-7
→ Cross, Gillian. *Wolf*. Oxford: Oxford University Press, 1990. 0-19271-633-6
→ Deane, Seamus. *Reading in the Dark*. London: Jonathan Cape, 1996. 0-37570-023-4
→ Derry, Terry. *Horrible Histories: Ireland*. London: Scholastic, 2000. 0-43901-436-0
→ Foreman, Michael. *War and Peas*. London: Hamish Hamilton, 1974. Puffin, 1978. 0-14-050243-2
→ Friel, Maeve. *Distant Voices*. Dublin: Poolbeg Press, 1994. 1-85371-410-0
→ Gébler, Carlo. *Frozen Out*. London: Mammoth, 1998. 0-7497-2874-4
→ Lingard, Joan. *The Twelfth Day of July*. London: Puffin Books, 1995, 0-1403-7175-3
→ Madden, Deirdre. *Hidden Symptoms*. London: Faber and Faber, 1987. 0-57115-074-8

→ McBratney, Sam. *The Chieftain's Daughter*. Dublin: O'Brien Press, 1993. 0-86278-338-0
   McBratney, Sam. *You Just Don't Listen*. 1994. 07-497-1699-1
→ McCaughren, Tom. *Rainbows of the Moon*. Dublin: Anvil Press, 1989. 09-479-6251-4
→ McCaughren, Tom. *In Search of the Liberty Tree*. Dublin: Anvil Press, 1994. 09-479-6289-1
→ McIvor, Philip. *An Ulster Wean's A to Z*. Belfast: Blackstaff Press, 1996. 0-85640-581-7
→ Mitchell, Gary. *In a Little World of our Own*. 1997.
→ Patterson, Glenn. *Burning Your Own*. 1993. 0-70113-291-4
→ Quinn, John. *One Fine Day*. Dublin: Poolbeg Press, 1996. 1-85371-612-X
→ Scoil Íosagáin and St Mura's National Schools. *I Am*.
   Buncrana: Scoil Íosagáin, 1999. 09-53-61440-9

PART II: FOCUS ON JOAN LINGARD AND CATHERINE SEFTON

A prolific and popular author, Joan Lingard is probably best known for her *Kevin and Sadie* series, which portrays the relationship between a Catholic boy, Kevin McCoy, and a Protestant girl, Sadie Jackson, who meet in the back streets of Belfast in the midst of the Troubles. The first novel, *The Twelfth Day of July* (1970), is broadly optimistic, portraying a movement from determined enmity towards sympathetic friendship, and from preconceived stereotypes towards understanding and compassion. The themes encompassed by the book and the questions it considers are wide-ranging, complex and universal, giving – like Shakespeare's 'Romeo and Juliet', whose theme is echoed in the second novel – a sense of a much greater timescale than the six days of the text itself. Here there exists the possibility of happiness, perhaps even peace for the children and, through them, we sense, for the province as a whole. Tragedy comes close when Kevin's younger sister, Brede, is hurt in the warfare between Catholic and Protestant children, but the accident leads to friendship rather than an escalation of violence, and the novel hints that children can escape the violence that permeates their community. *Across the Barricades* (1972) is, however, a much bleaker novel. Although it shows that the possibility of interdenominational friendship exists between individuals, it also makes manifest the impossibility of sustaining such a relationship in working-class Belfast.

The Twelfth Day of July opens with a description of the two families, the McCoys and the Jacksons, living in similar houses only a few streets apart from one another. The alternating chapters provide an account of life on either side of the sectarian divide. Although the depictions, here as elsewhere in the series, draw upon stereotypes – the overcrowded and chaotic Catholic household, the nagging Protestant mother concerned with the keeping up of appearances – these stereotypes evolve to give a convincing portrayal of two sets of similar characters living in comparable circumstances and sharing the same concerns and preoccupations. Each side is openly hostile toward the other, and Kevin and Sadie themselves accept, without question, the dogma absorbed since childhood. In the opening lines of the book, Sadie's father encourages his children in a ritual chant that is steeped in prejudice, and they are drawn into his game unthinkingly, enjoying the repetition of the old formula and returning happily to childish behaviour. Meanwhile, in the contrasting scene set in the Catholic streets at the same time on the same day, Kevin and his friends are so angered by the militant drum-beating of the Protestants preparing for their annual twelfth of July march that they plan direct action, in this case the defacing of a mural commemorating William of Orange.

When Sadie retaliates, daubing orange paint on Catholic walls, she and Kevin become sworn enemies. We sense, however, that, initially at least, the children are excited by the rivalry. Even the peaceable Brede enjoys the thrill of occasional risk-taking and Kevin and Sadie take pleasure in challenging one another, each attracted by the other's love of danger. There is almost an atmosphere of holiday-time adventure running through the early part of the novel, despite the serious nature of the rivalry between the two groups. In the end though, the danger inherent in their behaviour is brought home to the children when Brede is seriously hurt in their sectarian feuding. Nevertheless, the overall mood remains one of optimism, for both individuals and State, and the novel ends with Protestant and Catholic children spending the twelfth of July in friendship together.

The Twelfth Day of July, cover photographs by Andy Kingsbury.

Across the Barricades is, by contrast, much less optimistic in outlook. First published in 1972, it was written partly in response to the escalating violence in Northern Ireland at that time. It presents a picture of Belfast as a place in which it is impossible for working-class children on either side to escape involvement with paramilitary organisations. Here the division between the communities has terrible and far-reaching consequences, and the book depicts escalating and inescapable violence: Kevin is mugged and badly wounded, the local shopkeeper is killed when her shop is bombed, then the kindly ex-teacher who has befriended Kevin and Sadie dies when a petrol bomb is thrown into his house – a direct result of his sanctioning of their relationship.

In both communities violence is unavoidable; to ignore the conflict is to be seen as at best cowardly, and at worst traitorous. Kevin is first threatened and then beaten by his former friend when he refuses to join the Provisional IRA. Even Tommy's father is disappointed by his son's refusal to join the Orange Lodge. Kevin and Sadie try to escape the city streets for their meetings. We see them walking on Cave Hill, going to Bangor for the day, or meeting by the river. Meanwhile, Belfast itself is littered with reminders of battle: burnt-out cars and buses and armoured vehicles, torn-up paving stones, barbed wire coiled to form barricades. And along the streets went soldiers on patrol with fingers on the triggers of their guns ...

Kevin and Sadie are attracted to one another partly through their shared sense of adventure and out of a desire to challenge, even to thwart, authority. Their relationship is strengthened through adversity and, perversely, the very people who seek to drive them apart bring them closer together. The novel's ending is a pessimistic one, both personally and politically. After the death of Mr Blake, it seems that there is no future in Northern Ireland for Kevin and Sadie. Unemployed and unable to meet safely in their own country, the novel ends as they set off together for England, hand in hand, in a scene that ironically recalls Milton's Adam and Eve leaving the Garden of Eden.

The three later novels in the quintet, *Into Exile* (1973), *A Proper Place* (1975), and *Hostages to Fortune* (1977) are set mainly in England, and are concerned primarily with domestic rather than political life, although occasional episodes still act as reminders of the horror and violence that Kevin and Sadie have left behind them, most notably when Kevin's father is killed by a bomb and Kevin has to return to Northern Ireland.

In his trilogy of thematically related novels for older readers, Martin Waddell, writing as Catherine Sefton, also explores the impact of the Troubles on life for teenagers growing up in Northern Ireland. The first novel, *Starry Night* (1986), which was winner of the Other Award, portrays an adolescent Catholic girl living with her family in a rural area close to the border with the Republic. Family history and political background are woven together as Kathleen discovers secrets about her past, but in the main the Troubles remain in the background of the novel.

Frankie's Story, illustration by Caroline Binch.

The second and third books of Waddell's trilogy are, however, directly concerned with the effects of the conflict on ordinary families. Set in urban areas where passions run high and involvement in the conflict seems unavoidable, both novels feature protagonists set apart from their communities, their first-person narratives voicing their alienation from the political dogma and religious fervour that grips those around them. These novels, like those of the *Kevin and Sadie* series, show the near impossibility of escaping involvement in the Troubles, the immorality of both sides and the harm that each inflicts upon itself as well as on its 'enemies'.

Frankie's Story (1988) concerns a young girl distanced from her Catholic community, partly through her own rebellious nature and partly as a result of her father's decision to leave his family and live with another woman. His actions both provoke Frankie's desire to rebel and encourage the outside world to see her as a non-conformer, a potential threat to their close-knit community. Frankie has a Protestant boyfriend and her cynical first-person narrative draws comparisons with 'Romeo and Juliet'. However, this is not a love story but a story about growing up, which depicts the young heroine's increasing personal and political understanding. A self-aware young woman, she examines the interplay between her personal situation and the political background, her parents' broken marriage mirroring the fractured society in which she lives. Here, as in *Across the Barricades*, the cycle of violence seems unbreakable. Frankie is wrongly suspected of involvement with the police and is severely wounded in a petrol bomb attack. She ends the novel, like Kevin and Sadie, living in England, away from the Troubles, physically and mentally scarred by the attack, which leaves her unable to find peace in her own country.

Brian Hanna, protagonist of *The Beat of the Drum* (1989), has grown up determined to remain aloof from the religious and political arguments that fracture his community, although he himself is wheelchair bound, the victim of a paramilitary bomb that killed his parents. Like the Catholic Frankie, Protestant Brian remains aloof from the sectarian divisions that mark family and friends. His attitude is contrasted with that of his contemporary, Val, a conscientious and caring young woman who pushes Brian around in his wheelchair and believes in 'good work', but whose religious and political views are both bigoted and cruel. Val cannot see the illogicality inherent in her preacher father's attitudes, and she herself 'doesn't see anything odd in spouting Jesus Loves Me stuff one minute and Final Solution Politics the next'. Her father lacks compassion and is devoid of integrity, his presence drawing attention to the involvement of the Church in the paramilitary organisations. The novel is brutally graphic in its portrayal of the Troubles, depicting, like *Frankie's Story*, both the physical threat and the mental cruelty inflicted by the community upon outsiders. In the most horrific episode of the trilogy, a young and ill-educated informer – a childhood friend of Brian's – is cruelly murdered by his own side. The grotesque nature of his death is powerfully conveyed in Brian's gradual realisation of what has happened to his former friend. Unlike Frankie, Brian resists the desire to leave Ulster: 'I'm staying because I think I ought to stay. If I go, and all the others who think like me go, what'll happen to the people who are left?' His decision suggests a degree of optimism about the future of the province, the possibility that change can be effected if enough people learn, like him, not to hate.

Thirty years after *The Twelfth Day of July* was first published, the political situation in Northern Ireland remains tense and the need for readers to learn the value of compassion and tolerance is as great as it ever was. These two sets of novels, both written with the conscious intent of informing and educating their readers, continue to be popular with children and adults alike. In the autumn of 2000, Walker Books will republish Martin Waddell's trilogy, a sad tribute perhaps both to the power of the novels themselves and to the continuing need to convey to young people that violence and misery go hand in hand with prejudice and bigotry.

REFERENCES

→ Lingard, Joan. *Across the Barricades*. Britain: Puffin, 1995. 0-1403-7179-6
→ Lingard, Joan. *Hostages to Fortune*. Britain: Puffin, 1995. 0-1403-7400-0
→ Lingard, Joan. *Into Exile*. Britain: Puffin, 1995. 0-1403-7213-X
→ Lingard, Joan. *A Proper Place*. Britain: Puffin, 1995. 0-1403-7192-3
→ Lingard, Joan. *The Twelfth Day of July*. Britain: Puffin, 1995. 0-1403-7175-3
→ Sefton, Catherine. *Beat of the Drum*. London: Mammoth. 0-7497-0402-0
→ Sefton, Catherine. *Frankie's Story*. London: Mammoth. 0-7497-0588-2
→ Sefton, Catherine. *Starry Night*. London: Walker Books, 2000. 0-7445-7274-6

DIFFERENCE AND CONFORMITY: WHAT DO WE TELL THE CHILDREN?

In a society that still reserves the right to restrict what adults are allowed to read, the question of the nature of the material we produce for our children is an interesting one. As John Rowe Townsend points out, between the child and the story stand three adults: the writer, the editor and the person who makes the book available to the child. Therefore, what children read has been produced and sanctioned by adult society. What children's books contain says much about how we view the young. In the didactic tool that children's books almost inevitably are, what are we eager to reveal to our children and, conversely, what do we wish to suppress?

In the context of Irish children's literature the answer to that question is not a simple one. It is complicated by differences in the nationality of the authors who contribute to the body of Irish writing for children. The first Irish teenage novel is commonly thought to be Margrit Cruickshank's *Circling the Triangle*, written by a Scot. Marilyn Taylor, who has written a popular trilogy of 'Irish' books for teenagers, is English. Ireland's most prolific children's author is Ulsterman Martin Waddell, whether writing under his own name or as Catherine Sefton. In an interview with *Books Ireland* in April 1999, Waddell spoke of what he feels is his lack of recognition in the Irish Republic: 'I'm not into nationality at all as a political concept, but I feel Irish, my Irishness is something that's in me and it's disconcerting to be treated in my own country as somebody who in some way is not of it.'

Yet it is no accident, nor can it be explained by ascribing it to mere personality, that Waddell has a different social perspective from his colleagues born and raised in the Irish Republic. Of all Irish authors only Waddell, with his tradition of addressing social issues in fiction, could have written the intensely political *Tango's Baby*. The author's commitment to the portrayal of urban social deprivation can be gleaned from the book's dedication: 'This one's for me.'

Tango's almost inevitable decline from a disadvantaged childhood, through an unimaginative and hard-pressed education system, teenage fatherhood and eventually prison, mirrors the neglected and disintegrating society the book portrays. While the pages are peopled with those whom society may dismiss as social deviants – petty criminals, drug pushers, a prostitute, an adulterer and an abusive brother – there is no stereotyping. It

► *All the Way from China,* illustrated by Stewart Curry.

is the characters' humanity and individuality that allows them on a human, if not on a social level to rise above their circumstances. Although it is intrinsically an immensely sad story, it is told with a humour and lightness of touch that places its author, despite his nationality, in the British rather than the Irish tradition of children's writers; its British rather than Irish setting lends weight to this view.

Although different in concept, both John Quinn's *Duck and Swan*, published in 1993, and Frank Murphy's *Lockie and Dadge*, released two years later, have their own individual political radicalism. The two novels have a similar structure in which a young male protagonist, failed by society, is cared for illicitly by a childless elderly couple living on the margins of society. Both authors denounce the power of authority over the lives of the impotent. Murphy's Pasha firmly points the finger of blame at '*them*', the italicisation of the word not merely suggesting the vehemence of the attack, but also the strength of 'their' ubiquitous power, and, by inference, their opposition to 'us', the inconsequential poor. At the end of novel it is a judge and a social worker who legalise the family condemned as unsuitable and inappropriate by the Church and the proponents of respectability, a fact which suggests radical social reappraisal.

Duck and Swan features the first black Irish character in Irish children's literature, but, like Murphy, Quinn places his anger at social wrongs in the mouth of an elderly character, Granny, as she weeps for her stolen youth, quashed by a society that demanded retribution for youthful indiscretions: 'we had sinned, so we had to be punished'. Her extramarital pregnancy merited incarceration, for so Quinn describes it, in 'the Magdalen', where they took away the child she still mourns. There is here an implication that the negation of individuality and freedom of the young, which underpinned Granny's inhuman treatment, still finds an echo in the experiences of Martin Oduki, the 'Duck' of the title.

If Waddell's view of society is articulated by Catherine Sefton's narrator in *The Cast Off* when she describes it as 'the world that looks after people who can stand up for themselves and manage their own problems and ignore the rest', it is profoundly different from the one described by either Quinn or Murphy, where those at the margins of society, instead of merely being ignored, are persecuted.

The traditional people of 'difference' in Irish society are the travellers. That society within a society has featured in stories for children certainly since 1934 and the publication of Patricia Lynch's *The Turf-Cutter's Donkey*. The mixture of fear and romantic attachment with which the young protagonist, Eileen, views the travelling community finds resonances in their portrayal by Mike Scott in the *Spider and Judith* trilogy, and in Tony Hickey's *Joe* novels. Alongside the violence perpetrated by travellers, in good causes and in bad, Scott's depiction of the central relationship of a rich girl and a handsome, chivalrous traveller exudes romance and the almost mythic element of the traditional ballad, 'The Gypsy Rover', with its notion of winning 'the heart of a lady'. Similar stereotyping is seen in Marita Conlon-McKenna's *The Blue Horse* when Paddy's inability to settle at school is attributed to his nature as a nomad: 'being free and being a traveller [is] in your blood'. It is an easy explanation.

Alongside the clichés, however, the physical hardship of the travellers' life-style and their worries about the education of their children are portrayed. Scott, Hickey and Conlon-McKenna all depict travellers' attempts to settle. Despite these attempts at assimilation, and Maggie MacCarthy's assertion in *Joe in the Middle* that 'we're Irish people', the fiction in which they appear revolves around their status as largely despised outsiders.

There is a sense in which the position of travellers in Irish children's litera-ture, as at once of society yet a race apart, has been usurped by the adolescent who, while no longer a child, is suspended in a social limbo before he/she can rejoin soci-ety as an adult. This period of transition is often characterised in books for the young by dissatisfaction with the world and uncertainty of their place in it. Increas-ingly, adolescent discontent spills over into social alienation, often precipitated by abuse. While the protagonist in Cruickshank's *Circling the Triangle*, published in 1991, fights against the restrictions he feels are being imposed upon him, he does so from the comfort of his home and under the loving, if exasperated, protection of his parents. Dahy in Tony Keily's *The Shark Joke* (1994) is temporarily sleeping on his sister's sofa, and his estrangement from the community is reflected in the profanity of his language and the recurring images of blood and punishment. Sefton's fifteen-year-old protagonist, Marie, in *The Cast Off* (1993) and Siobhán Parkinson's squat-ters in *Breaking the Wishbone* (1999) have opted out of adult care and supervision, pre-ferring the precarious existence of the homeless. While Parkinson's Johnner, described as being hardly out of national school, is promised a future as the quasi-child of two of his fellow squatters, Marie's adulthood, we are to assume, is to be spent on the streets.

While Parkinson's young homeless are all in some respect victims, Waddell sees his protagonist as being responsible, at least in part, for her own fate, and cul-pable in respect of her parents' misery. In the area of bullying, in addition to being victims the young are portrayed as perpetrators of malicious acts, but, as in Maeve Friel's *Charlie's Story*, the miscreants' behaviour is usually chal-lenged and repentance ensues. It is to the uncom-promising vision of Ré Ó Laighléis and his short story 'Ecstasy' that we turn for the depiction of real evil in the sphere of bullying, and, significantly, this story ends not with the submission of the per-petrators to the rule of law, but with the threat of disclosure. In 'Heredity', in the same collection, we are confronted with the moment when a young vic-tim, exposed to the beating of his mother since childhood, turns perpetrator. The young as drug takers and as drug pushers feature both in Ó Laighléis's often graphic novel *Hooked* and in Scott's *Good Enough for Judith*.

Hooked, cover by Alanna Corballis.

While the habits, status and lifestyle which are outside the norm are not unusual in Irish children's books, the portrayal of inherent difference is. In a period when there is unprecedented concern in the country about the influx of refugees, there are few black characters in literature for the young, although one of the very few books for the under-nines that portrays difference, Pat Boran's *All the Way from China,* features a Chinese boy. Two novels feature young people in wheelchairs, and in the case of Catherine Sefton's *The Beat of the Drum,* disability is used as an authorial device to enable the narrator, Brian, to gain a unique perspective on the Ulster Protestant neighbourhood in which he lives. As he says, 'I'm a kind of King's Fool in my chair, given licence by being so obviously different.'

Two novels have sexual orientation as their main theme: Tom Lennon's *When Love Comes to Town,* first published by O'Brien Press for adults but since transferred to their 'young adult' list, and an import, also from O'Brien, Tatiana Strelkoff's *Allison – A Story of First Love,* dealing with a lesbian relationship. The two books share a similar approach, both dealing with parental outrage and non-acceptance. While on a literary level Lennon's novel is far stronger than its lesbian counterpart, both books abound with stereotypical images. Great play, for example, is made of the attractiveness of one of the young gay women and the plainness of the other. *When Love Comes to Town* includes campness, transvestism and a youth dying of Aids. Acceptance comes for the two protagonists only when Neil attempts suicide and Karen is the victim of an attempted gang rape.

This stereotypical treatment is consistent with that of the working-class in Irish children's fiction, where even in books written with warmth, humour and a degree of authenticity, like Peter Gunning's *Reaching the Heights,* the poor are still dogged by money-lenders or, as the symbol of dysfunction changes, abusive male characters. It is this view of the poor, after all, which forms the basis of *Lockie and Dadge.* One notable exception is the undervalued *View from a Blind Bridge* by June Considine.

Difference, generally, in Ireland's books for the young, and especially those written by writers native to the Republic of Ireland, is almost always seen as negative. The corollary to this must be the attachment to, if not reverence for, conformity – or is that just what we tell the children?

Is Anybody Listening?, cover by Slick Fish Design.

REFERENCES

→ Kelly, Shirley. 'Can't You Write, Father Bear!' In *Books Ireland.* No. 221. April 1999.
→ Townsend, John Rowe. 'Standards of Criticism for Children's Literature'. In *Children's Literature – The Development of Criticism,* edited by Peter Hunt. London: Routledge, 1990.

RECOMMENDED TITLES

Eoin Colfer
BENNY AND OMAR
O'Brien Press

This is that rarest of commodities in the realm of Irish children's literature: an intelligent and wonderfully written comic novel. The humour is engendered by the manipulation of language, and it is language that suggests both the gulf and the affinity between Benny, the Wexford boy newly arrived in Tunisia, and Omar, his African counterpart. Communication is through the familiar phrases emanating from the television set illegally beamed into the African boy's makeshift shelter. The growing intimacy underlying this hilarious mode of dialogue allows the boys not merely to indulge their mutual attraction to dangerous escapades undertaken despite the sanctions of the adult world, but also eventually to share Omar's poignant secret, the revelation which begins with 'a little brown hand' that is 'rubbing streaks in the glass'. Through those streaks, between the bouts of the reader's laughter, can be glimpsed a world of utter destitution, of institutional neglect – what Benny describes as 'real life'. This insight into the world beyond the carefreeness of childhood is reflected in the writing, where hilarity gives way to gentle humour and the reminder that reality is not totally bleak, containing as it does idealism, determination and a love so strong that it can overcome lack of affection and a profound trauma.

Josephine Feeney
MY FAMILY AND OTHER NATURAL DISASTERS
Puffin Books

Asked to write an autobiography in English class, twelve-year-old Patrick cannot persuade either of his newly separated parents to talk about the family's history. Not only does this lead to trouble at school, but Patrick is unable to understand the disintegration of his parents' relationship because 'grown-ups are clinging to all the information'. (It is no accident that the letters which punctuate the narrative are all written by adults.) Even on holiday in Ireland he finds that old certainties, exemplified by the Church, are undermined by harsh realities, such as the person lying drunk on the pavement. With references to the homeless and the marginalised, the protagonist's familial hurt and upheaval are seen as symbolic of a wider social malaise, one which causes Patrick's gran to cry as old values disintegrate. Tears, we are told with a wit characteristic of the narrator, 'fell off her face and onto her "Céad Míle Fáilte" apron'. It is only when his family's past is revealed that the boy can begin to answer the question: 'how would I fit into my life story?' Patrick must return to school and, like his gran, find a way to adapt to the pain of reality.

Elaine Forrestal
SOMEONE LIKE ME
Puffin Books

'All our good times are all gone ...'; 'The summer's gone and all the leaves are falling ...' The messages of the tunes Tas plays on his mouth organ reflect the musician's fear of growing up, a fear that infuses his dreams with images of Peter Pan and the 'dream cliff' above the menacing 'black water'. Part of his reluctance to change is his happy existence in rural Australia, with his secure home, his beloved dog, Reebok, and his school life, which is characterised by frequent fights. Into Tas's raucous existence comes the calm and unruffled Enya, fleeing the Ulster Troubles. Her close relationship with him is almost ended when the violence she thought she had escaped twice threatens the life of her friend. Following his brush with death, Tas, significantly, embraces a more serious kind of music, the love and pursuit of which leads him not only to accept the transience of life, but also to look forward to the future and independence. With an echo of Kemp's *The Turbulent Term of Tyke Tiler*, the boy's difference, hinted at teasingly on several occasions, is revealed in the book's final sentence, as he reacts joyfully to a letter of congratulation from the music college that has awarded him a scholarship.

Someone Like Me,
illustration by Richard Jones.

Carlo Gébler
FROZEN OUT
Mammoth

While set in County Fermanagh, this is not a novel depicting the Troubles, but a skilful and intelligent depiction of the process of growing up. On the verge of her teenage years, Phoebe moves with her family from London to Northern Ireland. The threatening glimpses of the tensions there, which permeate the innocent normality of Phoebe's life, intermingle with the growing uncertainty and pain which characterise the passage from childhood to maturity. Northern Ireland, with its combination of the mundane and the dangerous, is, in a sense, used as a metaphor for adolescence – that period torn between the warmth, protection and com-

Frozen Out, illustration by David Axel.

parative certainty of childhood and the darker, more frightening emotional life of adulthood. Given the constraints of Northern Ireland, it is no accident that it is in the relative freedom of Donegal that the protagonist is able to divest herself of constraining allegiances. With childish impetuosity she ends her relationship with her first boyfriend, and on the beach she is cruelly excluded from the intimacy of her erstwhile companions. It is in the arms of her mother that she is at last reconciled to what she sees as the betrayal of her friends. In a beautifully crafted moment, which perfectly encapsulates the essence of adolescence, Phoebe and her mother share feelings of sadness, loss and hurt, allying the girl to the adult world. Yet Phoebe is relieved and comforted that her mother, as throughout Phoebe's childhood, can still 'read her mind', still know, love and understand her.

Larry O'Loughlin
IS ANYBODY LISTENING?
Wolfhound Press

Laura's mind is invaded by the voice of Sanjid, a six-year-old boy chained to a loom in an Indian carpet workshop, who, through the medium of thought transference, introduces her to Rosa, a survivor of a Brazilian massacre of children. Their plight exercises Laura's compassion and awakens her political awareness. Her concern and her exposure to the suffering of others radically changes her life, forcing her to reassess the superficial friendships of her childhood and to re-evaluate the quiet and thoughtful Declan. Her empathy with Sanjid is so profound that when his workplace is set alight, Laura, an asthmatic, almost dies of smoke inhalation. As in a ghost story, the successful portrayal of the paranormal depends on an authentically depicted reality, and the strength of O'Loughlin's novel lies in the characterisation of Laura, her family and friends, which resonates with warmth, insight and humour. For example, he describes a quartet of girls as 'the Four Horsemen of the potato crisp'. It is this authorial skill that lends credibility to Laura's telepathic experiences.

Mark O'Sullivan
WHITE LIES
Wolfhound Press

Nance is black and middle-class, OD, her boyfriend, is white and working-class. Both find facing the truth of their position in their respective families devastatingly painful. Nance is afraid to ask her adoptive parents about her origins, and OD cannot accept his mother's desertion nor the love of Jimmy, his feckless father. It is, though, not merely 'lies, other people's lies' which obscure the truth, but their youthful idealism which weaves romantic notions around the past. While fantasies protect them from an actuality that might prove injurious, they also blind them to the love that surrounds them. It is only when his dad's life is in danger that OD allows his feelings to surface, reciprocating Jimmy's devotion. Then 'Father' replaces 'Jimmy' as OD reclaims their true relationship. Nance, too, regains a parent and relinquishes a romantic idea. Both maturing narrators begin to accept the grey areas, the imperfections of the world they inhabit and of themselves.

Mark O'Sullivan
SILENT STONES
Wolfhound Press

award-winning
Mark O'Sullivan

The sins of Sean Wade, who died 'for Ireland only' at the age of nineteen, haunt his son, Robbie. They explain why he lives with his misanthropic great-uncle, Eamon, instead of his mother and her new husband. They are the reason Razor McCabe, an escaped terrorist, chooses their farm as a sanctuary. Into this disturbing situation comes Mayfly and her New Age family, attempting to avert the fate of her terminally ill mother, Andy, by exposing her to the healing power of the standing stones of the title. The two worlds are drawn together by their disparate values of violence and healing. (Robbie's poisoned dog, ordered by Eamon to be shot, is healed by Mayfly.) The love that grows between the young people is put at risk by Eamon's lie to the police about Robbie being endangered by the newcomers' drugs. It is an action that results in Andy's death, her partner's imprisonment, and her daughter and Eamon being held hostage while Robbie is sent to lure his stepfather to his death. Before the dangerous mythology of the past can be dispelled, Mayfly has to perpetrate an act of absolute abhorrence that leaves the way open for new beginnings. The world O'Sullivan portrays in his two novels is one where pain is ubiquitous. In neither book is there a person free from torment, nor an individual who is prosaic. Hurt seeps up from the past, rendering it more invasive, more tenacious, and the courage and desperation the characters need to extricate themselves from its slavery threatens lives and relationships.

Siobhán Parkinson
THE MOON KING
O'Brien Press

This superbly written novel depicts the events surrounding the introduction to the Kellys' home of the disturbed and silent Ricky. Parkinson's at times breathtakingly energetic and visual prose is interspersed by Ricky's contrasting, stilted internal monologue. Its disjointed quality, and the dubbing of himself as 'Spiderboy', suggests a lack of confidence and a self-image that equates him with insect life, allowing him the security of scuttling off and hiding when perceived dangers threaten. This need for self-preservation arises from the boy's frequent beatings by Ed, his mother's boyfriend, the resulting trauma of which has rendered the child dumb. In his kingdom in the attic, ensconced upon his throne, he shows his subject, a tailor's dummy, a tolerance unknown to him before he came to his foster home. We are told: 'He raised his hand graciously to show her he was listening, ready to consider her request, but she was too shy to speak. '"Never mind," said Ricky to her. "You don't have to speak if you don't want to. Some other time perhaps."' Ricky's speech slowly returns in the loving household, but it is only when young Helen Kelly replaces jealousy with loving acceptance that Ricky is sure of his own worth and of his place in the world – of his status as the moon king.

Siobhán Parkinson
BREAKING THE WISHBONE
O'Brien Press

Purportedly four young homeless people face the television cameras in turn and tell their story. While their speech patterns are a little too choreographed, the first-person narrative, free from authorial description and comment, does give the impression of personal confession, of intimate accounts of deprivation and suffering recollected with childlike vulnerability. Stories are told of paternal beatings, of the unbearable existence in a children's home, of the inability to cope with the death of parents. But the squat they share is no safe haven. Its piercing cold symbolises the loss of the care and love a child should be heir to. It is the place where drug dealer and pimp, Beano, stabs his pregnant girlfriend on the night of little Johnner's party and from which she has to escape to a place of safety. This is no mere social document, however. While it might be, as Sr Stanislaus Kennedy maintains, an 'absolutely accurate' account of child homelessness, it is also an imaginative, sensitive and well-written testament to how, despite external forces, the human spirit survives and fulfils the need and desire in us all to love and be loved.

◆

Silent Stones,
cover by Slick Fish Design.

The Moon King,
illustration by Finbarr O'Connor.

TITLES REFERRED TO IN ARTICLE AND IN RECOMMENDED LIST

→ Boran, Pat. *All the Way From China.* Dublin: Poolbeg Press, 1998. 1-85371-853-X

→ Conlon-McKenna, Marita. *The Blue Horse.* Dublin: O'Brien Press, 1992. 0-86278-305-4

→ Considine, June. *View From a Blind Bridge.* Dublin: Poolbeg Press, 1992. 1-85371-244-2

→ Cruickshank, Margrit. *Circling the Triangle.* Dublin: Poolbeg Press, 1991. 1-85371-137-3

→ Feeney, Josephine. *My Family and Other Natural Disasters.* London: Puffin Books, 1995. 0-140-36511-7

→ Forrestal, Elaine. *Someone Like Me.* London: Puffin Books, 1996. 0-140-38644-0

→ Friel, Maeve. *Charlie's Story.* Dublin: Poolbeg Press, 1995. 1-85371-183-7

→ Gébler, Carlo. *Frozen Out.* London: Mammoth, 1998. 0-7497-2874-4

→ Gunning, Peter. *Reaching the Heights.* Dublin: Blackwater Press, 1995. 0-86121-810-8

→ Hickey, Tony. *Joe in the Middle.* Dublin: Poolbeg Press, 1988. 1-85371-021-0

→ Hickey, Tony. *Joe on Holiday.* Dublin: Poolbeg Press, 1991. 1-85371-145-4

→ Hickey, Tony. *Where is Joe?* Dublin: Poolbeg Press, 1989. 1-85371-045-8

→ Keily, Tony. *The Shark Joke.* Dublin: Martello Books, 1994. 1-86023-005-9

→ Lennon, Tom. *When Love Comes To Town.* Dublin: O'Brien Press, 1993. 0-86278-361-5

→ Lynch, Patricia. *The Turf-Cutter's Donkey.* Dublin: Poolbeg Press, 1998. 1-85371-808-4

→ Murphy, Frank. *Lockie and Dadge.* Dublin: O'Brien Press, 1995. 0-86278-424-7

→ Ó Laighléis, Ré. *Ecstasy.* Dublin: Poolbeg Press, 1996. 1-85371-611-1

→ Ó Laighléis, Ré. *Hooked.* Ballyvaughan: Moinin, 1999. 0-9532777-1-2

→ O'Loughlin, Larry. *Is Anybody Listening?* Dublin: Wolfhound Press, 1999. 0-86327-721-7

→ O'Sullivan, Mark. *Silent Stones.* Dublin: Wolfhound Press, 1999. 0-86327-722-5

→ O'Sullivan, Mark. *White Lies.* Dublin: Wolfhound Press, 1997. 0-86327-592-3

→ Parkinson, Siobhán. *Breaking the Wishbone.* Dublin: O'Brien Press, 1999. 0-86278-635-5

→ Parkinson, Siobhán. *The Moon King.* Dublin: O'Brien Press, 1998. 0-86278-573-1

→ Quinn, John. *Duck and Swan.* Dublin: Poolbeg Press, 1993. 1-85371-317-1

→ Scott, Mike. *Good Enough for Judith.* Dublin: Wolfhound Press, 1994. 0-86327-396-3

→ Scott, Mike. *Judith and Spider.* Dublin: Wolfhound Press, 1992. 0-86327-347-5

→ Scott, Mike. *Judith and the Traveller.* Dublin: Wolfhound Press, 1991. 0-86327-299-1

→ Sefton, Catherine. *The Beat of the Drum.* London: Hamish Hamilton, 1989. 0-241-12642-8

→ Sefton, Catherine. *The Cast Off.* London: Hamish Hamilton, 1993. 0-241-13362-9

→ Strelkoff, Tatiana. *Allison – A Story of First Love.* Dublin: O'Brien Press, 1998. 0-86278-559-6

→ Waddell, Martin. *Tango's Baby.* London: Walker Books, 1995. 0-7445-4304-5

IRISH CHILDREN'S BOOKS IN TRANSLATION

> *In dieser Geschichte spielt das Kleine Volk eine große Rolle.*
> *Dazu gehören die Elfen, die noch heute im Alltag vieler Iren le-*
> *bendig sind* – The Little People play a major part in this story.
> Especially the elves, still a vivid element in the everyday lives
> of many Irish people today.

This comment on contemporary Irish life can be read in the introduction to the
German translation of Patricia Lynch's *Pat O'Brian und die Zaubermelodie* (*Brogeen
follows the Magic Tune* (1952)); the translation was published in 1996. It would seem
to indicate that the perception and presentation of Irish children's literature abroad
was, in the mid-1990s, still stuck in a time warp, oblivious to the unprecedented
growth of home-grown books for Irish children from the early 1980s on. Since that
time, Irish children's writers have been embracing themes both Irish and international and developing exciting ways of telling stories, old and new, to a modern
audience. Could it really be that Tony Hickey's statement, in 1982, about overseas
publishers tending 'to want only their notions of Irishness, the land of leprechauns'
still held true in 1996 or still holds true today?

The brief and fortunate answer to this question is 'no'. However, it takes
time and a lot of effort from Irish publishers for the international children's book
scene to register modern Irish children's literature. To this end, a tremendous opportunity was offered when Ireland was the Focal Theme of the Frankfurt Book
Fair in 1996. Several books and brochures on Ireland, its people, history, culture and
publishing industry were produced for – or at least in time for – the event. For our
purposes, the most important one was the *Big Guide To Irish Children's Books*, which
introduced recent developments and books to an international audience, as well as
to the domestic audience. The flurry of journalistic activity leading up to and during
the Fair focussed extensively on Irish literature, especially books published in
German translation. It was an ideal chance for Irish children's literature to present
itself to the international publishing world.

Before going on to look at how Irish children's books of this period have
fared abroad, two authors have to be mentioned who, until then, almost exclusively
flew the Irish flag in international circles: Patricia Lynch and Eilís Dillon. Both were
and are well-known in other English-speaking countries and have been translated
into several languages; Dillon's *The Lost Island* can be enjoyed as far away as China.

In many countries, Lynch remains a 'historical' phenomenon. In France, for
instance, six of her novels were published between 1947 and 1954, but none since

then; in Germany, on the other hand, no fewer than three new translations appeared in the 1990s. However, the German publisher's risk would not seem to have paid off. Olaf Hille, who admirably set out to make English-language 'classic' children's literature available in German (Norman Lindsay's *The Magic Pudding*, Mary Norton's *The Borrowers*, etc.), sadly had to close down his press.

Eilís Dillon's books have been more successful in Germany. There her name is linked to Heinrich Böll, author of the still popular *Irisches Tagebuch* (*Irish Diary* (1957)), which sent young Germans in their droves to 'find themselves' in the west of Ireland. Heinrich and his wife, Annemarie Böll, also translated Irish authors into German: Brendan Behan, Tomás Ó Crohan, Flann O'Brien and Eilís Dillon. *The Island of Horses* was translated, as it says on the cover, 'out of affection for Ireland by A. und H. Böll' in 1963, during the initial phase of the post-war German love affair with Ireland. It was a great hit and was nominated for the prestigious Deutscher Jugendliteraturpreis (German Children's Literature Prize) a year later. The German critic Horst Künnemann wrote in 1996, 'even 40 years after publication [it] has lost none of its lively freshness, linguistic precision and intense atmosphere.' In all, fifteen of Dillon's children's books have been translated into German, five of those by Annemarie Böll. Two of them are still selling well today: *Die Insel der Pferde* (*The Island of Horses*) – the hardcover edition ran to twelve printings, the paperback has had eight reprints; and *Im Schatten des Vesuv* (*The Shadow of Vesuvius*), an historical novel about the last days of Pompeii – popular in German schools, the paperback edition is in its eleventh reprint.

But who are the most internationally acclaimed and successful representatives of contemporary Irish children's books? If we take 'Irish children's books' to mean (as consensus mostly has it) books published in Ireland or books published abroad by Irish authors, then at least six names come to mind: Martin Waddell, Joan Lingard, Marita Conlon-McKenna, Tom McCaughren and Mark O'Sullivan. The sixth is not an author but an illustrator, Belfast-born P.J. Lynch – an illustrator of international acclaim who has won many awards. He was shortlisted for the Kate Greenaway medal for *A Bag of Moonshine* (1986) and *East O' The Sun and West O' The Moon* (1991), and finally awarded the medal for *The Christmas Miracle of Jonathan Toomey* (1995) and again in 1996 for *When Jessie Came Across the Sea*.

Martin Waddell is one of the most prolific and most successful contemporary authors of children's books, with over one hundred titles to his credit. He has found international recognition primarily for his picture books, which deal with 'wheel of life' themes that cut through all linguistic and cultural boundaries: 'birth, death, loving, caring, families, ageing'. He has said that books should reach out to basic childhood emotions, like fear of the dark (*Can't You Sleep, Little Bear?*) or separation (*Owl Babies*), feelings that relate directly to events and experiences in a young child's life. This explains, in part, the universal attractiveness of the picture books that he has authored. This appeal is

Run to Earth, cover for Japanese edition.

also due to his style – text pared down to the absolute minimum and often infused with great humour, and pictures by some of the best names in children's illustration. Waddell's picture books have been translated into most European languages and have won many prestigious awards: the Smarties Grand Prize and the Kate Greenaway Medal in Britain; Le Prix des Critiques de Livres pour Enfants in Belgium; nominated on a couple of occasions for the Deutscher Jugendbuchpreis (German Children's Literature Prize); and awarded a Parents' Choice Honor in the USA in 1992. Less known abroad are the books he has written under his pseudonym, Catherine Sefton, including the books set in Northern Ireland (*Starry Night, The Ghost Girl*, etc.).

The children's writer who has put Northern Ireland on the international map, both as a setting and as a topic, is Joan Lingard. Her *Sadie and Kevin* series (*Across the Barricades, The Twelfth Day of July, Into Exile, A Proper Place* and *Hostages to Fortune*) about a young couple who fall in love across the divide, first published in the 1970s and 1980s, has been widely translated. The series has been praised in reviews abroad for painting a picture of everyday life in Belfast with its strict segregation. Her even-handed treatment of the subject, her lack of pathos and her ability to make the situation understandable while offering no easy solutions has also been noted by foreign critics. The *Kevin and Sadie* books are not only read in foreign languages abroad, the books are also used in schools by those teaching English as a foreign language; a special school edition of *The Twelfth Day of July*, in English, was published in Berlin.

The major international success story in Irish children's publishing in the first half of the 1990s was Marita Conlon-McKenna's *Under the Hawthorn Tree*, published by the O'Brien Press in 1990. The first book for children to deal with the Great Famine, it marked a new approach to the writing of historical fiction for that audience, and showed how the survival of three children owed everything to their strength and determination in a society – in a universe, even – where nobody could help them but themselves. Praised in *The White Ravens* for the 'the lovely cadence of Irish speech and the (vivid depiction of) warm relationships within the family and among neighbours despite the depressing, but real background of disease and poverty', *Under the Hawthorn Tree* is a prime example of how skilfully the specific can be shown – and perceived – to be of universal relevance, enabling a transfer beyond the Irish context. It has been translated into Dutch (*Onder de Meidoorn*), French (*Les Enfants de la Faim*), German (*Folgt immer dem Fluss*), Danish (*Den store Sult-Den*), Swedish (*Den svåra vandringen*), Spanish and Japanese, and was also published in Britain by Viking Penguin and in the USA by Holiday House. It received the accolade of an International Reading Association Book Award in 1991, was on the honours list of the Österreichischer Kinder- und Jugendbuchpreis (Austrian Children's Literature Prize) in 1993 and was nominated by *The White Ravens* in 1992.

The other two books in Conlon-McKenna's *Children of the Famine* trilogy travelled well too, even if they didn't enjoy the same spectacular success of the first book. *Wildflower Girl* was translated into Danish, German and Dutch and *Fields of*

Home was translated into German. Both books were also published in the USA and in Britain.

Under the Hawthorn Tree was the first wide-scale international success following the Pick Report in the late 1980s. That report established that the domestic market alone was too small to support the Irish publishing industry and recommended a stronger international orientation – specifically that Irish rights to foreign titles should be bought and the rights to Irish publications be sold to foreign publishers (especially to publishers in other English-speaking countries). The recommendations in the report were widely followed with the result that while more and more British publishers bought the British rights to Irish books, the option on the author's next book remained with the original publisher. This meant that an Irish author such as Marita Conlon-McKenna could enjoy international sales while remaining with the O'Brien Press, her Irish publisher. In the past, Conlon-McKenna

Under the Hawthorn Tree,
cover for German edition.

would have had to seek publication in Britain to have enjoyed comparable international distribution. Irish publishers could now legitimately say, as Michael O'Brien did in a newspaper interview in 1989, 'we are now in a position to offer authors a world market'.

Another international success story that started during the early phase of the recent developments in Irish children's literature was the first volumes of Tom McCaughren's 'fox' novels. The wildlife series – *Run with the Wind* (1983), *Run to Earth* (1984), *Run Swift, Run Free* (1986), *Run to the Ark* (1991), *Run to the Wild Wood* (1996), *Run for Cover* (1999) – was initially published by the Wolfhound Press in Dublin, but the British and Commonwealth rights were then bought by Penguin UK. *Run with the Wind* has been translated into German, Japanese, Latvian, French and Swedish; *Run to Earth* into German, Japanese and Swedish (the Swedish translations of the first two volumes in the 1980s were reissued in 1996 and 1997); *Run Swift, Run Free* was recommended by *The White Ravens* in 1991 and has been translated into Japanese. McCaughren's Northern Ireland novel, *Rainbows of the Moon*, published by the Children's Press in 1989, has also been translated into French, Danish and Dutch and was published in Britain.

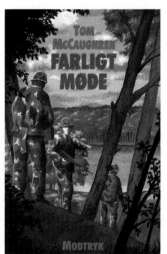

The most recent shooting star amongst Irish children's authors abroad is Mark O'Sullivan, all of whose novels to date, published by Wolfhound Press, have attracted interest on the continent. *Melody for Nora* (1994) merges the personal and political in a story set against the backdrop of the Irish Civil War.

Rainbows of the Moon, cover for Danish edition.

The *White Ravens* nomination in 1996 characterised this novel as follows: 'this timely, balanced novel explores complex political allegiances, the horror of war and

Angels Without Wings,
cover for Greek edition.

difficult family circumstances through the eyes of its central character ... This novel is as much about Irish life in that turbulent period as it is about growing up in hard times.' The balance between local interest and universal appeal is struck well in this novel, which has been translated into Swedish, German and French, and won the prestigous Prix Des Lecteurs Du Mans in 1999, an international competition judged by the teachers, academics and readers from the Le Mans district in France. The sequel to Nora's story, *Basin Street Blues* (1995), has appeared in Swedish and French. The novel about a German-Irish family, national and cultural identity and competitive sport, *More than a Match* (1996), has been translated into German as has *Angels without Wings* (1997), a cleverly plotted story that departs from an Irish setting and plays sophisticated games with the notion of fiction: the characters of a book come alive in order to try to prevent the manipulation of their story according to the dictates of Nazi ideology. *Angels without Wings* has also been translated into Greek. *White Lies* (1999), O'Sullivan's second 'intercultural' Irish novel after *More than a Match*, is about an adopted black Irish teenager who begins to doubt the details of her adoption in Africa. It was selected by *The White Ravens* in 1998 and has, to date, been translated into Italian, Turkish, Dutch and French. The English-language edition of *White Lies* is also used quite extensively in the Dutch school system; according to Seamus O'Reilly, sales and marketing manager at Wolfhound Press, a large number of copies were sold to a specialist schools distribution company.

Irish authors tackling non-Irish subjects, especially in historical novels, is a relatively recent feature of home-grown Irish fiction. The Second World War period and the Holocaust have featured prominently in European and British children's literature for some time now, giving scope for writing about persecution, about bravery in the face of unimaginable adversity, about loyalty, betrayal, suffering and endurance. This period of history has been discovered by Irish children's literature only in recent years. Eilís Dillon's final novel, *The Children of Bach* (1993), set in central Europe during the 1930s, is one of the earliest examples. Mark O'Sullivan's *Angels without Wings*, mentioned above, is another. Bill Wall's *The Boy Who Met Hitler* (1999), set in Cork during the Second World War, deals with the impact of that war on two friends, some of whose relatives are involved in the war against the Germans. It is currently being translated into Italian. The rights to Gregory Maguire's *The Good Liar* (1995) – a moving story about the recollection of a childhood in a village in occupied France and the complications involved when the boy befriends a German soldier – have been sold to publishers in Australia, Canada, Holland, New Zealand and the USA.

Subjects from Irish history, when given the appropriate treatment, can prove of great interest for overseas readers. Morgan Llywelyn's books have international appeal. Her *Strongbow* (1992) sells in Canada, Catalunya, Spain and in the USA; the rights to *Brian Boru* (1990) have been sold to Canada and the USA.

Of the individual titles which have done exceptionally well abroad, Sam McBratney's *Guess How Much I Love You?* (1994), a simple celebration of love between father and child, has to be mentioned. It has been translated into several languages. Siobhán Parkinson's books have also achieved foreign recognition: *The Leprechaun Who Wished he Wasn't* (1993), a comical story about two opposites who are dissatisfied with themselves and their appearances, has been translated into French, *Sisters ... No Way!* (1996), the book which can be read from either end depending on whose side of the story the reader wishes to hear, can now be read in French, Italian, Portuguese and German, while her most recent prize-winning title, *Four Kids, Three Cats, Two Cows, One Witch (maybe)* (1997), has so far been translated into Danish and German.

The books and authors mentioned so far have enjoyed international attention, have been translated into several languages and published in other English-speaking countries. There are several books which have not (yet) enjoyed, but which deserve, similar attention. Critics are often at a loss to explain why certain books do well – witness the amazement at the 'Harry Potter' phenomenon – and why others which deserve widespread attention are overshadowed by their more mediocre colleagues. Acclaim – even international critical acclaim – doesn't always translate into books or rights being sold. For example, warm praise was given to Mary Beckett's *Hannah Or Pink Balloons* (1995) and to Elizabeth O'Hara's historical novel *Blaeberry Sunday* (1994) in *The White Ravens 1996*, but neither title has been translated as a result.

Which aspects of Irish children's literature are favoured by which countries? It is difficult to see absolute trends, but generally speaking it could be said that the southern European countries – Italy, Spain and, to a large extent, France – tend to go for light-hearted, humorous stories, such as Siobhán Parkinson's *The Leprechaun Who Wished he Wasn't* (1993) (translated into French), Una Leavy's *No Shoes for Tom* (1997), a story about a child who has fun with his bare toes and is reluctant to wear shoes (translated into Spanish), Margot Bosonnet's *Up the Red Belly* (1996) about the adventures of a gang of children, which is doing well in France and the humorous stories of family life and strife in Creina Mansfield's *My Nasty Neighbours* (1995), which has been translated into French, Italian and (Brazilian) Portuguese.

The serious, larger themes tend to be favoured by the northern European countries – hence a thought-provoking (and rewarding) novel like John Wood's *In a Secret Place*, a fantasy novel about the power of imagination, which is an elusive, atmospheric story that was nominated for the Carnegie Medal and, as the *Big Guide To*

Sisters ... No Way! (flipper cover), cover for Italian edition.

Irish Children's Books said, 'demands close reading', was translated into German. More controversial themes in adolescent novels, such as Tom Lennon's *When Love Comes to Town* (1993), about a teenager coming to terms with his homosexuality, have been translated into languages of countries known for their progressive attitude towards reading matter for children and young adults. This particular book has been translated into Dutch and Danish.

But exceptions prove the rules, and a serious author like Mark O'Sullivan can be appreciated in France, and Hugh Galt's action-packed tale of thieves, kidnappers and first love, *Bike Hunt* (1988), in Germany, Holland and Denmark. Michael Scott's horror stories, *October Moon* (1992), *Wolf Moon* (1995) and *House of the Dead* (1993), seem to thrill readers all over Europe, the USA and beyond – he has been translated into Catalan, Dutch, French, Spanish, Italian and Chinese.

Apart from horror stories, American readers seem to favour topics on Irish history and time-travel fantasy. Yvonne MacGrory's *The Secret of the Ruby Ring* (1991) is selling well in the USA and Canada – a favourable review there even compared it to Philippa Pearce's *Tom's Midnight Garden*, and it was made into a two-hour TV film. MacGrory's *Ghost of Susannah Parry* has also been translated into Japanese.

New markets are now opening up in Eastern Europe and Irish children's books have made some inroads there. Orla Melling's contemporary children's fantasies with Celtic elements, *The Druid's Tune* (1992)and *The Singing Stone* (1993), for example, have been translated into Czech. In the Far Eastern countries of Malaysia, Singapore, Vietnam, Cambodia, Brunei, Hong Kong, Laos, Thailand, Burma, Taiwan and Indonesia, readers of English could, if they felt so inclined, giggle at some Irish fun books, for example, Don Conroy's *The Owl Who Couldn't Give a Hoot*, *The Tiger Who Was a Roaring Success* or Patricia Forde's *The King's Secret*. Both O'Brien Press and Wolfhound Press have a worldwide network of distributors and agents. Wolfhound can boast of modest success in Australia, where their distributor sells books, according to sales and marketing manager Seamus O'Reilly, 'usually those with an environmental slant'. An increasingly significant sector of the English language market is in the 'English as a foreign language' sector. More and more books for children and young adults are being discovered and accepted for use in schools abroad for English language classes.

The scope of modern Irish children's books is large; it ranges from humorous, fun books for younger readers, undemanding, lively stories, through more thoughtful offerings such as time-slips, etc., to the problems dealt with in novels for adolescents. Entertaining, amusing or thought-provoking, many of these have found publishers abroad. For a book to succeed abroad, factors other than content (or even than quality) play a significant role – finding the foreign-language publisher with the most compatible list, for example, securing good translations, good marketing and distribution are paramount.

◆

Ghost of Susannah Parry,
cover for Japanese edition.

The two Irish publishers most active and successful in placing their titles abroad are doubtlessly O'Brien Press and Wolfhound Press. They both work with literary agents and have developed a network of international distributors. On its web page the O'Brien Press proclaims: 'In recent years the number of O'Brien Press books sold into translation has increased significantly – an indicator of their quality and broad appeal'. (see: www.obrien.ie) Many of these sales are negotiated at the Frankfurt and Bologna book fairs. O'Brien again: 'We decided to operate on the world stage as far as possible, thus hoping to create the situation whereby authors of children's fiction published in Ireland would have as good a chance as any of being published abroad.'

Irish children's books have, within the past fifteen to twenty years, become an important factor in the international market. But what about the other side of the coin? Which books from which languages can be found in translation published in Ireland or even distributed by an Irish publisher? The answer to this question is, at the present time, quickly given – there have been very few, with the exception of books translated into the Irish language. In the spirit of international exchange, it would be nice to think that by the time *The Big Guide 3: Irish Children's Books* is published there might just be the need for an article on 'Books from abroad published in Ireland'.

White Lies, cover for Italian edition.

REFERENCES

→ Hickey, Tony. In Loughborough 1981. *Conference Proceedings of the 14th Loughborough International Conference on Children's Literature, Dublin 1981*, pp.32–37. Dublin: Dublin Public Libraries, 1982.

→ Künnemann, Horst. 'Rückkehr zur Insel der Pferde.' In *Bulletin Jugend & Literatur*, pp.8, 16. 1996.

→ *The White Ravens 1992. A Selection of International Children's and Youth Literature*. Munich: International Youth Library, 1992.

→ *The White Ravens 1996. A Selection of International Children's and Youth Literature*. Munich: International Youth Library, 1996.

The White Ravens is an annual catalogue which presents a selected number of books from over forty countries deemed to be striking in their literary or graphic qualities and hence worthy of international attention (the white ravens amongst the black). They are selected by the International Youth Library in Munich, the home of the most comprehensive collection of international literature for children and young people available worldwide, and displayed during the Bologna Children's Book Fair. Ireland first featured in 1992 as one of the countries represented; two to three Irish books are nominated each year. *The White Ravens* of the past few years can be found at www.ijb.de

AWARDS AND RESEARCH

BOOK AWARDS

'Awards are an irrelevant impertinence, a distorting imposition on a book, and I want every one I can get,' writes British author Alan Garner. Though he spends the remainder of the article (originally an address to IBBY) reappraising his own misgivings about book awards, I do think that his statement resonates with the genuine ambivalence that many of us feel about children's book awards. That notion of 'the best' is a very absolute one and indicates that all the other members of that class are somehow inferior.

Fierce Milly, illustrated by Leonie Shearing.

American artist and illustrator Marcia Browne remarks that 'prizes and awards are gifts from the gods unless they are given for measurable performances, such as jumping.' Can an act of creation, such as writing or illustrating for children, be put on a measurable scale? Many writers and critics would say 'No!'

Indeed, the critic Eleanor Cameron writes: 'doesn't it seem burningly unfair to writers, not to speak of the almost impossible burden of judgement on the committee members, that they are trying to decide among bananas, lemons, oranges, plums and peaches as to which is the "one" finest fruit of the year?'

This raises questions about the need for, or value of, any book award. This in turn begs the further question: 'what is a "good" children's book?' And indeed the next obvious question: 'good for whom?' Ethel Heins considers this question in detail and concludes that 'the subject does not submit to being encapsulated in a formula or a theorem, it's very elusiveness may prove to be its glory.'

The act of reading is more than decoding and understanding a text. The creation of the best possible text and image is the onerous task of the writer and the artist. Bringing that book to life, finding its 'glory' – the space where it can matter, where it can live in the life of the reader – has to be the focus of literature, especially literature for children.

Those who bring books to the children – writers, illustrators, editors, publishers, booksellers, parents, teachers and librarians – endeavour, each in their own way, to pass the interest and passion for books on to them. We see the necessity of having as rich and varied a selection of books available for them as is possible. Part of passing on this interest has to include the notion of books that are worthy of our recommendation to children – and therefore we end up creating a hierarchy of sorts. In recommending a book, do we not 'award' it with our approval in some way? Are not book awards a kind of 'collective approval'? I certainly would not agree with Bláithín Gallagher's contention in *Children's Books in Ireland* that 'awards signify society's seal of approval'. 'Society' is a very large concept and I really wonder if it is that concerned about children's reading material?

Not every worthwhile book has been given the accolade of an award. American author William Sleator, in a conversation following his keynote address at this year's American Library Association Conference, reminded us that E.B. White's *'Charlotte's Web* did not receive the Newbery Award when published in 1953 ... This, despite being considered by many as the most significant American novel for children in the past century. It was in fact an Honour Book! Some other book called *Secret of the Andes* by Ann Nolan Clarke won the Newbery that year. How many of you have read and reread that one?' he asked.

'Also-rans' make interesting reading and have given rise to a unique award for children's writing: the aptly named Phoenix Award. Set up in 1985 in the USA, it honours books published in English that were not considered worthy of major award in the year of their publication. The recipients of this well-regarded award include a veritable who's-who of children's writers: Jill Paton Walshe, Robert Cormier, Alan Garner, Nina Bawden and Katherine Paterson.

The existence of the Phoenix Award echoes the sentiment of author, critic and one-time member of the Caldecott Committee, Gregory Maguire: 'I no longer trust that a committee, including any I am on, will ever give a prize to a "best" book,' he says. 'I merely hope against hope that we will manage to select a good book, and let the best book, with luck, find its own way into the hearts of readers.' Indeed, Martha Vaughan Parravano, senior editor of *The Horn Book* magazine, echoes this sentiment when she says, 'we will try to keep the "fine" books that went unrecognised alive – by holding them in our own memories, by sharing them with others.'

Is that the best award of all, that the book lives in the heart of the reader? Is Ireland ready for some version of the Phoenix Award I wonder – perhaps the 'Aiséirí Award'? Or is the fact that we may not have the need for such an award reason for concern? Does anyone feel that a certain book published here was overshadowed and not given due recognition?

An Rógaire agus a Scáil, illustrated by Piet Sluis.

Ireland currently has two children's book awards. Both have commercial sponsorship and produce a shortlist of possible winners. Both are open to books written in English or in Irish. Both can be withheld if suitable titles are not submitted. The Reading Association of Ireland (RAI) presents a book award and a merit award every two years for a book written by an Irish author and published in Ireland. The Bisto Awards, under the auspices of Children's Books Ireland, present five annual awards, the best-known of which is the Bisto Book of the Year Award. But it also includes three Merit Awards and the Eilís Dillon Memorial Award for a first time author. Any author and/or illustrator born or resident in Ireland is eligible for these awards.

The RAI book award was instigated in 1985 with the primary objective of encouraging the publication of children's books in Ireland. It was the first such award in

Ireland, and is presented on a biennial basis. In 1989 a second award was instigated, the Special Merit Award, to honour a specific contribution to publications for children in Ireland. The prizes are non-monetary and are sponsored by the EBS Building Society.

In 1984 the RAI executive committee set up a sub-committee to oversee the administration of the awards. The sub-committee looked at the criteria for book awards in other countries and came up with a set of criteria, which are furnished to Irish publishers. Following each award, the committee re-examines the award criteria and recommends any changes to the executive committee. This allows the conditions to reflect the changes in publishing for children in Ireland. A panel of twelve jurors reads and discusses the books. Discussion and ballot constitute the main selection procedure for the generation of a shortlist. Jury members tend largely to remain unchanged from year to year, which, according to chairperson Maureen Colfor, allows for a consistency of opinion when it comes to the selection of winners. But this she feels may be something that might need to be re-examined prior to the next award.

In 1990 the Bisto Book of the Decade Award was initiated. Following its success it continues on as an annual event. A five-member jury with a non-voting chairperson is convened, with members serving for a maximum of three years. The 'pool' of books is far wider than that of the RAI, taking in books published outside Ireland by Irish writers and illustrators, as well as those of non-nationals resident in the thirty-two counties of Ireland. This has a two-fold effect in that it includes Irish authors and illustrators who are published overseas, but also allows overseas authors published in Ireland to be considered for the awards. This international aspect can allow for a richer and more varied 'pool of books' to be submitted for consideration. Each member of the judging panel reads all books submitted.

In comparison, the Bisto awards are monetary. The awards are sponsored by RHM Foods, Ireland. There are no formal criteria set down. This, according to Rosemary Hetherington, allows the members of the jury to arrive at a consensus as to what should or should not be considered for the shortlist. As with the RAI, the ballot is used to generate the shortlist and the winners.

Both awards coexist happily and hold each other in high regard. There has been a high correlation in the choice of winners over the years. Both have been set up to encourage publication of quality children's books in Ireland. This sentiment is echoed in many children's book awards worldwide – though interestingly the Australian Book Council's stated focus is 'to encourage children's reading'.

Both awards were set up at a time when publishing for children in Ireland needed to be encouraged. But the industry is now well-established and thriving. Is there a need, therefore, for two awards claiming to encourage quality publications for children? Should they rethink their *'raisons d'être'*, or change their focus?

Donna Norton cites three different types of children's book awards: literary awards, popular appeal awards and human awards. Worldwide there is a proliferation of each type of award. Here in Ireland, we have only those based on literary value.

Certainly popular appeal awards ('best-sellers' and 'children's fa-vourites') tend to be less well received and tainted with the consideration of commercial gain. I do think that this lack of credibility for children selecting their own award-winners is one that we need to consider seriously. Certainly the chil-dren's book market can be manipulated by the media, taste or fashion, and so can any other market. Yet, if we care enough about our children as readers, should we not be educating them to be critical readers, to hold opinions and values about what they are reading and ultimately to become discerning readers, critics and, in-deed, consumers?

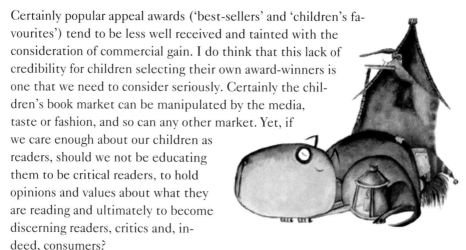

Tales of Wisdom and Wonder, illustrated by Niamh Sharkey.

No real debate has taken place on the RAI book awards outside committee level. Press interest has been limited to photographs of the prize ceremony and scant column inches of description. A detailed account of the award ceremony and the award-winning books is carried in *Reading News,* the RAI's official journal.

Bisto, on the other hand, has managed to find its way into print on several occasions. As already cited, Bláithín Gallagher's questioning of the 1993 awards pro-voked reaction, but it was short-lived. In the same year, Eilís O'Hanlon, writing in the *Irish Times,* questioned the idea of 'political correctness' in children's literature. Her article, 'What Shall We Tell The Children?', provoked quite an interesting re-sponse in the letters page of the *Irish Times,* which went on for several weeks. More recently, the position of Irish-language books was the subject of a comprehensive ar-ticle by Helen Ryan in *Children's Books In Ireland.*

I wonder had the spirit of this debate been nurtured, might it have pro-vided the genesis of a forum where real literary debate could take place on a regular basis? We really do need to have something other than the *Harry Potter*-type phe-nomenon to have children's books taken seriously by the mainstream media.

Until something does change, I wonder can we seriously consider any real change in the nature of our current awards? Certainly, I believe that we could invite winning authors and publishers to address their work at conference level – provide a forum where they can debate the literary merits of their art. One of the highlights of the RAI Spring Conference 2000 was an outstanding address from Seamus Cashman, publisher at Wolfhound Press, regarding the moral implications of new technologies for his profession.

Both Colfor and Hetherington are dismayed by how little use is made of shortlists for awards. A considerable amount of deliberation goes into generating these lists and both feel that books making it to the shortlist stage are in fact de-serving of a lot more attention than that given to the ultimate winners. I wonder could we stop at the shortlist stage and not take it any further or are we caught up in the 'winners-and-losers' syndrome?

Robert Dunbar, in conversation with Shirley Kelly in *Books Ireland*, says: 'But there are aspects of the world of children's books in this country of which I am openly critical. I do detect a little parochialism, for instance, which I find a wee bit numbing … we now have far too many children's books coming from Irish publishers and in this respect I think it's time for publishers to think about retrenching.'

Should both RAI and Bisto in fact consider retrenching a little themselves? Is it time for them to acknowledge that publishing is alive and well here in Ireland, due in no small part to their efforts at encouraging excellence? And furthermore to find mechanisms within their award schemes to arrive at a more critical kind of award? Should we not wonder why no one has publicly asked, 'Well, why did such-and-such a book not make it to the shortlist?' Is it that we are too polite for such a question or indeed do we now feel that we have a fixed notion of what constitutes an award- winner here? Has the time arrived for an 'Aiséirí Award'?

The Blue Horse, illustration by Katherine White.

I know that the Irish market is limited and so will not support a plethora of awards for every type of book published. But there are glaring omissions – Martha Vaughan Parravano, in examining the Newbery Award, poses some interesting questions which can be asked equally about awards here. 'Why not create an award for books published for younger children? Or an award specifically for illustration? Or for poetry or non-fiction? Or for books for the newly independent reader? Should we not have an award for writing for older children so that books for younger children are not eclipsed by the sheer size and scope of the bigger books?' she asks.

Should there not be an award for school textbooks? 'After all,' says Colfor, 'these are the texts that children have to encounter and engage with in schools. Many school texts will now be literature based at primary level and may comprise original work. Why not reward the best of these?' Should not each type of book have its own distinctive award, which could be withheld should a book of suitable quality not be submitted?

White Lies, cover by Slick Fish Design.

Following from this, there is another aspect that may need to be addressed. Martha Vaughan Parravano talks about the 'shroud of secrecy surrounding awards'. Maybe it is time that the award committees here had more to say than simply '… and the winner is …?' I am not sure that I am buying into the need for accountability here, so much as the need for transparency about the qualities found in a particular book which made it worthy of note. Perhaps we could make the shortlist for each award more relevant and noticeable were this to be done for all the books on it?

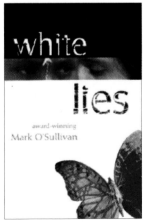

I have been privileged to work on both the RAI and Bisto Awards and could not finish this essay without attesting to the enthusiasm and dedication of those involved. I earnestly hope that these awards continue, but also that they grow and remain relevant. I will leave the final word to Alan Garner: 'The work must merit the award, if the award is to merit the work.'

An Eala Dhubh, illustrated by Cormac Ó Snodaigh.

REFERENCES

→ Browne, Marcia. 'One Wonders'. In *Lotus Seeds*. New York: Charles Scribner's Sons, 1986.
→ Cameron, Eleanor. 'On Criticism, Awards and Peaches'. In *The Seed and the Vision*. New York: Dutton Children's Books, 1993.
→ Colfor, Maureen. In conversation with the author. 2000.
→ Gallagher, Bláithín. 'Sexing The Bisto'. In *Children's Books In Ireland*. No 9. December 1993.
→ Garner, Alan. 'Purlock Prizes'. In *The Voice That Thunders*. London: Harvill Press, 1997.
→ Heins, Ethel. 'Go and Catch a Falling Star: What is a Good Children's Book?' In *Innocence and Experience: Essays and Conversations on Children's Literature,* B. Harrison and G. Maguire. New York: Lothrop Lee and Shepard Books, 1987.
→ Hetherington, Rosemary. In conversation with the author. 2000.
→ Kelly, Shirley. In conversation with Robert Dunbar. *Books Ireland*.
→ Maguire, Gregory. In conversation with the author. 2000.
→ Norton, Donna. *Through the Eyes of a Child*. Ohio: Colombia, 1987.
→ O'Hanlon, Eilís. 'What Shall We Tell The Children?' Dublin: The *Irish Times*, 8 May 1993.
→ Parravano, Martha Vaughan. 'Alive and Vigorous: Questioning the Newbery'. In *The Horn Book Magazine*. July/August 1999.
→ Ryan, Helen. 'Bisto and The Year 2000'. In *Children's Books In Ireland*. No 21. 1999.
→ Sleator, William. In conversation with the author. 2000.

AWARDS FOR CHILDREN'S BOOKS

BISTO BOOK AWARDS

BISTO AWARDS 1996–1997

Bisto Book of the Year Award

Parkinson, Siobhán. *Sisters … No Way!* O'Brien Press.

The Eilís Dillon Memorial Award

Whelan, Gerard. *The Guns of Easter*. O'Brien Press.

Bisto Merit Awards

Cussen, Cliodna/Ó Snodaigh, Cormac. *An Eala Dhubh*. Coiscéim.

Friel, Maeve. *The Lantern Moon*. Poolbeg Press.

Whelan, Gerard. *The Guns of Easter*. O'Brien Press.

Also Shortlisted

Ó Raghallaigh, Colmán/Carroll, Anne Marie. *Drochlá Ruairí*. Cló Mhaigh Eo.

Kissane, Dan/Johnston, Aileen. *The Eagle Tree.* O'Brien Press.

Lynch, P.J. *The King of Ireland's Son.* Poolbeg Press.

Ó Laighléis, Ré. *Gafa*. Comhar.

Ó Raghallaigh, Colmán/ Ní Raghallaigh, Aoife. *Róisín ar Strae*. An Gúm.

O'Sullivan, Mark. *More than a Match*. Wolfhound Press.

BISTO AWARDS 1997–1998

Bisto Book of the Year Award

Whelan, Gerard. *Dream Invader*. O'Brien Press.

Eilís Dillon Memorial Award

Miliano, Ed. *It's a Jungle Out There*. Wolfhound Press.

Bisto Merit Awards

Lally, Soinbhe. *The Hungry Wind*. Poolbeg Press.

Lynch, P.J. *When Jessie Came Across the Sea*. Poolbeg Press.

Parkinson, Siobhán. *Four Kids, Three Cats, Two Cows, One Witch (maybe)*. O'Brien Press.

Also Shortlisted

FitzGerald, Mairéad Ashe /Hall, Stephen. *The World of Colmcille, also known as Columba*. O'Brien Press.

Kissane, Dan/Clarke, Angela. *Jimmy's Leprechaun Trap*. O'Brien Press.

Kissane, Dan/Clarke, Angela. *The Eagle Tree*. O'Brien Press.

O'Loughlin, Larry/Leonard, John. *The Gobán Saor*. Blackwater Press.

O'Sullivan, Mark. *Angels Without Wings*. Wolfhound Press.

O'Sullivan, Mark. *White Lies*. Wolfhound Press.

BISTO AWARDS 1998–1999

Bisto Book of the Year Award

Sharkey, Niamh. *Tales of Wisdom and Wonder*. Barefoot Books.

Eilís Dillon Memorial Award

Hastings, Caitríona. *Dea-Scéala*. Cló Iar-Chonnachta.

Bisto Merit Awards

Fitzpatrick, Marie-Louise. *The Long March*. Wolfhound Press.

Parkinson, Siobhán. *The Moon King*. O'Brien Press.

Rosenstock, Gabriel/Sluis, Piet. *An Rógaire agus a Scáil*. An Gúm.

Also Shortlisted

Boran, Pat/Curry, Stewart. *All the Way from China*. Poolbeg Press.

McBratney, Sam. *Bert's Wonderful News*. Walker Books.

McCaughren, Tom. *Ride a Pale Horse*. Anvil Press.

Murphy, Mary. *Please Be Quiet*. Methuen.

Sharkey, Niamh. *The Gigantic Turnip*. Barefoot Books.

BISTO AWARDS 1999–2000

Bisto Book of the Year Award

Taylor, Marilyn. *Faraway Home*. O'Brien Press.

Eilís Dillon Memorial Award

McLaughlin, Marilyn. *Fierce Milly*. Mammoth/Egmont.

Bisto Merit Awards

Arrigan, Mary. *Siúlóid Bhreá*. An Gúm.
McLaughlin, Marilyn. *Fierce Milly*. Mammoth/Egmont.
O'Sullivan, Mark. *Silent Stones*. Wolfhound Press.

Also Shortlisted

Colfer, Eoin. *Benny and Babe*. O'Brien Press.
Whelan, Gerard. *Out of Nowhere*. O'Brien Press.
O'Loughlin, Larry. *Is Anybody Listening?* Wolfhound Press.
Sharkey, Niamh. *Jack and the Beanstalk*. Barefoot Books.
Lawrence, Louise. *The Crowlings*. Collins.
Wall, Bill. *The Boy Who Met Hitler*. Mercier Press.
Rosenstock, Gabriel/Sluis, Piet. *Paidín Mháire Mhuigín*. An Gúm.

READING ASSOCIATION OF IRELAND CHILDREN'S BOOK AWARDS

AWARDS FOR 1997

RAI Award

Lynch, P.J. *The Christmas Miracle of Jonathan Toomey*. Poolbeg Press.

RAI Special Merit Award

The O'Brien Press.

Also Shortlisted

Friel, Maeve. *The Lantern Moon*. Poolbeg Press.
Lally, Soinbhe. *A Hive for the Honey Bee*. Poolbeg Press.
Llywelyn, Morgan. *Cold Places*. Poolbeg Press.
Maguire, Gregory. *The Good Liar*. O'Brien Press.
Whelan, Gerard. *The Guns of Easter*. O'Brien Press.

AWARDS FOR 1999

RAI Award

O'Sullivan, Mark. *Angels Without Wings*. Wolfhound Press.

RAI Special Merit Award

Fitzpatrick, Marie-Louise. *The Long March*. Wolfhound Press.

Also Shortlisted

FitzGerald, Mairéad Ashe. *The World of Colmcille, also known as Columba*. O'Brien Press.
Miliano, Ed. *It's a Jungle Out There*. Wolfhound Press.
Parkinson, Siobhán. *Four Kids, Three Cats, Two Cows, One Witch (maybe)*. O'Brien Press.
O'Sullivan, Mark. *White Lies*. Wolfhound Press.
Whelan, Gerard. *Dream Invader*. O'Brien Press.

RESEARCHING IRISH CHILDREN'S BOOKS

In recent years Irish children's literature has attracted an increasing amount of attention from researchers. As yet there is no comprehensive history of the subject, but the fruits of research are appearing in periodicals, international publications about children's books and through the work of a number of organisations. The following list is not necessarily complete, but it represents an attempt to draw together at least some of the sources of information about Irish children's books.

ORGANISATIONS AND LIBRARIES

Children's Books Ireland, Autumn 1998, No.19.

- **Children's Book History Society**, 25 Field Way, Hoddesdon, Herts, EN11 0QN.
  A UK-based organisation. Its regular *Newsletter* carries information of Irish relevance from time to time.
- **Children's Books Ireland**, 19 Parnell Square, Dublin 1. (Details in section on 'Organisations', p.150.)
- **Children's and Schools' Section**, Dublin Public Libraries, Kevin Street Library, Kevin Street, Dublin 2. Holds a collection of books of Irish relevance (mainly twentieth century). Access on application to the Librarian.
- **Church of Ireland College of Education Library**, 96 Upper Rathmines Road, Dublin 6.
  The collection contains books of Irish interest, and the college also houses the publications of the Kildare Place Society. Access on application to the Librarian.
- **The National Library of Ireland**, Kildare Street, Dublin 2.
- **St Patrick's College Library**, Drumcondra, Dublin 9. A collection of the works of Patricia Lynch and other works of Irish interest are contained in the college library. Access on application to the Librarian.

BOOKS

Enchanted Journeys: Fifty Years of Irish Writing for Children, illustrated by Aileen Johnston.

- Brown, Stephen J. *Ireland in Fiction: a guide to Irish novels, tales, romances and folklore, 1915*. Vols. 1 & 2. Irish University Press, reprinted 1969.
- Coghlan, Valerie and Keenan, Celia (eds). *The Big Guide to Irish Children's Books*. Dublin: Irish Children's Book Trust, 1996. 1872917011
- Cotton, Penni. *Picture Books Sans Frontières*. Stoke-on-Trent: Trentham Books, 2000. 1858561833
- Dunbar, Robert (ed.). *Enchanted Journeys: Fifty Years of Irish Writing for Children*. Dublin: O'Brien Press, 1997. 0-86278-518-9

- Dunbar, Robert, (ed.). *Secret Lands: the World of Patricia Lynch.* Dublin: O'Brien Press, 1998.
- *Loughborough '81 Conference Proceedings.* Dublin: Committee of the 14th Loughborough International Conference on Children's Literature, 1982. 0950813400
- Reece, Leslie and Rosenstock, Gabriel (comps). *Irish Guide to Children's Books: Decade 1980–1990.* Dublin: Irish Children's Book Trust, 1990. 1872917003
- Taylor, Anne. *Catherine Sefton/Martin Waddell.* Swindon: School Library Association, 1993. 0900641681
- Taylor, Anne. *Joan Lingard: From Belfast to the Baltic.* Swindon: School Library Association, 1992. 0900641

PERIODICALS

- *Books Ireland.* Dublin. Occasional articles and reviews related to children's books.
- *Children's Books in Ireland.* Dublin: CLAI (Children's Literature Association of Ireland), No.1, December 1989–No.15, December 1996; Dublin: CBI (*Children's Books Ireland*), No.16, Summer 1997 – ongoing.
- *The Lion and the Unicorn,* Vol.21 (3). Special edition on Irish children's literature, guest edited by Celia Catlett Anderson and Robert Dunbar. 1997

The Lion and the Unicorn, Volume 21, No.3.

IRISH CHILDREN'S LITERATURE

ARTICLES

- Anderson, Celia Catlett. 'Stories for Every Child: the Books of Martin Waddell/Catherine Sefton'. In *Teaching and Learning Literature,* Vol.6 (4). March/April 1997.
- Brown, Stephen. 'Irish Fiction for Boys'. *Studies,* Vol.18.
- Coghlan, Valerie. 'Children's Leisure Reading.' In *Words Alone: the Teaching and Usage of English in Contemporary Ireland,* edited by Denis Bates et al. Dublin: University College Dublin Press, 2000. 1900621339
- Coghlan, Valerie. 'Ireland' (Country Survey). In *Bookbird,* Vol. 36 (2), pp.46–52. Summer 1998.
- Coghlan, Valerie. 'Ireland.' In *Routledge Companion Encyclopaedia to Children's Literature,* edited by Peter Hunt, pp.695–698. London: Routledge, 1996.
- Coghlan, Valerie. 'Looking Forward, Looking Back'. In *Childhood Remembered: Proceedings from the 4th Annual IBBY/MA Children's Literature Conference at Roehampton Institute London,* NCRCL Papers 3, pp.163–172, edited by Kimberley Reynolds. London: National Centre for Research in Children's Literature, 1998.
- Donlon, Patricia. 'Irish Children's Fiction'. In *Linen Hall Review,* pp.12–13. Autumn, 1985.
- Dunbar, Robert. 'Children's Fiction and the Ulster 'Troubles''. *Proceedings of the 12th Annual Conference of the Reading Association of Ireland,* pp.73–91. Dublin: RAI, 1987.
- Dunbar, Robert. 'Children's Literature: the Contemporary Irish Dimension'. In *European Children's Literature, Kingston Hill Papers in Education,* pp.77–85, edited by Penni Cotton. Kingston Upon Thames: School of Education at Kingston University, 1996. 1899711058
- Flanagan, Frank. 'Children's Literature in the Republic of Ireland: Historical Background'. In *European Children's Literature, Kingston Hill Papers in Education,* pp.67–76, edited by Penni Cotton. Kingston upon Thames: School of Education at Kingston University, 1996. 1899711058
- Griffin, Seán. 'Celebrating the Dublin Millennium through Children's Fiction'. In *Proceedings of the 5th Annual Drumcondra Educational Conference,* pp.37–45. Dublin: INTO, 1988. 07905076

- Hetherington, Rosemary. 'Recent Irish Publishing for Children'. In *An Leabharlann/The Irish Library*, Second Series, Vol.12 (1), pp.31–36. 1995.
- Lake, Wendy. 'A Question of Identity: Some Aspects of Historical fiction for children Set in Ireland'. In *Children's Literature in Education*, Vol.18 (1), pp.13–19.
- Madden, P.J. 'Children's Books in Ireland'. In *An Leabharlann*, Vol.13 (1), pp.33–44. 1995.
- Marriott, Stuart. 'Culture, Identity and Children's Literature in Northern Ireland'. In *European Children's Literature, Kingston Hill Papers in Education*, pp.87–96, edited by Penni Cotton. Kingston upon Thames: School of Education at Kingston University, 1996.1899711058
- Reddin, Kenneth. 'Children's Books in Ireland'. In *Irish Library Bulletin*, Vol.7, pp.74–76. 1946.
- Rolston, Bill. 'Escaping from Belfast: class, ideology and literature in Northern Ireland'. In *Race and Class*, pp.41–55. January 1978.
- Ryan, Helen. 'Children's Literature'. In *Dictionary of Irish Literature*, Vol.A–L, edited by Robert Hogan. London: Aldwych Press, 1996.
- O'Sullivan, Emer. 'The Development of Children's Literature in Late Twentieth-Century Ireland'. In *Signal*, Vol.81, pp.189–211. September 1996.
- Webb, Jean. 'A Comparative View of Children's Literature: a Discussion Paper'. In *Other Worlds, Other Lives: Children's Literature Experiences*, Vol.2, pp.1–16. Pretoria: Pretoria University Press, 1996.
- West, Máire. 'Kings, Heroes and Warriors: Aspects of Children's Literature in Ireland in the Era of Emergent Nationalism'. In *Bulletin, John Ryland's Library, University of Manchester*, Vol.76 (3), pp.165–183. 1994.

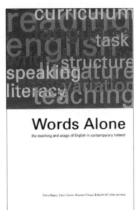

Words Alone: the Teaching and Usage of English in Contemporary Ireland, cover by Origin Design Associates.

WEB SITES

- www.irishbooks4kids.com
- Stephanie Dagg www.booksarecool.net
- Eilís Dillon http://homepage.eircom.net/~writing/01.Biobiblio.html

AUTHORS

Articles about individual authors are to be found in the following publications:

- Berger, Laura Standley (ed.). *Twentieth-Century Young Adult Writers.* Detroit: St. James Press, 1994. 1558622020
- Prendergast, Sara and Prendergast, Tom (eds). *The St. James Guide to Children's Writers.* 5th edition of *Twentieth-Century Children's Writers.* Detroit: St James Press, 1999. 1558623698
- Watson, Victor (ed.). *The Cambridge Guide to Children's Books.* Cambridge: Cambridge University Press, to be published 2001.
- *Wordsmiths: Contemporary Authors from Denmark, Ireland and Portugal.* CD-ROM, Dublin Corporation Public Libraries, Cumberland House, Fenian Street, Dublin 2.
- Zipes, Jack (ed.). *The Oxford Companion to Fairy Tales.* Oxford: Oxford University Press.

ORGANISATIONS

CHILDREN'S BOOKS IRELAND (CBI)

Children's Books Ireland was formed in 1996 through the amalgamation of the Children's Literature Association of Ireland (CLAI) and the Irish Children's Book Trust (ICBT). It is a limited company with charitable status. It is funded by the Arts Council, membership subscriptions, activities and sponsorship. The aims of CBI are:

- ▶ To promote reading
- ▶ To provide information on all aspects of children's literature
- ▶ To provide a forum for discussion
- ▶ To liaise with other organisations
- ▶ To promote research
- ▶ To encourage excellence in text and illustration for children

CBI seminars, conferences and summer schools are targeted at those professionally involved with children and reading. Its magazine, *Children's Books in Ireland*, appears three times per annum. In addition, CBI has published *Book Choice (1999)* in conjunction with the Department of Education and Science, and with the Youth Library Group publishes an annual book guide to coincide with the Children's Book Festival, which is co-ordinated by CBI. The Bisto Book Awards, sponsored by RHM Foods, are organised by CBI, as is the biennial CBI Summer School Award for outstanding services to children's literature in Ireland. CBI is a focus for research into children's books and reading in Ireland.

Contact: The Administrator, Children's Books Ireland, 19 Parnell Square, Dublin 1.
Tel/Fax: 01-872 5854   childrensbooksire@eircom.net

IBBY IRELAND

IBBY Ireland is the Irish section of the International Board on Books for Young People (IBBY). It is a voluntary, non-profit organisation that promotes children's books at an international level. It endorses the aims and objectives of IBBY. The aims of IBBY Ireland include the development and promotion of relevant expertise relating to children's books at national and international levels, and the development of networks linking Ireland and other countries in the area of children's books. IBBY Ireland organises seminars, lectures, exhibitions and other events.

Contact: IBBY Ireland, 20 Victoria Road, Rathgar, Dublin 6.

THE LIBRARY ASSOCIATION OF IRELAND SCHOOL LIBRARY DEVELOPMENT COMMITTEE

The Committee reflects the concern of the Library Association of Ireland to foster effective libraries in schools through the encouragement of school libraries and local authority School Library Services. Committee members have contributed to *School Libraries: Guidelines for Good Practice* (LAI, 1994) and *Library File: Making a Success of the School Library* (Coghlan, Quigley, Walton: LAI, 1999).

READING ASSOCIATION OF IRELAND (RAI)

The Association aims to stimulate and to promote an interest in reading. To do this, it holds conferences and workshops relating to the development of reading and to the professional development of teachers in the areas of reading and language. It encourages research into new trends in reading and into finding solutions for reading problems. It also publishes a magazine, *Reading News*.
Contact: Reading Association of Ireland, Educational Research Centre, St Patrick's College, Drumcondra, Dublin 9.

THE SCHOOL LIBRARY ASSOCIATION REPUBLIC OF IRELAND BRANCH (SLARI)
THE SCHOOL LIBRARY ASSOCIATION NORTHERN IRELAND BRANCH (SLANI)

SLARI and SLANI support all those committed to the promotion and development of libraries and information literacy in schools. They provide access to conferences, seminars, training days, library visits, a quarterly journal, *The School Librarian*, and a series of practical publications on all aspects of school libraries.
Contact: The School Library Association Republic of Ireland, The Library, St Andrew's College, Booterstown, County Dublin.

THE YOUTH LIBRARY GROUP (YLG)

The Youth Library Group of the Library Association of Ireland aims to encourage reading through the provision of seminars, workshops and conferences. It plays an active part in many children's book events and cooperates with CBI in the production of a reading guide for the annual Children's Book Festival.
Contact: The Honorary Secretary, YLG, The Library Association of Ireland, 53 Upper Mount Street, Dublin 2.   youthlibrariesgroup@ireland.com

CONTRIBUTORS

KATE AGNEW is a children's bookseller in London. She has contributed articles to many publications. She is a current judge for the Whitbread Book Award and the Smarties Book Prize, and has a won a 'Nibby' for services to the National Year of Reading.

RO AITKEN is Head of English at St Paul's School, Greenhills, Dublin.

IRENE BARBER is a learning support teacher in two Dublin primary schools. She was a school principal for fourteen years and taught in a college of education. She writes teachers' guides for novels.

VALERIE COGHLAN is the Librarian at the Church of Ireland College of Education, Dublin, and is currently Vice-President of IBBY Ireland.

JANETTE CONDON is a graduate of University College Dublin and NUI Galway. She has a M.A. in Culture and Colonialism, and received a doctorate in 1999 for a study of the politics of children's literature in nineteenth-century Ireland.

ROBERT DUNBAR lectures in English at the Church of Ireland College of Education, Dublin. He has edited three anthologies of Irish writing for the young and, with Gabriel Fitzmaurice, an anthology of poetry, *Rusty Nails and Astronauts*.

CELIA KEENAN is director of the M.A. in Children's Literature and lecturer in English at St Patrick's College, Drumcondra, a college of Dublin City University.

P.J. LYNCH has received international acclaim for his picture book art. He has won many awards, including the CBI Bisto Book of the Year Award, and is twice winner of the Library Association's Kate Greenaway Award.

LIZ MORRIS is a primary school teacher who taught for twenty years in Rathmichael School, Dublin. She currently works in publishing.

LUCY O'DEA has worked as a primary school teacher and is currently a lecturer in English Methods and Education in Froebel College, Dublin.

FINIAN O'SHEA is currently Assistant Co-ordinator for the Learning Support Programme at the Church of Ireland College of Education, Dublin. He is a member of the executive committee of the Reading Association of Ireland and of IBBY Ireland.

EMER O'SULLIVAN lectures and researches at the Institut für Jugendbuchforschung (Institute for Children's Literature Research) at the Johann Wolfgang Goethe-Universität in Frankfurt. Her area of specialisation is comparative children's literature.

GILLIAN PERDUE has been working as a primary school teacher for fifteen years, ten of which were spent in St Maelruain's NS in Tallaght. She was chairperson of the Bisto Book Awards from 1999–2000. She is currently writing for children.

CAROLE REDFORD is a doctoral student of children's literature at St Patrick's College, Drumcondra, a college of Dublin City University.

MARY SHINE THOMPSON is a lecturer in English at St Patrick's College, Drumcondra, Dublin, where she also teaches on the M.A. in Children's Literature. She is a former primary school teacher.

ALAN TITLEY is one of Ireland's best-known writers in the Irish language. He is a critic, broadcaster and Head of the Irish Department at St Patrick's College, Drumcondra, Dublin.

INDEX: AUTHORS

INDEX: ILLUSTRATORS

Index: Titles